Mark's Guide

for

Alberta Paddlers

2007

Mark Lund

Canadian Cataloguing in Publication Data

Lund, Mark E. R. (Mark Ernest Robert), 1951 -

Mark's guide for Alberta paddlers

ISBN 0-9682326-1-2

1. Canoes and canoeing
2. Kayaks and kayaking
3. Alberta guidebook - Description and travel

Includes bibliographical references.

GV776.15.A4L89   1997   797.1'22'0971233   C97-900624-4

© June 2007 by Mark Lund

with minor revisions and updates to August, 2009

Published by:

Mark Lund
5404 - 114 A St.
Edmonton, Alberta
T6H 3M7
780.436.4253
e-mail: *marklund@shaw.ca*

Photographs by Mark Lund   (except as noted)
Edited by Lois Samis Lund and Anna Lund
Production by Mark Lund

1st Printing - 2000 copies
2nd Printing - 2500 copies - August, 2009

Printed and Bound in Canada

Front cover photo: Lois and Mark Lund (& Gimli) in "the Bump" on the Waterton River, early July 2006, Photo by David Whitten

"... no paddler has ever drowned on the portage trail."

DISCLAIMER

The authors of this guide have taken care to insure that the information is accurate at the time of publication, BUT rivers and lakes DO CHANGE! Public access to our rivers and lakes come and go, dams are built, weirs are periodically removed, rapids are scoured out by one flood, and filled in by the next, rivers meander, change channels, wash out old log jams and create new ones. Our paddling environment constantly changes and paddlers must be alert at all times when on the water.

All paddlers must take full responsibility for insuring their own safety.

ALL PADDLERS must take precautions to insure that all their equipment is in good working order. When planning trips, they are responsible for ensuring that the water level is safe and that the trip itself does not exceed their abilities as paddlers or the capabilities of the group with which they are travelling. During a trip, each paddler must continuously evaluate the water, the rapids, and the weather, and determine if they have the ability to continue the trip, or to run a particular rapid, drop or other natural or man-made hazard. All trip participants must review and seriously consider the *Safety Code of the American Whitewater Affiliation*, which can be found in this guide as Appendix A. All paddlers must consider the *Paddler's Self Rating Guide* on pages 8 to 10 of this guide, and then select only trips that match their abilities and experience.

Acknowledgments

Any project, even a small guide like this is not done without assistance. I would like to acknowledge the previous work of my many colleagues from the *Canoe Alberta* projects of 1972 & '73, the late Bernice Parry for her work with the 1978 *Canoe Alberta* revisions, and the work of various Alberta Wilderness Association and Alberta Canoe Association members in helping with the Janice MacDonald, *Canoeing Alberta* (1985) edition. The American Whitewater Affiliation has again allowed the use of their Safety Code. Without the editing of my wife Lois and daughter Anna, this would be a much more difficult read. Many other paddlers have contributed to this guide through the submission of reach reports, photographs, and technical reviews. I have tried to acknowledge these contributions at the appropriate place, with their pictures, or with their submission. And, I must thank all those many, many paddlers with whom I have paddled and shared the lakes and rivers of this province, and across Canada. Without all your assistance this project could not reach publication, and I thank you all! And may we get back to paddling!

River, Lake and Report Locations

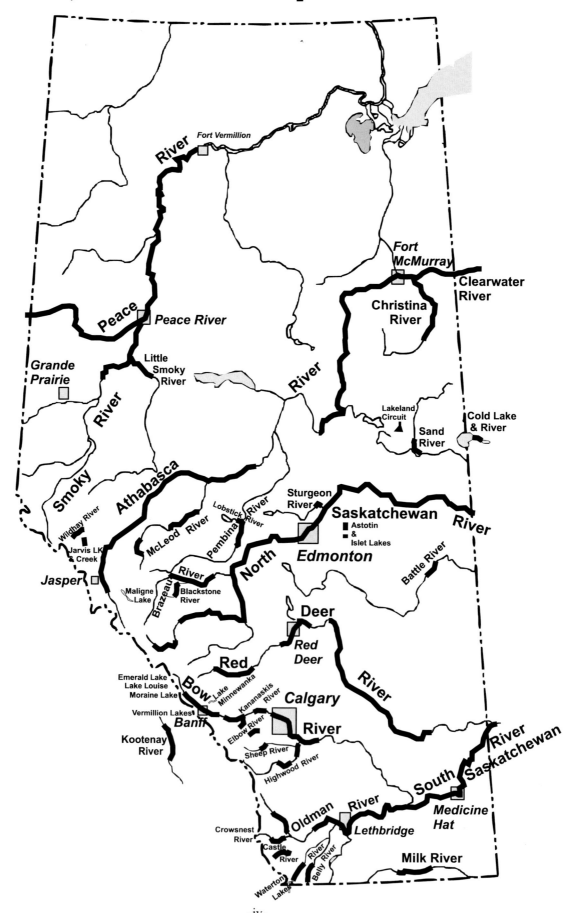

Contents

Contents (cont'd)

Introduction

Paddling in Alberta

Alberta is a province blessed with good paddling resources. We have it all: the whitewater of the mountains and foothills, great lake trips both in the mountains and the boreal forest, multi-day river trips in nearly all parts of the province, and near our population centers -- good day tripping, and both ponds and flowing water to initiate new paddlers. And, our paddling sports are well developed: we have the Alberta Whitewater Association to support those who like to play and compete in the "big rapids", Paddle Alberta (formerly ARCA the Alberta Recreational Canoeing Association) to support those with a less competitive bent in both canoe and kayak, and the Alberta Sprint Racing Canoeing Association to support those who have competitive flatwater aspirations. Each of these province wide associations supports and is supported by a host of local community clubs. Check out Appendix E for a list of the active clubs, and their web site addresses for contact. Over this past decade we have also seen the further development of the commercial side of paddling: more paddling specific shops, more map and guide stores, more shuttle services, more outfitters, and an even a greater variety of craft with which to explore and play on our rivers and lakes.

This Guide

Canoeing guides for Alberta have been an ongoing concern of mine since the late Herb Benthin made the suggestion at an early meeting of the Alberta Whitewater Association: "...*what canoeing in this province really needs is a good canoe guide!*" With Herb's prod, and the subsequent announcement of the 1972 *Opportunities for Youth Program*, I was soon deep into paddling, researching and preparing the first version of *Canoe Alberta* with a group of college friends. Since then I contributed to each subsequent version of *Canoe Alberta*, in 1973, and 1978, and then to Janice MacDonald's *Canoeing Alberta* (1985). In 1996 I self-published my first guide, *Mark's Guide for Edmonton Paddlers*, and in 1997 an expanded version, *Mark's Guide for Central Alberta Paddlers*. Over the past decade this guide sold over 2200 copies across Canada.

When I started writing our first guide over 35 years ago I thought, write a guide and it will last forever. NOT SO! Rivers, roads and other geographic features change, often in over very few years. Some changes are small, the erosion into a bank, and new sweepers appear; or larger changes like the cutting off of a meander bend, these change the course of a stream. We humans put roads in, take bridges out, dam streams, and even re-chanlize streams. This is one of the prime reasons for my decision to cease publishing the "Central Alberta guide," too much had changed. And over this past decade I have prepared new reports for rivers in the south, and in the north and the best decision seemed to be to prepare a guide for the whole province.

My "Edmonton Guide" had 13 reports, my "Central Alberta Guide" 30 reports, and this new "Alberta Guide" 60 reports. Again some will ask: "Hey Mark, why not a report on every river and every reach in the province?" My answer is again: "Too much, too big, changes too fast!" My goal over the next few years will be to try to add a few reach reports that deserve to be included, and to bring out a revised edition in less than a full decade! And as I stated in 1997, I do believe that many paddlers do like to do their own research, their own map and air photo (often now Goggle Earth) study, their own gradient calculations and earn their own sense of exploration.

I greatly enjoy my contact with paddlers who forward comments, suggestions and up-dates. I will do my best to incorporate these into future revisions, and I will try to post up-dates as completed to my web site for this guide. My contact information is:

> web site: http://members.shaw.ca/marksguide/index.htm
> e-mail: marklund@shaw.ca
> Canada Post: 5404-114a Street, Edmonton, Alberta, T6H 3M7

This is a guide to a selection of the rivers and lakes of Alberta – it is **NOT an instructional manual**. I have included in Appendix C an annotated list of paddling manuals, and in Appendix D a list of relevant web/internet resources. If you are unsure of your paddling ability it is best to review the *Paddler's Self Rating Guide* on pages 8 to 10. The clubs listed in Appendix E are often your best source of instruction in the paddling skills, and others to trip with. **Most paddling accidents can be attributed to either poor skill, or poor judgement! You should avoid both!**

How to Read a Reach Report

This guide can be used for planning canoe trips ranging in length from a few hours to many days. The following is an annotated review of the Reach Reports and has been prepared to help you to interpret the information contained. Interpretation requires some background and I have tried to give an indication of how each reach report section has been developed. This is a guide to the selection of a canoe trip appropriate to the skills, interests, and available time frame for paddlers. These reports should NOT be the only research an interested paddling party does; stream flows will need to be checked, better maps acquired, and other local paddlers should be consulted for a paddling conditions up-date.

Title
This is the name for the river or lake.

Reach
This is the part, section or *reach* of the river or lake contained in the report.

Why Go
A brief description of why you may want to paddle this reach: the scenery, the whitewater, the camping, the wildlife, etc.

Each report includes a photo of a typical, or a special scene .

Duration of Tours(s)
This section includes two pieces of information:

*The overall distance in kilometers. These have either been measured using Garmin's *Topo Canada* as a "route" measure, or from an actual GPS "track". Any measure of a reach is an estimate. In the days when I manually measured distances from 1:50,000 NTS maps I found that with repeated measures of long distances I could get the variance down to about 2-3%. I find that even with repeated GPS "tracks" there is a small a variance of 1-2% and from a "track" to a "route" measure a variance of 2-4%. So please take each reach measure with a "grain of salt" and let me know of any variance (error?) greater than 5%.

* A conservative estimate of the time required, usually ½ day, day or multi days. Many of the reach reports include the possibility of intermediate access, and thus sub-reaches.

A Location Map
This is only a location map and is designed to give a general overview of the river, and to help you locate possible access & shuttle routes, public or commercial campground locations, and local communities. The maps are all drawn with the "top" as north. There is no scale, but take a look at the length of the reach for a scale estimate, on some maps the reach is only a few kilometers long and on others hundreds of kilometers long.

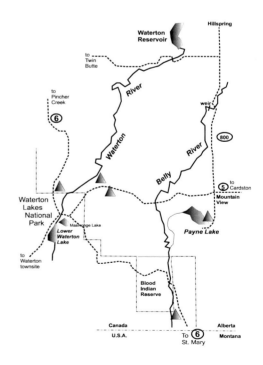

Classification

Each reach is rated according to the American Whitewater Association's version of the International Canoe Federation *International Scale of River Difficulty*. This rating **primarily applies to the rapids** on the reach. It does not account for many of the other common dangers and factors that increase risk on Alberta's foothills streams such as: logjams and sweepers, cold water, inaccessibility, weather and even wildlife.

In addition to the river ratings, I have suggested what level of paddling skill and experience is required for paddlers to safely complete the reported reach or lake run. Please use the next section of this guide to rate your skill and experience level before attempting any reach reported in this guidebook. On many reaches that have historically been used for the training of new paddlers, I have suggest a paddler rating for "self lead" groups, with no experienced leader who has been down the river recently, versus a group that does have experienced leaders (instructors, guides) who do know the river well and how to teach and lead less experienced paddlers.

Start

This section provides some details about the first access location, and when appropriate, other access points that are commonly used to start sub-reach tours.

Finish

Similar to start, just the other end!

Intermediate Access and Distances

ie:

Location	Elevation	Km down	Km up	Km between	Access / Bank or Rapid / Class	MGRS datum	Gradients m/km
	meters					NAD 1927	
						Zone 12 U	

Locations
The various location and features along the river from start to end.
Elevation
The height in meters or feet above sea level. These elevations are all based on the NTS Topographic maps. But *Topo Canada*, the source for much of my data converts the actual "feet" on the older NTS sheet to meters and thus the numbers seem a bit odd at times. I have an ongoing concern that the placement of contour line crossings on streams, especially those in canyons or deeply entrenched valleys, is an imprecise science. This imprecision then has implications for the calculation of the average gradients between the contour lines. In many of the reports you will see again my expression of this concern that the calculated gradient does not match the experience of paddling the reach.
Km (down)
This is a calculation of how far you have left to paddle to the last access point or finish of the report - km 0.
Km (up)
This is a calculation of how far you have gone with the start as Km 0.
Km (between)
This is a calculation of the distance between the more popular access points and thus the distance for popular sub-reaches.
Access / Bank or Rapid Class
For each "location" I try to provide some description. For access locations this is either the right or left bank (as always taken facing downstream) and often upstream or downstream of "the bridge" or confluence where the access is. For rapids that are located on a reach, a rating range for the difficulty is expressed, as per the ICF River Classification system (see Appendix A).
MGRS (datum)
I have provided in this guide a grid reference for GPS users, and map users that understand grid reference, for access points, most significant river features. I have chosen to use the "Military Grid Reference System" (MGRS) and to provide the grid reference to 100 m. I find MGRS is the system that coordinates best with the Canadian Topographic maps at 1:50,000 (see http://maps.nrcan.gc.ca/topo101/mil_ref_e.php). All Canadian Topo Maps at 1:50,000 include the MGRS (or UTM) grid to 1000 m, and one can easily interpolate the 100 m reference.

The reported grid references in this guide come from: actual waypoints taken on site, waypoints generated from *Topo Canada* or waypoints from map interpolation. Given the error inherent in our topo sheets (see example at http://maps.nrcan.gc.ca/topo_metadata/topo_metadata_e.php), and errors in locating waypoints, my goal has been to try to provide a reference that most folks will find to be within 100 to 200 m of the actual location. Anyone paddling these reaches MUST be able to recognize the signs of an upcoming river hazard such as a logjam, weir, ledge, falls, or rapid within the next 100 to 200 m.

Remember that MGRS references are in three parts: first a two letter coordinate that references a 100 km grid, then a three digit "easting" that is read from west to east across the map, and then the three digit northing that is read from south to north on the map. I have also provided the larger Zone reference for the 100,000 km grid. All NTS Topo sheets will have a small example on the side of the map of how to interpolate the last 100 m reference. One essential item that all GPS users MUST set correctly is the "Datum" year. This is either NAD 1927 Canada, or NAD 1983 (or WGS 1984). The wrong datum setting will provide an additional error of well over 100 m, and the two letter coordinate maybe off by 1000 km (see http://maps.nrcan.gc.ca/topo101/correction_e.php).

Natural Resources Canada provides further excellent information about the NTS Maps at: http://maps.nrcan.gc.ca/topo_e.php

I would also encourage paddlers unfamiliar with map use to work their way through "Topo 101" at: http://maps.nrcan.gc.ca/topo101/index_e.php .

Gradients
The last or right column is the calculated mean gradient between each noted elevation. This must be taken "with a grain of salt". As noted above and many times again, contours are not perfect representations, and river difficulty is determined by **not** just gradient, but also by river volume and the geology of the river bed.

Gradient

This brief paragraph reviews the gradients, notes discrepancies, and highlights what sections may be more difficult. Big rivers like the North Saskatchewan in Edmonton flow along quite nicely for novice paddlers at a gradient of .5 to 1 m/km and a flow of 150 to 300 cms, whereas smaller foothill streams like the Red Deer are exciting white water with gradients of 7 to 10 m/km with just 30 to 70 cms. With more volume, less gradient is required to make exciting, or more dangerous rapids! The Nordegg to Rocky Mtn. House run on the North Saskatchewan river is a popular white water run and has a gradient of less than 3 m/km, but a volume of 150 to 300 cms through much of the summer.

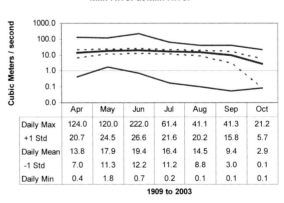

River Volume and Flow Rate

Each report includes a hydrograph similar to the *Milk River at Milk River* graph and table to the right. Some key points to note are:
- the Y scale is a logarithmic scale and provides flow in Cubic metres per second (cms). 1 cms is approximately 35 cubic feet per second (cfs).
- Daily maximum & minimum. flows are for a full day's flow, not an instantaneous measure.
- Daily mean flow is a full day's average flow.
- +1 Standard Deviation (Std) and -1 Std approximates the Alberta definition of normal flow from the 25 to 75 percentile of all recorded flows.
- the table below the graph is the actual data as provided by Environment Canada - Water Survey of Canada through the HYDAT Program (http://www.wsc.ec.gc.ca/products/main_e.cfm?cname=products_e.cfm)

In addition to the graph each report includes a brief paragraph of recommended flows for safe and enjoyable paddling, often other volume facts, and estimates of the stream velocity at the reporting station for various flows. These velocities have been estimated from the Alberta Environment (1996) *Stream Flow Fact Sheets*.

Small rivers like the Wildhay, Belly or Sheep, may be a fun paddle at 20 Cms, or a medium sized river like the Red Deer at Red Deer may require 40 cms as a minimum, or an even larger stream like the North Saskatchewan in Edmonton 100 cms is a minimal flow. BUT with: 40 cms in the Wildhay, Belly or Sheep rivers, 200 cms in the Red Deer or 1000 cms in the North Saskatchewan at Edmonton, these streams all become dangerous even for experienced paddlers.

Flow reports are published on-line by the Alberta Environment River Forecast Center and are available at: http://environment.alberta.ca/apps/basins/default.aspx . These on-line flow reports are up-to-date, often within the last three to four hours! One can get a pretty good feel for what is happening, or likely to happen to stream flows by checking both the reports for the monitoring stations on the reach you hope to paddle, and the stations upstream of where you hope to paddle.

In addition Alberta Environment publishes a flow forecast each week at: http://environment.alberta.ca/forecasting/.

The River forecast Centre also tracks and reports on precipitation and storm events at: http://environment.alberta.ca/6.html .

Environment Canada flow reports can be found online at: http://scitech.pyr.ec.gc.ca/waterweb/main.asp?lang=0

Maps (& Guides)

Next is a listing of recommended maps, and the requisite National Topographic System maps for the reach. Suggested NTS scale is reach appropriate, only 1:250,000 sheets for the big northern rivers, both 1:250,000 and 1:50,000 sheets for the middle size rivers of central and southern Alberta and just the 1:50,000 sheets for the foothills and mountain streams. Where appropriate and available I have also provided reference to other useful guides and supporting materials.

As I go to press with the August 2009 revisions I would like to recognize to the readers of this guide my developing dependence on my GPS. I've worked through three generations of Garmin GPS units and presently use a model 76 CSX. Both this and my earlier model 60C have the ability to upload Garmin maps and I've been using their Topo Canada maps for some time now. It is a good system! But you must have back-up... I have had my GPS crash and batteries die. Extra batteries and a back-up map are essential. It is now possible to download all Canadian NTS topo maps for free from
http://geogratis.gc.ca/geogratis/en/whatsnew.html#toporama-20090630
Use the Toporama link and I find it quickest to know what sheet I am interested in and work through the FTP download link. These can be rather large .tif files!

Camping

For most reaches I list, locate and provide a contact phone number for the popular public and commercial campgrounds on or near the reach. Also indicated is whether the reach is appropriate for wilderness or "random" camping on crown land.

Again as I go to press with the August 2009 revisions I find that both National and Provincial Parks have in place reservations systems for most of their campgrounds:
National Parks phone: 1.877.737.3783 and on-line at: http://www.pccamping.ca/parkscanada
Alberta Provincial Parks on line at: http://reserve.albertaparks.ca
and Travel Alberta maintains a good campground directory with reasonably up-to-date phone numbers at:
http://www1.travelalberta.com/
and then click on the "campground" link.

Wildlife

In a paragraph or two I highlight likely wildlife sightings, locations for, and past experiences with wildlife along the reported reach.

Trip Notes

This section may be a brief paragraph highlighting the pleasures of the reach, other interesting facts, or for some foothill's whitewater streams a fairly lengthy report on the difficulties, hazards and options.

Other Reaches

I have given up trying to write a comprehensive paddling guide to all reaches, for every river or lake in Alberta. These two paragraphs, one for the upstream reach, and one for the next downstream reach, are either a "teaser" for the next run, or a warning. Some brief information is provided: distance, and character of the adjacent reaches, and maybe the prime reason to paddle on, or start higher. BUT you will have to do some additional research before paddling these reaches. Yes, I do truly believe that all fully competent paddlers should be able to research and plan their own trips. Heck, half the fun of paddling is doing the research and planning! This is what winter is for, if not for skiing!

Other local Activities or Destinations

Over the years as a father, club trip leader and troop scouter, not everyone shares my enthusiasm for paddling, even in "ugly" conditions. Crews have mutinied, revolted, even refused to paddle. Then the question becomes what else may you do? I try to answer that question in this section.

Rentals and Shuttles

Where available and known, I have tried to list the available canoe and paddling rental agencies that are handy to the reach, and then the various available shuttle services. I was once told I should write a PhD. thesis on the organizing of canoe trip shuttles, but as I've grown older I've come to see the wisdom of contracting out, and I have in recent years made good use of local taxi services. Not too many years ago a shuttle from Drayton back to Rocky Mtn. House in the "town limo" worked out to less than $10 per paddler who benefitted – cheap for a long weekend of paddling! And it saved everyone the extra 3 hour wait of a "double shuttle."

As I prepare these revisions and corrections in August 2009 I am finding that shuttle and taxi services are changing almost as often as campground phone number and useful web sites. DO NOT plan on finishing a trip and being able to depend on immediate service from a local cab company. It is best to call ahead and book your shuttle. In many small communities a canoe shuttle requires that an extra driver be brought in and thus these arrangements require time and planning.

****

This guide has been written conservatively, both with consideration to classification of rapids, recommendation for paddling skills required and to the time-distance estimates. A paddler new to the rivers and lakes of this guide, or a new novice paddler should start with the less difficult, the smaller, low gradient streams, and then work one's way up in both gradient, volume and difficulty. Each reach report lists gradients and volumes and you will soon come to recognize those that match your comfort level, skill and experience. In addition, each report suggests the required level of skill and experience. How do your skills and experience measure up? Complete the *Paddler's Self-Rating Guide* in the next section.

One of the hardest thing to consider is when should a river trip be cancelled because of high water. For this 2007 version of my guide I have chosen to use the federal government calculation of plus or minus one standard deviation to define normal flow, these flow numbers are very similar to our provincial governments definition of normal flow as being between the 25 and 75 percentile of flows on record. Once stream volumes exceed about the 75th percentile, or +1 Std for early summer (June through July), or the stream is brimming, overflowing the normal banks, and is running through the willows on the inside of most corners, the hydraulics within the stream become chaotic, dangerous, even on small rivers and creeks. Paddlers should consider cancelling or changing their trip to another run, or even staying home! In June 2005 I cancelled Ceyana Canoe Club trips three weekends in a row! We stayed home, the province suffered through three major "storm events" that year, and all streams within a reasonable weekend distance of Edmonton suffered multiple floods!

But do remember, that there is good chance (50% of the time by the Alberta government definition) that the river volumes will be reported as below or above normal -- the key is the early summer (flood season - June to July on most Alberta streams) "normal" volumes. At the other end of the volume spectrum I have consulted a variety of sources beyond my own experience in trying to determine minimal flows. Again for some streams and some paddlers the provincial 25 percentile for late summer flows on many streams is considered low, other paddlers are prepared to go slower, walk more often and paddle with less water flow. For each run I have provided a guideline for optimal water flows; they are just that, a guideline.

Paddler's Self-Rating Guide

Instructions: for each group of statements below (i.e. *Flatwater Paddling Skills)*, select *the most advanced statement* that best reflects your present skills, or experience, for each **Venue** you have paddling experience in, in your *boat-of-choice*. You may give yourself a partial score (an intermediate value) on any one statement. Total your maximum score for each paddling venue and use the rating table to determine your level of paddling skill & experience.

Paddling Venues: FW = Flatwater, Riv = River, WW = Whitewater

For **Example** an *Intermediate* Paddler with **some** Lake/Flatewater and River Experience but **no** whitewater experience may complete the *Other Rescue Skills* category as: (Note that in this example the paddler has not given themselves a full score for the throw bag rescue.)

Rating Statements	Max. Value	Score by Paddling Venue		
		FW	Riv	WW
Other Rescue Skills				
Complete a T- Rescue in flat water.	1	1		
Toss a throw bag to a floating & moving person, at 12 m distance, on two of three trials.	2	■	1	
Complete a towing rescue of boat-of-choice and or a paddler in Class II rapid.	3	■		

****

Please Complete the table below now.

Rating Statements	Max. Value	Score by Paddling Venue		
		FW	Riv	WW
Swimming Skills:				
Swim at least 200m on front and back	1			
Swim in a river current, can ferry when swimming on back with feet-up	2	■		
Swim in class III rapid with some control of direction of travel.	3	■	■	
Self-Rescue Skills				
Able to pull self back into an upright canoe or kayak in flat water.	1			
Have rescued myself and my paddling gear and boat in moving water, on a stream of less than 100 cms.	2	■		
Have rescued myself and my paddle and boat in a Class III rapid.	3	■	■	

Rating Statements	Max. Value	Score by Paddling Venue		
		FW	Riv	WW
Other Rescue Skills				
Complete a T- Rescue in flat water.	1			
Toss a throw bag onto a floating & moving person, at 12 m distance, on two of three trials.	2	█		
Complete a towing rescue of boat-of-choice and or a paddler in Class II rapid.	3	█	█	
Flatwater Paddling Skills				
Know the canoe forward stroke, draw stroke, cross-draw, and basic duties of a "bow" paddler, or in a kayak, able to paddle in a straight line for 100m and turn the boat where to and when desired.	1			
Use the J-stroke and/or can keep the boat-of-choice on a straight line in a light breeze. Most of the time can provide useful steering directions to partner or another paddler in boat-of-choice.	3			
Use more than one J-stroke and/or can keep the boat-of-choice on a straight line in a modest to strong breeze. Rarely make an error when providing steering directions to a partner, or another paddler in my boat-of-choice. If a tandem canoeist can confidently paddle both ends of the canoe with less skilled paddlers.	5			
River Paddling Skills				
Occasionally miss an eddy turn or ferry in a current of less than 5 km/hr. Can keep boat-of-choice going in desired direction.	1	█		
Occasionally miss eddy turns or ferries in strong currents >5 km/hr, can back ferry (or sct). Can pick out a river channel through sand and gravel bars, and can predict, recognize and avoid sweepers and logjams.	3	█		
Rarely miss an eddy turn, ferry or set, even in a very strong current of >8 km/hr. Am confident at "reading the river" and directing other paddlers through difficult passages in gravel bars and around log jams and sweepers in their boat-of-choice.	5	█		
Whitewater Paddling Skills				
Know the AWA/ICF River & Rapid Rating system, and have practiced the river skills of eddy turns and ferrying in moving water.	1	█		
Can read the navigable channel in up to a Class III rapid and rarely miss an eddy turn or ferry, generally successful in bracing into and out of small "holes", likes to "play" in most river features on modest streams of up to 100 cms. If a "closed boater" can generally roll boat-of-choice in the current.	3	█	█	
Confident leading others through Class III rapids and can scout the navigable channel in Class IV rapids. Generally try to "play" most river features in small and large streams (>100 cms) and rarely miss a roll in the current, holes, wave train or along an eddy line.	5	█	█	

Rating Statements	Max. Value	Score by Paddling Venue		
		FW	Riv	WW
Experience				
Have paddled for less than two seasons and on less than ten lakes, streams or reaches of longer rivers.	1			
Have paddled for more than two seasons and on more than ten lakes, streams or reaches of longer rivers. Have been involved in less than ten rescues as part of the rescue team.	3			
Have paddled for many seasons on a wide variety of lakes, rivers AND rapids, been involved in more than 20 rescues, completing a variety of rescue tasks (i.e. - T-Rescue, other re-entry rescues in flat water, throw-bag, towing to safety a boat or swimmer in a river and or rapid, picking up lost gear, etc.), and have taken the lead roll in the majority of these 20 rescues.	5			
Your Maximum Score for each category above				
Swimming Skills				
Self Rescue Skills				
Other Rescue Skills				
Flatwater Paddling Skills				
River Paddling Skills				
Whitewater Paddling Skills				
Experience				
Total Score				
Paddler Self Rating	**Score**			
Novice		>5	>10	>15
Intermediate		>9	>18	>21
Skilled		= 13	= 24	= 29
		FW	Riv	WW

Paddlers with experience may find themselves scoring as Skilled Flat Water paddlers, and Intermediate River and White Water paddlers. A number of result combinations are possible depending on when, where, with whom and for how long you have been paddling. Please note that a brand new paddler, some one with no experience is NOT a Novice. **The Novice rating indicates that a paddler has some minimal experience and skill.**

These results are just estimates, and should give you some idea if you are adequately prepared to tackle the different lakes and rivers included in this guide. New paddlers, and paddlers new to Alberta should start with some of the lower rated rivers first and "work their way up" to streams and reaches of greater difficulty. And no paddler should forget that the volume of water in a stream will change the difficulty!

Milk River

Town of Milk River to Highway #880

Why Go
Badlands scenery, hoodoos, pictographs, and whitewater for a number of the reaches. These reaches offer great day tripping, and there are opportunities for camping on the river.

Duration of Tour(s)
* 104 km
* 3 to 5 days or a series of 1 day trips

in Writing-on-Stone Provincial Park

Classification
1. Rapids: Class I to II+ at most water levels, easy III at higher (65 to 80th percentile) water levels
2. Skill of Paddlers: Intermediate, open canoe river skills and river reading skills required, lots of rocks to dodge! We have had reports of aluminum and plastic canoes wrapped around rocks on these reaches.

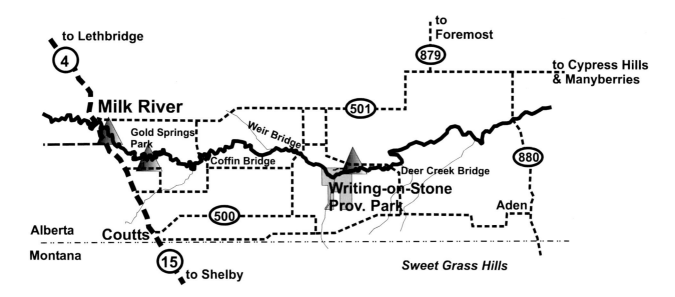

Start
Each of these sub-reaches of the Milk has a bridge or campground at the start of each day. In the town of Milk River paddlers can put in at the campground just downstream of the Highway #4 bridge. Both Gold Springs Park and Writing-on-Stone Park have beaches along the river that require minimal hikes from parking spots, and Coffin, Weir and Deer Creek Bridges all have dedicated access.

Finish
This reach allows one to finish at any of the intermediate access points, or the final bridge on Highway #880. In good weather shuttles are direct along the country roads. In 2004 with the Ceyana Canoe Club we stayed at Gold Springs Park. On the first day local roads were very wet and muddy and for the shuttle to Coffin Bridge we went back through town before heading east. Later in the weekend, after a hot day or two, we were able to use the local gravel roads south and east of Gold Springs Park to return from each day's paddle.

Intermediate Access and Distances

Location	Elevation meters	Km down	Km up	Km between	Access / Bank or Rapid / Class	MGRS datum NAD 1927	Gradients m/km
	3425		-2.5			Zone 12 U	
Milk River - #4 Bridge		104.7	0.0		downstream, left bank	VK 211 438	
	3400	98.0	6.7				0.8
	3375	94.8	9.9				2.4
						NAD 1983	
	3350	89.3	15.4				1.4
Gold Spring Park		88.3	16.4	16.4	right bank	VV 277 386	
	3325	86.1	18.6				2.4
	3300	82.3	22.4				2.0
	3275	79.9	24.8				3.2
	3250	77.6	27.1				3.3
Red Creek		72.2	32.5		right bank	VV 341 370	
	3225	71.4	33.3				1.2
	3200	70.3	34.4				6.9
Coffin Bridge		68.6	36.1	19.7	downstream right bank	VV 352 392	
	3175	68.4	36.3				4.0
	3150	66.2	38.5				3.5
	3125	60.5	44.2				1.3
	3100	57.4	47.3				2.5
	3075	54.8	49.9				2.9
Poverty Rock		54.7	50.0		right bank	VV 420 399	
	3050	52.8	51.9				3.8
Verdgris coulee		50.1	54.6		left bank		
	3025	49.0	55.7				2.0
	3000	44.3	60.4				1.6
Weir Bridge (#500)		44.2	60.5	24.4	upstream on right bank	VV 488 392	
Enter Writing-on-Stone Park		39.5	65.2			VV 520 373	
Van Cleeve Coulee		37.9	66.8		right bank		
Police Creek		36.1	68.6		right bank		
	2975	36.1	68.6				0.9
Writing-on-Stone Campground beach		34.5	70.2	9.7	left bank	VV 551368	
Leaving Writing-on-Stone Park		33.7	71.0			VV 554 370	
Deer Creek Bridge		26.6	78.1	7.9	upstream on left bank	VV 607 374	
Deer Creek		24.7	80.0		right bank		
	2950	22.7	82.0				0.6
	2925	11.9	92.8				0.7
Macdonald Creek / Black Coulee		7.4	97.3		right bank		
	2900	4.5	100.2				1.0
Highway #880 Bridge		0.0	104.7	26.6	right bank, downstream of	VV 776 436	

Gradient

Calculated gradients range from a low of less than 1 m/km to a high of nearly 7 m/km. As is often the case on small streams in canyons I am skeptical of these map based gradient estimates, but there is no doubt that the higher gradient stretches shown above do have more, and more difficult rapids. The reach below Gold Springs Park, and particularly the reach from Coffin Bridge to Verdigis Coulee offer the greatest whitewater challenges.

River Volume and Flow Rate

The best paddling flows are between approximately 15 and 25 cms. This river has enhanced flows to support irrigation through the spring and summer and then the water is turned off by mid August most years. Peak flood flows have been over 330 cms. Velocities range from less than 2 km/hr at approximately 15 cms to over 6 km/hr at nearly 200 cms.

Milk River at Milk River

	Apr	May	Jun	Jul	Aug	Sep	Oct
Daily Max	124.0	120.0	222.0	61.4	41.1	41.3	21.2
+1 Std	20.7	24.5	26.6	21.6	20.2	15.8	5.7
Daily Mean	13.8	17.9	19.4	16.4	14.5	9.4	2.9
-1 Std	7.0	11.3	12.2	11.2	8.8	3.0	0.1
Daily Min	0.4	1.8	0.7	0.2	0.1	0.1	0.1

1909 to 2003

Maps

1 - *A Paddler's Guide to the Milk River: Whiskey Gap to Deer Creek* from ARCA should be one's first choice on these reaches.
2 - NTS 1:50,000
    72 E/4 - Coutts
    72 E/3 - Aden (only required for the run down to Highway #880 below Deer Creek)

Camping

Campgrounds in the area include: the town campground next to the Highway #4 bridge in Milk River, Gold Springs Park (403.647.2277), and in Writing-on-Stone Provincial Park (403.647.2364, group campsite reservations 403.893.3777) On-river camping can be had in many places, but paddlers must remember that all of the land along the river is either privately owned or park, and campers must stay below the "high water line". Wilderness camping is not allowed in Writing-on-Stone Park. Local paddlers have arranged with the land owner for a campsite at Poverty Rock, and this is a popular site for paddling groups, as it provides some shelter and rough toilets.

Wildlife

Paddling in the open country of the Milk River allows one great views of the topography and wildlife. Unfortunately the most common sighting will be the red & white of Herford cattle, but mule deer, great blue herons, cliff swallows and various hawks can also be seen. During our 2004 Ceyana excursion we were fortunate to come across both rattle and bull snakes during one side excursion off the river to check out some pictographs. Then just after getting back into our canoes those of us at the back of the pack also came across another rattlesnake swimming in the river. Many of the reported sighting of rattlesnakes that I have from paddlers, is of the rattlers swimming in the river. Paddlers with kids and dogs must keep both under close scrutiny in this country. People of all ages must be most conscious of avoiding the placement of hands and feet in any place that cannot be clearly observed for snakes.

On our last evening at Gold Springs Park in 2004 we had a pleasant hour watching a mamma great horned owl give her two offspring flight lessons from the cliff just down stream of the campground.

Trip Notes

I first visited Writing-on-Stone Park with my family in 1965. I did not get back to paddle these reaches until 2004 – big mistake! I don't think you've really paddled in Alberta until you've paddled on some of these southern rivers. The scenery is spectacular and the paddling is interesting. Maybe too interesting for some. During our 2004 trip with the Ceyana Canoe Club we met two different Scout groups on the water. One had taken the time to prepare properly, had their leaders properly trained through our provincial recreation canoe association (Paddle Alberta), and the group had a thoroughly enjoyable time. The second group was less well managed and prepared, had difficulties with the river and rapids, damaged their canoes, and were evacuated, with some difficulty, from Poverty Rock. Other relatively inexperienced paddlers have also told me that this was the most difficult paddling they have ever done, and reports of canoe damage are common. On the other hand, with modestly good river skills, this is a fun river! I'm going back soon.

In 2004 our group camped at Gold Springs Park, and shuttled each day to the river. Our first reach was from Gold Springs park down to Coffin Bridge, then the next day Coffin to Weir Bridge, and finally on the Monday of the long weekend, we did the run through Writing-on-Stone Provincial Park -- Weir Bridge to Deer Creek Bridge. The extra driving was a fair trade off for the fine group campsite we were given along the river in Gold Springs Park.

Other Reaches
Upstream: the ARCA river guide provides good information for the runs from Whiskey Gap all the way into town, about 116 km.

Downstream: the Milk River becomes difficult to access and arrangements must be made in advance to access the grazing lands along the river in Alberta. To enter Montana, one must check-in, in advance with a border crossing.

Other Local Activities or Destinations
Writing-on-Stone Provincial Park is the prime attraction in this area. To see the largest gallery of the pictographs in the park you must join one of the regular park tours. You must also join a guided hike to visit the old police post across the river on the south bank.

Rentals and Shuttle Services
Local Shuttle Services include:

Milk River Raft Tours
403.647.3586

Gold Springs Park looking SE to the Sweet Grass Hills

North West Mounted Police Buildings, Police Coulee in Writing-on-Stone Park

Waterton Lakes

Why Go
Great mountain scenery, crystal clear water, wonderful side hikes, and wilderness camping.

Duration of Tour(s)
* ½ day to multi-day tours are available. The length may depend on side trips or hikes that you undertake, being wind-bound, or just how long you choose to camp at some spots to take in the view!

Looking west across Middle Waterton Lake

Classification
Lake trip: Intermediate Flatwater paddlers with experience in windy conditions and big, rough waves. Be prepared to be "wind bound" and you may need to paddle very early or very late in the day to make up for lost time.

Starts & Finish
All distances below are from the marina in the townsite. The picnic site on the south-west corner of the townsite makes a good starting point as does anywhere along the beach of the town campsite.

Trips south into the upper lake are "out and back" trips. A trip down to the middle and lower lakes may end at Knights Lake picnic site or the Maskinonge Lake picnic site.

Intermediate Access and Campsite Distances

Access Points & Campgrounds	Comments	Approximate km from Start	MGRS *datum 1927*
1 - heading south along the west shore on Upper Waterton Lake			
Town site Marina		0	TK 877 372
Picnic Site	To access take the Cameron Falls road and keep heading south past the falls and along the west side of the campground.	1.6	TK 871 362
Bertha	Wilderness Campsite	3.5	TK 873 345
Boundary Bay	Wilderness Campsite	6.8	TK 875 312
Goat Haunt	Wilderness Campsite, USA Warden Station and Tour Boat Dock	12.3	TK 886 267
2 - heading south along the east shore on Upper Waterton Lake			
Crypt Landing	Boat Dock	3.4	TK 874 346
3 - heading east through the Bosporus straits, into Middle Lake, along the south shore, through the Dardanelles, into Lower Lake and along the west shore to the Maskinonge picnic site.			
Bosporus		0.6	TK 872 376
Wishbone		2.2	TK 895 366
Dardanelles	start	6.2	TK 916 387
Marquis Hole	picnic site - can be hard to access from river, check and flag before commencing if planning to end here.	6.8	
Dardanelles	picnic site - can be hard to access from river	7.8	
Lower Waterton Lake	start	8.3	TK 919 405
Knights Lake	picnic site - west shore, just off of main park road	11.0	TK 919 426
Maskinonge	picnic site - south or right shore - in from highway 5/6 just south of the bridge	12.4	TK 928 434

Maps

1 - 1:50,000 - Waterton Lakes National Park - this is a park map and the only map that you should need for any of these trips.

Camping

Car Camping: is available in the park at the townsite (for information 403.859.5133, for townsite campground reservations 1-877-737-3783 it fills quickly and early!), and out of town along Blakiston Creek at Mount Crandell (reservations NOT taken). East of the park there is a Provincial Recreation Area on Crooked Creek (403.653.1100) and private operations at Waterton Riverside east of the park on Highway #5, and just north of the park gate there is Waterton Springs (403.859.2247).

Wilderness Camping: As listed above there are five wilderness campsites on the Upper and Middle Waterton Lakes. Wilderness camping permits are required and are available from the Trail Office at the Parks Information Center (403. 859.5133). In addition, permits are available at the park information centre for camping at Goat Haunt in Glacier Park, Montana.

Trip Notes

I'll confess right from the start – my only trip to the south end of Upper Waterton Lake was some years ago, on the tour boat! However, in August '99, Lois and I had a wonderful day trip from the town picnic site, around the town site, through the Bosporus, along the south shore of Middle Lake, through the Dardanelles, and down Lower Lake to Knights Lake picnic site. I have never been wind bound on the big lake. But, during our '99 visit to the park we did enjoy a most pleasant supper in the Prince of Wales hotel dining room, which overlooks the lake. Throughout our supper we were able to watch numerous rain squalls blow down the lake. It was grand to be able comment on how glad we were that we were not fighting our way up the lake against the wind and waves, or struggling to hold a loaded canoe surfing homeward. It was doubly grand because we were camped down in the campground and it sure was dry and warm in the dining room, and the meal ... Mmmmm!

Our day paddle across the lakes was picture perfect – it was dead calm until mid-afternoon. Only one motor boat disturbed us all morning. Our closest brush with fear was when passing the Wishbone dock, we noted that the campsite was closed due to a bear in the area. We ate lunch on the other side of the outlet at the start of the Dardanelles! These lakes should be paddled at least once, just for the scenery!

Stewart Rood, from Lethbridge, reports that he regularly brings University environment students on this Middle and Lower Lakes paddle. He reports that trout can often be spotted in the big eddy on river left at the exit from Middle Lake. He also notes that his students often stop for a swim in Middle or Lower lake, and that the Upper Lake deserves great respect from paddlers – in part because the water is so much colder all season long!

Good side hikes are available from the Crypt, Bertha and Boundary campsites. Crypt Lake is possibly the classic Waterton Park hike, with the trail following up a mountain stream, along a ledge, through a tunnel and finishing with views of both a waterfall and a mountain tarn.

Other Local Activities and Destinations

On most trips to Waterton we manage to find time for an evening drive up to Red Rock Canyon, and take the hike around and enjoy the evening light on the red shales, and the surrounding mountains. Waterton Park is known for it's great day hiking, much of it very close to town. And if the weather is really poor, it is only an hours drive to Cardston and the Remington Carriage Museum.

Red Rock Canyon, July, 2006

Belly River

Highway #6 to Highway #800

Why Go
Great spring and early summer whitewater, and the open scenic vistas of the mountains and ranch lands.

Duration of Tour(s)
* 29.8 km
* ½ to 2 days

early July 2000, just above Highway #5

Classification
1. Rapids: up to Class III+
2. Skill of Paddlers: Intermediate River Paddlers in WW kayaks, or Skilled River Paddlers, if paddling open canoes.

Start
There are two starts, at the Highway #6 bridge in the Southeast corner of Waterton Lakes National Park, or at the Highway #5 bridge east of the Park. In dry weather both accesses allow one to drive to the river bank. The Highway #6 access does require permission of local Indian Band; this can usually be acquired at their store just north of the access, by the bridge. The Highway #5 access does require 200 m of driving down the north highway ditch to save the extra carry. Each start provides for an excellent ½ day to a full day paddle, depending on your propensity to "play" the river.

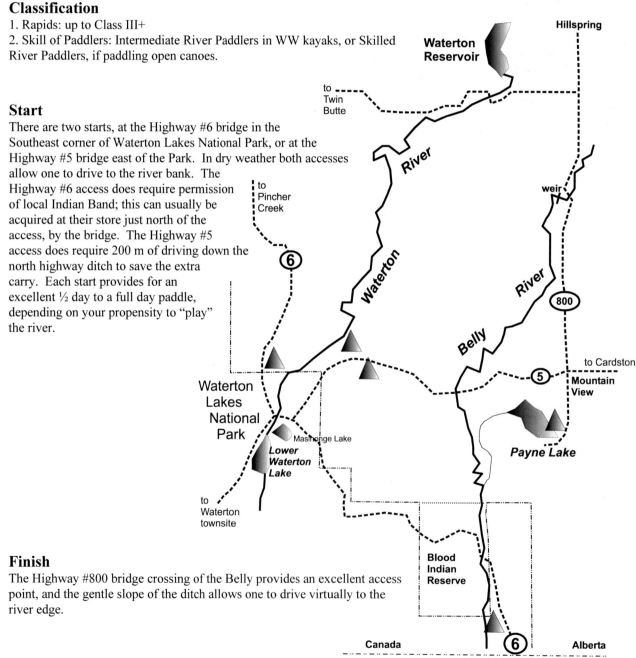

Finish
The Highway #800 bridge crossing of the Belly provides an excellent access point, and the gentle slope of the ditch allows one to drive virtually to the river edge.

Intermediate Access and Distances

Location	Elevation meters	Km up	Km down	Km between	Access / Bank or Rapid / Class	MGRS datum NAD 1983 Zone 12U	Gradient m/km
	1372	-0.9					
Start		0.0	29.8		left		
Highway #6 Bridge		0.1	29.7			UV 035 362	
Paine Lk canal headworks		4.5	25.3		right bank	UV 036 397	
	1341	7.4	22.4				3.7
	1311	12.1	17.7				6.4
#5 Highway Bridge over Belly		12.6	17.2	12.6	right bank	UV 019 447	
	1281	15.7	14.1				8.3
	1250	19.6	10.2				7.9
abandoned bridge site		21.1	8.7			UV 067 491	
	1219	24.3	5.5				6.6
	1189	29.0	0.8				6.4
Weir		29.0	0.8		right bank	UV 079 546	
#800 Highway bridge		29.8	0.0	17.2	right bank	UV 085 549	

Gradient

Gradients range from an easy 3.7 m/km for the first bit, to a very challenging 8.3 m/km for the stretches just above and below the Highway #5 bridge. Due to the challenging water just above and below the #5 bridge, both runs require good paddling skills, especially for those paddling open canoes.

River Volume and Flow Rate

Peak flows have exceeded 330 cms in floods.
In the early summer the good paddling can be had when the river flow is from 12 to15 cms and right through to 40 cms.
Velocities as measured at the Mountain View station range from less than 2 km/hr at 15 cms to nearly 8 km/hr at 100 cms.

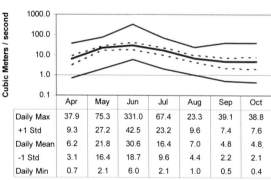

Belly River near Mountain View

	Apr	May	Jun	Jul	Aug	Sep	Oct
Daily Max	37.9	75.3	331.0	67.4	23.3	39.1	38.8
+1 Std	9.3	27.2	42.5	23.2	9.6	7.4	7.6
Daily Mean	6.2	21.8	30.6	16.4	7.0	4.8	4.8
-1 Std	3.1	16.4	18.7	9.6	4.4	2.2	2.1
Daily Min	0.7	2.1	6.0	2.1	1.0	0.5	0.4

1911 to 2003

Maps

1. - 1:50,000 NTS: *Waterton Lakes* 82 H/4
2. - 1:125,000: *Adventure Guide and Topographic Map of Southwest Alberta*, available from Southwest Alberta Business Development Centre

Camping

Numerous public and commercial campgrounds are available in the area. Payne Lake and Waterton Riverside are two of the closest campgrounds to the Highway #5 Bridge. The Belly River Campground in Waterton Lakes National Park (403.859.2224) is just 2.5 km upstream of the Highway #6 Bridge. Both times I've been down south to paddle these reaches I've stayed at the Waterton Riverside campground and made it a long weekend of paddling on the Waterton and Belly rivers.

Trip Notes

On the July 1 long weekend in 2000, a number of Ceyana Canoe Club members joined Lois and I, for a series of day trips on the Waterton and Belly rivers. Our long time paddling friend, Frank, repeatedly asked throughout the weekend; *Why are these rivers not more popular?* Both rivers were running clear, the open prairies allowed wide scenic vistas of the mountains, the rivers were fun with just the appropriate degree of challenge for our mixed group of experienced paddlers, some with young partners, and some with new partners.

In 2000 we ran the #5 to #800 reach with the river flowing at 19 cms. As the older guides and the SW Alberta Map indicate, this run starts with a bang! Two Class III rapids in the first couple of kilometres. The first is a short drop. When we returned in 2006 we found that the second rapid which had been a long boulder garden that swept around a "S" bend and island was virtually dry at 20+ cms. The new channel was now to the left of the island, and we paddled in with inadequate scouting. We found three good ledges, and the Lund canoe was our group's only swim, in the last ledge. As we were collecting ourselves at the bottom of the island, we were in good position to rescue the next party's canoe crew that tipped in the second ledge. The river continues to be a mix of boulder gardens and broken ledges most of the way to Highway #800. As the river first approaches #800 it becomes "depositional" and we found many new logjams and sweepers on the last third of this run. Just above the finish is a 3 m weir. This weir is on a long right bend, and the water flows diagonally across the top of the weir. We scouted this weir from about 200 m upstream. The levee and the concrete headworks on the left bank should provide good warning, except at very high flows. There are signs, but too few! Be on your toes! We portaged on the right after walking our boats the last 100 m or so down the right side gravel bar.

In 2000 we left the Highway #6 to #5 run for our last day, as the old *Canoeing Chinook Country Rivers* guide book reported this as an easier run. It is shorter, and we had a long drive back to Edmonton! I did want to complete this run as I had mixed reports about the former weir on this reach. We began the paddle in a thundershower, and me without rain gear! We worked our way through the logjams in the first stretch. This stretch, from above our Highway 6 start, and for the first 7 or 8 km is also depositional for debris collected upstream, and there are many logjams and sweepers that one must remain alert for. The channels have changed somewhat from what the map shows, and the weir has been removed and replaced with a channel side headworks on the right bank. It now presents no danger as long as one passes on the left, or the far side of the river from it. This headworks provides water for Payne Lake (spelled Paine on the topo!). The last three kilometers or so provides some real excitement. The floods of the mid '90s have really scoured three or four of the last drops, and at least two of them are quite challenging! I'm certain that these two runs will hold most paddlers attention, at most water levels. At above normal flows, this river, like most, can become downright dangerous.

At the Highway #6 access, the left bank, both above, and below the bridge for 4 km, is the boundary for the Blood Indian Reserve (#148a).

Not far below Highway #5

Other Reaches

Paddlers camping at the Belly River Campground in Waterton Park may choose to paddle right out of the campground. This will add approximately 2.5 km. Like the first stretch below the Highway #6 Bridge, watch out for logjams and sweepers.

There are many more kilometers of paddling on the Belly below Highway #800. It is approximately 31 kilometers to Highway #505. Beware of the entry of the canal from the Waterton reservoir approximately 20 kms downstream, and then the impoundment and dam. The recommended portage is on the left shore. Other authors have rated this run as a Grade 2 run with rapids to Class II+.

Other Local Activities or Destinations

This is southern Alberta, everything is close. If it is not a good day for paddling: consider the drive east to the Remington Carriage Museum in Cardston, or the day hiking to the west in Waterton National Park, or even just the tourist drive south into Montana, and Glacier National Park (remember your passport!).

Waterton River

Waterton Lakes to the bridge east of Twin Butte

"the Bump" at 40 cms, July 1, 2006

Why Go
I've been down to paddle this run about four times and each time I have been impressed with the clear water, the open prairie scenes, the mountains views and the fun whitewater.

Duration of Tour(s)
* 28.1 km
* 1 day

Classification
1. Rapids: to Class III-
2. Skill of Paddlers: intermediate river paddlers

Starts
The primary start for this run is in Waterton Lakes National Park, at the Picnic site just across the river from the park gatehouse. Use the picnic site on the south side of the river, west of the highway #6. Paddlers camped at Waterton Riverside Campground, 5.6 km downstream may start there.

Finish
This run finishes at the bridge just upstream of the Waterton Reservoir, and approximately 13 kilometers east of Twin Butte.

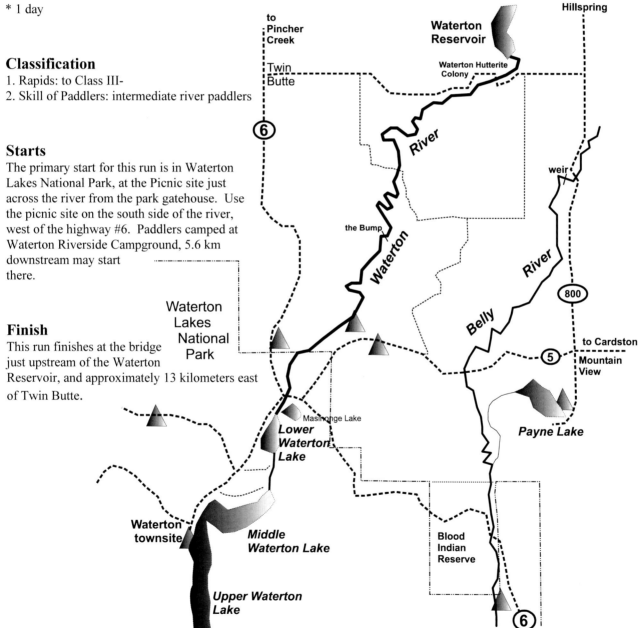

Intermediate Access and Distances

Location	Elevation ft	km down	km up	km between	Access / Bank or Rapid / Class	MGRS datum NAD 1983 Zone 12U	Gradient m/km
Highway #5/6 Bridge		28.1	0		right bank above bridge, in picnic site	TV 927 437	
Waterton Riverside Camground		22.5	5.6	5.6	right bank	TV 959 480	
	4100	16.4	11.7				2.3
Old Bridge Shoderee Ranch		10.5	17.6	12		TV 992 564	
	4000	6.2	21.9				3.0
	31950	3.3	24.8				5.3
						NAD 1927	
Bridge - E. Of Twin Butte		0	28.1	10.5	right bank, above bridge	UV 045 595	
	3900		28.5				4.1

Gradient

Gradients range from approximately 2.3 m/km to as much as 5.3 m/km. The reach starts gently, and then picks up after about kilometer ten. At approximately kilometre twelve, or a sharp left hand bend there is the one drop on this reach, *The Bump*, that may go Class III- at some levels. Below this rapid the river flows much swifter with many fun Class I to II+ rapids, that are composed of partial ledges, gravel bar chutes and boulder gardens.

River Volume and Flow Rate

On the July long weekend 2000, Ceyana paddlers had a very fun paddle at 36 cms, and two weeks later the local Pincher Creek group reported a good paddle at 23 cms. Canada Day weekend 2006 we were back with the river flowing at 40 cms – the waves were even bigger! The paddling was still great, even for our less experienced paddlers who were in our party. Normal summer flows range from less than 10 cms to more than 100 cms, and floods have exceeded 650 cms! At the hydro station near the park gates this river flows at 2 km/hr with approximately 20 cms, and up to 7 km/hr with 300 cms.

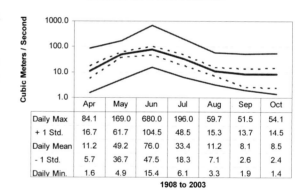

Waterton River near Park Gate

	Apr	May	Jun	Jul	Aug	Sep	Oct
Daily Max	84.1	169.0	680.0	196.0	59.7	51.5	54.1
+ 1 Std.	16.7	61.7	104.5	48.5	15.3	13.7	14.5
Daily Mean	11.2	49.2	76.0	33.4	11.2	8.1	8.5
- 1 Std.	5.7	36.7	47.5	18.3	7.1	2.6	2.4
Daily Min.	1.6	4.9	15.4	6.1	3.3	1.9	1.4

1908 to 2003

Maps

1 - 1:50,000 NTS:
  Waterton Lakes 82 H/4 3rd edition, with 1983 datum
  Pincher Creek 82 H/5 2nd edition, with 1927 datum
2 - 1:125,000:
  Adventure Guide and Topographic Map of Southwest Alberta, available from Southwest Alberta Business Development Centre and many book and map sellers in southern Alberta

Camping

Numerous public and commercial campgrounds are available in the area. Waterton Riverside has been a natural first choice as it is right on the river. I've had troubles in August 2009 confirming that this campground is still in operation. Crooked Creek (403.653.1100) is just up the hill from Riverside and Payne Lake is south of #5 near Mountain View. The Waterton Park campsites (403.859.2224) either in the townsite or at Crandell are good alternatives but they are popular and often very hard to get into.

Trip Notes

This is another wonderful southern Alberta river for late spring and early summer paddling. This run should appeal to those that like clear flowing water, mountain vistas, and many playful rapids. The Ceyana Canoe Club group that ran the river in early July 2000, consisted of five canoes, the Paton parents each taking a young daughter on their first trip with full bow paddler responsibilities, one member trying out a new solo canoe, and a couple of canoes of "old dogs." The day started almost clear and quite sunny. By early afternoon thunder showers threatened, but they held off until we were loading the canoes at the end. Waterton Lakes National Park advertises itself as "where the prairies meet the mountain," and these open prairies allow wonderful vistas back to the Rocky Mountains.

The first eleven kilometers or so are relatively flat with few hazards. Then, at approximately kilometer 12 from the Park (TV 982 521), the river makes a sharp right turn over a small ledge and into a short boulder garden. At 36 cms this Class II+ rapid appears mostly as a chute, at 23 cms the Pincher Creek group reported it as a 70 cm ledge. This rapid marks the transition from a lazy paddle to a fun paddle at most normal water levels. From here on, almost every corner provides a broken ledge, a steep gravel chute, or boulder garden to keep paddlers on their toes. In July 2000 we had one swim on the river, and the Pincher Creek group reported one "canoe wrapped boulder" on their run. This river does require experience and paddling skill, but it is not as difficult as the Belly, its sister stream just over the hill.

The Pincher Creek group paddled this run in the late afternoon and early evening and reported seeing a herd of elk, and a young grizzly bear crossing the old bailey bridge just before kilometer 18. On our Ceyana Canoe Club, mid-day runs, we have always seen a number of eagles, osprey and great blue herons along the river. In 2006 Lois and I got a little behind the others, near the above noted bridge, and when we caught up the others asked if we had seen the grizzly that had stood up to check us out. We had not, and it maybe best we didn't as we had passed within 20 m or so!

Other Reaches

Above this run are the Waterton lakes, reported on previously in this guide. Immediately below this run is the Waterton reservoir. There is a campsite on the west side of the dam, and road access is available to below the dam. There are some 28 km of paddling below the dam (Highway #505 crosses the dam) to Highway #810 north and east of Glenwood. This run has been rated as Grade 2 with rapids to Class II+ by other authors. There may also be a small weir or water diversion in the last few kilometers before #810.

Other Local Activities or Destinations

If you end up in camp suffering a heavy monsoon, and nobody wants to paddle, especially the kids and dog, there are some wonderful local alternatives! The Reynolds Carriage Museum in Cardston, is just 40 kms east of the park gates. This museum is well worth most of a day -- don't plan of blowing through it in a hour or so. To the west is Waterton Lakes National Park, with many scenic day and part-day hikes, including a very nice evening walk at Red Rock Canyon.

Looking back to the mountains, July 2006

Castle River

Castle Falls to Highway #3a

Why Go
Great whitewater day runs with some fine public campsites from which to base one's day trips!

Duration of Tour(s)
* 34.5 km
* ½ day to 2 day tours are possible, though this is usually a white water play stream, and done in short, one-day or half-day runs.

Classification
1. Rapids: Class I to IV
2. Skill of Paddlers: Intermediate River closed boat paddlers, Skilled River paddlers in open canoes. The rodeo grounds to Canyon Bridge makes a good training run at modest flows. The Falls & Canyon runs should be run by Skilled Paddlers only , or lesser paddlers with very good leadership and support groups.

Surfing immediately below Canyon Bridge

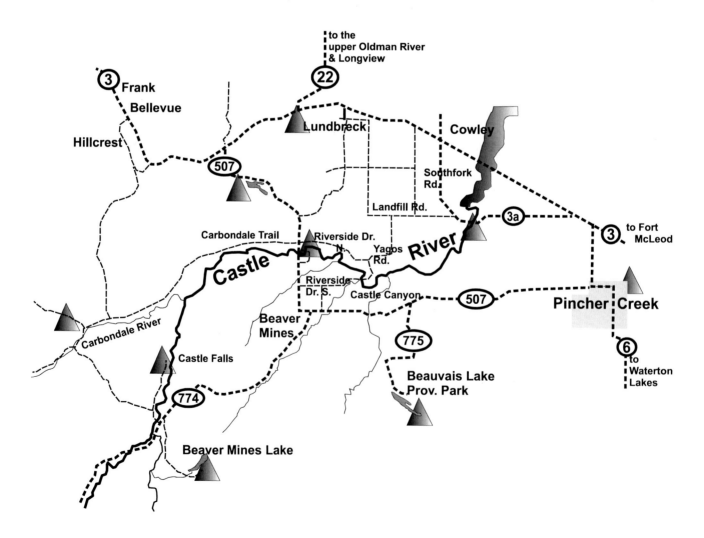

Starts

Each of the access points listed below provides an excellent start for a ½ to full day's paddling for playing and learning.

Castle Falls Campground is accessed by taking secondary highway #774 south from Beaver Mines. Just before crossing the Castle River, turn right (west) onto the forestry road, stay right at the next intersection and follow the signs into the campground. Access to the river is just beyond Castle Falls on river left.

The #507 bridge access is north of Beaver mines. At the top of the south bank, take the Rodeo/Campground access road. east of #507 and follow it down into the valley. The access to the river is just beyond the Rodeo & Campground gate.

Canyon Bridge is reached from either Riverside Road North, or Riverside Road South. Riverside Road South leaves #507 less than 2 km south of the Castle River Bridge. To reach Riverside Rd North, head west from the Castle River Campground on #3a (also called South Fork Road), turn left onto Landfill Rd at the top of the hill, then the next left, south onto Yagos Road, and finally left on to Riverside Road North and follow this road along the ridge and then down to the river.

Finish

The finish for this run is usually in the Castle River Campground, just above the #3a bridge. #3a maybe accessed either just west of Pincher Station, or right in Cowley, off of #3 -- the Crowsnest Highway. Castle River Campground is on river right and about half way between Cowley and Pincher Station, about 5-8 minutes either way!

Intermediate Access and Distances

Location	Elevation ft	km down	km up	km between	Access / Bank or Rapids / Class	MGRS datum NAD 1927 Zone 11U	Gradient m/km
	4300		-2.5				
Castle Falls			-0.1			PE 942 800	
Access below Falls		34.5	0		left bank		
Dave's Delight		33.3	1.2		Class III to III+		
	4200	32.7	1.8				7.1
Carbondale River		30.9	3.6		left bank	PE 948 830	
	4100	28.3	6.2				6.9
Switchback		24.2	10.3			PE 989 867	
	4000	22.1	12.4				4.9
#507 Bridge		19.2	15.3	15.3	below bridge, on river right, just beyond the access to the rodeo grounds and in the campground	QE 030 868	
	3900	12.9	21.6				3.3
Canyon Bridge		12.5	22		either side	QE 070 851	
	3800	6.9	27.6				5.1
#3a Bridge		0	34.5	19.2	right or left, campground is on river right just above the bridge	QE 147 894	
	3700		34.6				4.4

Gradient

Gradients for these runs range 3.3 to 7.1 meters per kilometre. The most difficult run, the Castle Canyon does not actually have the highest gradient stretch. The highest gradient is found on the next most difficult run here, the run below Castle Falls. The run from #507 to the Canyon Bridge has the lowest gradient.

River Volume and Flow Rate

Good paddling on the Castle can be had from as little as 20 cms to as much or more than 80 cms. In May '00 our Ceyana open canoe paddlers tackled the Canyon run at 43 cms and were able to find beaches for scouting and portaging. Much more water and these beaches would have been gone, and the hydraulics even more fearsome. The next day we ran from the Rodeo Grounds to Canyon bridge at 60 cms and it was a fun run that any paddler with basic river skills would have enjoyed.

This river has been known to exceed 550 cms, and in the '95 flood took out the Canyon Bridge – it used to be called the blue bridge and remains of it can be seen below the canyon! Rood & Tymesen (2001) report that most authors consider 15-20 cms about minimal flow for the Castle river for paddling. Flow velocities vary from approximately 2 km/hr at 15 cms to 8 km/hr at 240 cms at the station "near Beaver Mines."

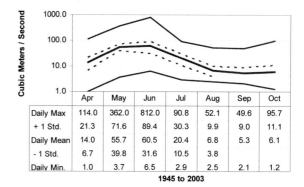

Castle River near Beaver Mines

	Apr	May	Jun	Jul	Aug	Sep	Oct
Daily Max	114.0	362.0	812.0	90.8	52.1	49.6	95.7
+ 1 Std.	21.3	71.6	89.4	30.3	9.9	9.0	11.1
Daily Mean	14.0	55.7	60.5	20.4	6.8	5.3	6.1
- 1 Std.	6.7	39.8	31.6	10.5	3.8		
Daily Min.	1.0	3.7	6.5	2.9	2.5	2.1	1.2

1945 to 2003

Maps

1. 1:125,000: *Adventure Guide and Topographic Map of Southwest Alberta*, available from Southwest Alberta Business Development Centre

2. 1:50,000 NTS: 82G/8 *Beaver Mines* and 82 G/9 *Blairmore*

I usually keep the *Adventure Guide* in the car and take the topo sheets with me on the river on these runs.

Camping

There are three campgrounds on the river, Castle Falls, at the Rodeo Grounds and Castle River on highway #3a. There are also nice lakeside campgrounds nearby at Beaver Mines Lake, and Beauvais Lake Provincial Park.

Trip Notes

This is a river that has earned the respect of most Alberta paddlers. In 1980, Buhrmann and Young in their guide, *Canoeing Chinook Country Rivers* reported that the Castle *... is probably the most challenging canoeable river in southern Alberta.* We Ceyana paddlers on our infrequent trips south, have far more often than not had the Castle remind us of our limitations.

The run below Castle Falls campground begins with bang. A class III rock garden, Dave's Delight (a ledge) at III to III+, and then at least another four named drops before the Carbondale river joins from the left side at km 3.6. Two of these ledges are often rated as Class IV drops. Below the Carbondale the Castle eases off, with Switchback (class II + to III) about ½ way along to highway #507 as the last named drop.

The Rodeo Ground run is an instructors delight, it starts easy, and the best rapids are just above the finish. At some water levels these final ledges may earn a class II+ to III- rating, and the run has a number of other class I to easy II rapids.

In 1980 Buhrmann and Young wrote that the canyon run was for experts in groups, or those with a "suicidal desire." Paddling has progressed a good deal in these last two plus decades, but for open canoeists this is still a very difficult run that should only be tackled at optimum water levels (see note above). One of my old paddling partners was on the river the same week as I in May, 2000, with a large and a well-supported group of relative novice teenage kayak paddlers. They suffered numerous swims, but no incidents. They ran the canyon at both 43 and 60 cms over the weekend. Yes, the river came up a lot overnight!

All of the real excitement in the canyon occurs after you are about 500 m into it, and then until about 2 km below the bridge. In May 2000, we open canoeists chose to run the first good drop, but then we lined and portaged two drops, and ran the last drop. Our fear was that a swim in either of the middle two drops meant a sure swim over the last drop. This last drop has a well earned reputation for "squirrely" hydraulics which we did not want to swim into and through -- if through is even possible. We found that it was quite easy to line up in the pool before the last drop so as to take the correct chute and miss the hydraulics. As mentioned above, I strongly suspect that with much more than 43 cms, there would be no eddy beaches, and scouting, lining and portaging these middle ledges would be virtually impossible. This is a reach that many a wise paddler, myself included, has "passed on" because the river was not at an OPTIMAL level.

Below the canyon the river's challenges ease off, but do not disappear. A number of broken ledges and some fast gravelly chutes make for some fun places to play! In 2000 one of our crews survived the canyon, only to let one of these easier drops remind them that in May the water is still cold!

Other Reaches
Above the falls there is 7.4 km of relatively easy paddling from the Highway #774 bridge, with no rapid rated more than class II+. Below the Castle River Campground the river flows for about two more bends, and then at most times of the year you are onto the reservoir. Prior to the construction of the dam, this was a most scenic run, with large cliffs, many fine cottonwood stands, and a number of fun gravelly chutes.

Other Local Activities or Destinations
If caught by an ugly day, or by partners that are just not keen, consider a trip to Waterton Lakes, just a short hour to the south, the Frank Slide Interpretative Center 40 minutes to the west, or the Head Smashed In Buffalo Jump Interpretative Center, 30 minutes to the north and east . There are short hiking trails at Beauvais Lake, and longer hikes out of Beaver Mines lake.

A near swim at bottom of first drop in the Canyon!

Looking over the middle ledge in canyon,
note paddler just over the drop, May 2000 at 43 cms!

Crowsnest River

Bellevue - Hillcrest
to the Oldman River Reservoir

Why Go
More good foothills whitewater that is appropriate for the developing paddler. Great training & teaching runs, with some interesting bits for the "old dogs."

Duration of Tour(s)
* 30.8 km
* ½ days to a 2 day tour are possible, but the "Crow" is a play stream for whitewater paddlers, who generally take short runs and "mess about"!

Classification
1. Rapids: to Class III - and Lundbreck Falls
2. Skill of Paddlers: Intermediate River Paddlers if in open canoe, or Novice River Paddlers in either closed boats or open canoes with good leadership. This is a fine teaching river at most average to below average flows.

Surfing a broken ledge on the lower run.
May, 2000

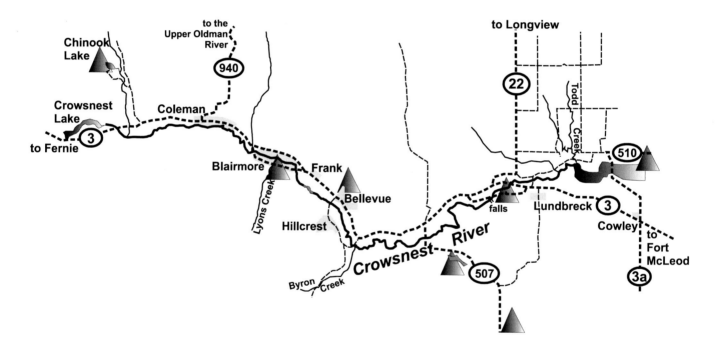

Starts
The start for the most upper reach included this report may be approached by taking the Crowsnest Highway (#3) into Bellevue, and then turning SW and taking the road to Hillcrest.

For the more popular run, the "Falls run," start at the Lundbreck Campsite. For this run follow the signs off of Highway #3, between Lundbreck and the Highway #22 intersection.

Finish

The finish for the lower reach is gained by taking the road north off of Highway #3 between Lundbreck and Lundbreck Falls access roads. This road almost immediately crosses the Crowsnest, and then strikes a "T" intersection, the west fork will take you out to Highway #22, and the east fork follows the Crowsnest down to the Reservoir. Todd Creek Picinic site is at the "top" of the reservoir.

Intermediate Access and Distances

Location	Elevation ft	km down	km up	km between	Access / Bank or Rapids / Class	MGRS datum NAD 1927 Zone 11U	Gradients m/km
Bellevue - Hillcrest Bridge	4100	30.8	0		left bank	PE 898 949	
Bridge near Byron Creek		26.2	4.6	4.6		PE 919 918	
	4000	25	5.8				5.3
		21.6	9.2		cut off meander bend		
	3900	19	11.8				5.1
old Burmis Bridge site		18.5	12.3				
#507 Bridge		18.1	12.7	8.1	access on river left, off of local road upstream of bridge	PE 968 925	
Railway Bridge just above Lundbreck Falls		8.1	22.7	10		QE 017 955	
	3800	8.05	22.8				2.8
Lundbreck Falls		8	22.8		Begin the portage on right bank just above the railway bridge, follow the road across the tracks and down to the campground.		
Lundbreck Falls Campground		7.8	23		River access from walk-in camp site parking lot right bank	QE 020 959	
Bridge NW of Lundbreck		4.5	26.3	3.3	either bank	QE 045 970	
	3700	4	26.8				4.6
Todd Creek Picnic Site		0	30.8	4.5	left bank	QE 078 983	

Gradient

Gradients for these reaches vary from 5.3 m/km for the top reach to 2.8 m/km for the long lazy run above the falls. The gradient of 4.6 m/km for the run below the falls takes into account much of the reported 12 m height of Lundbreck Falls.

River Volume and Flow Rate

In May '00 we paddled the run below the falls at a most pleasant flow of 9.6 cms. Local paddlers report that this river is enjoyable at as little as 6 cms. In 2006 we were back again and paddled "the Crow" with flows in the 18 to 22 cms range – it was much more exciting. On the run below the falls, it was all we could handle in open canoes! Like any river, when normal flows are greatly exceeded this river becomes very dangerous, and given the constricted nature of much of the of "the Crow" in many places, the hydraulics must be particularly awesome! The maximum flows reported for 1910 to 2003 exceed 90 cms.

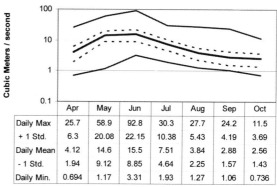

Crowsnest River at Frank

	Apr	May	Jun	Jul	Aug	Sep	Oct
Daily Max	25.7	58.9	92.8	30.3	27.7	24.2	11.5
+ 1 Std.	6.3	20.08	22.15	10.38	5.43	4.19	3.69
Daily Mean	4.12	14.6	15.5	7.51	3.84	2.88	2.56
- 1 Std.	1.94	9.12	8.85	4.64	2.25	1.57	1.43
Daily Min.	0.694	1.17	3.31	1.93	1.27	1.06	0.736

1910 to 2003

Maps

1 - 1:125,000: *Adventure Guide and Topographic Map of Southwest Alberta*, available from Southwest Alberta Business Development Centre
2 - 1:50,000 NTS: 82 G/9 *Blairmore*

Camping

The campground at Lundbreck Falls (403.563.5395) offers some very nice drive-in sites, and a number of walk-in sites. It can be a little noisy given the falls are just upstream, and the campsite is situated between the Crowsnest Highway and the railway. Ceyana paddlers often camp over on the Castle river, and make the short drive over the hill to paddle the Crow'! We have also camped at Cottonwood Campground (403.382.4097) on the Oldman just below the dam, or even up at Beauvais Lake Provincial Park (403.627.2021) – all are nice campsites, and for those used to northern Alberta distances, the drives are all short!

Trip Notes

The "Crow" is a pretty little river. Given the lakes in its headwaters the water most often runs clear. At normal flows the Crow' does not generate fearsome horsepower, and these are all easily run.

Below Bellevue, and on the first couple of reaches, the greatest dangers are the occasional log jams and sweepers. Some years ago, on a Ceyana trip, one log jam above Byron Creek had the river completely blocked. Depending on water levels one will encounter numerous Class I and easy Class II rapids on the run down to Lundbreck Falls. As you approach Lundbreck Falls, beware. There is a series of broken ledges above the falls that extends to the railway bridge. It is probably best to leave these be, and make for shore and the start of the portage. The portage can be easily made along the road on the right bank.

Below Lundbreck Falls is probably the favorite "play" run on the Crow'. Immediately below the campground is Lundbreck rapid, a series of ledges and broken ledges that can go Class III at higher water levels. Just down a bit, is fun chute with a couple of good surfing waves. Then there are a number of Class I and easy Class II rapids all the way to the final take out. In addition to the challenges of mother nature, "the Crow" has seen extensive fishery mitigation and there are many wonderful "wing dams" that make great eddies for practice. The only negative consideration though is all the fly fishermen – on a good day – one fisherman per eddy. Do try to leave their lines alone and graciously share the river. We paddlers can usually reach a greater variety of eddies and play spots than any one fisherman can in a day. But, you must promise to not teach them how to paddle!

Other Local Activities or Destinations

If caught by an ugly day, or cranky kids that are just not keen to paddle: consider a trip to Waterton Lakes just an hour to the south, the Frank Slide Interpretative Center twenty minutes to the west, or the Head Smashed In Buffalo Jump Interpretative Center forty minutes to the north and east. There are short hiking trails at Beauvais Lake and Allison Lake, and longer hikes are possible out of Beaver Mines lake.

Other Reaches

It is possible to paddle the Crowsnest above Bellevue. The primary hazard is the Frank Slide which has created some very significant rapids in "the Crow." Buhrmann and Young (1980) graded the Cascades as Class V & VI, and Smith (1995) has rated the lower and more difficult of the two drops as IV+ to -V, and the upper at IV.

In May 2006 we Ceyana paddlers tackled the run from Crowsnest Lake down to Frank – literally to the hydrology station near the water treatment plant. It was a mix of some very pleasant paddling, one reach full of log jams and sweepers, one double ledge near the west end of Coleman that we portaged, and then a sluice through Blairmore that took all the skill our group had, and at 20+ cms, the very limit for open canoes. The pictures below are from this paddle.

Logjams and sweepers not far below Crowsnest Lake, May 2006

Double ledge near the west side of Coleman,
note the log stuck in the centre and above the second ledge,
May 2006

Oldman River

Oldman River Campsite
to the Oldman River Reservoir

Why Go
Spring and early summer whitewater! Great day trips on whitewater with the Livingstone Range, the Whaleback, and the Porcupine Hills as scenic backdrops.

above Olin Creek

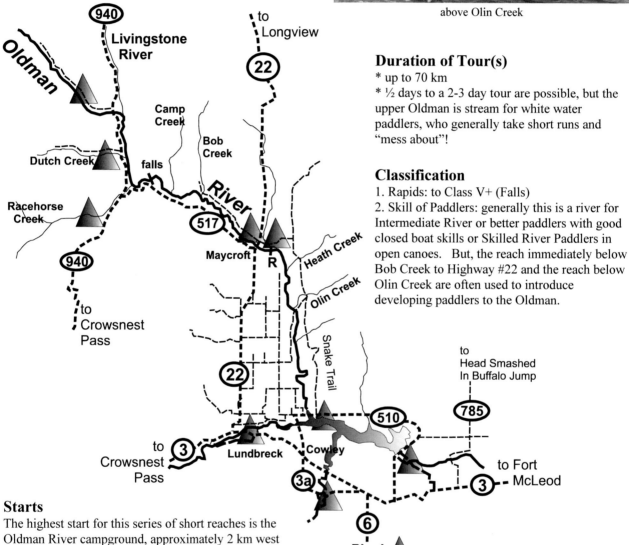

Duration of Tour(s)
* up to 70 km
* ½ days to a 2-3 day tour are possible, but the upper Oldman is stream for white water paddlers, who generally take short runs and "mess about"!

Classification
1. Rapids: to Class V+ (Falls)
2. Skill of Paddlers: generally this is a river for Intermediate River or better paddlers with good closed boat skills or Skilled River Paddlers in open canoes. But, the reach immediately below Bob Creek to Highway #22 and the reach below Olin Creek are often used to introduce developing paddlers to the Oldman.

Starts
The highest start for this series of short reaches is the Oldman River campground, approximately 2 km west of the Forestry Trunk Road (Highway #940) crossing of the river. Other common starts include: the Dutch Creek Meadows, in the Gap along Highway #517, Bob Creek on the north side access road, at Highway #22, at Waldron Flats/Falls/Campground, and finally the lowest start is at the Olin Creek Bridge.

Finish
The lowest finish for this reach is on the Oldman River reservoir, at the North Fork picnic site just below the Highway #510 bridge which passes over the Oldman reach of the reservoir. In May 2002, this access point was "back on" flowing water as the three years of drought had dropped the reservoir over 60 feet and left considerable mud flats for paddlers to cross.

Intermediate Access and Distances

Location	Elevation	km down	km up	km between	Access / Bank or Rapids / Class	MGRS datum	Gradients m/km
	feet					NAD 1927 Zone 11U	
	5000		-2.2				
Oldman River Campsite		70.0	0.0		left bank	PF 838 358	
	4900	68.9	1.1				9.2
FTR Bridge		67.8	2.2			PF 858 360	
	4800	66.2	3.8				11.3
Livingstone River Confluence		65.4	4.6		left bank	PF 872 351	
	4700	61.9	8.1				7.1
Dutch Creek meadow - access		61.2	8.8		right bank		
Dutch Creek		59.6	10.4	10.4	right bank	PF880 303	
	4600	57.3	12.7				6.6
Race Horse Creek		55.8	14.2		right bank	PF 889 270	
	4500	52.8	17.2				6.8
Oldman Falls		52.5	17.5	7.1	Recommended portage is on river right.	PF 908 277	
	4400	49.6	20.4				9.5
Camp Creek		48.2	21.8		left bank	PF 937 263	
Ernst Creek		47.5	22.5		right bank	PF 941 260	
	4300	43.4	26.6				4.9
Bob Creek		43.1	26.9	9.4	left bank	PF 976 261	
	4250	40.8	29.2				5.9
Coyote Creek		40.4	29.6		left bank	PF 992 253	
Eagle Coulee		39.1	30.9		left bank	PF 999 247	
	4200	37.4	32.6				5.1
Tetley Creek		33.7	36.3		right bank	QF 026 216	
	4150	32.8	37.2				3.3
	4100	30.5	39.5				4.8
#22 Bridge & Campsite		29.6	40.4	13.5	left bank	QF 051 199	
Waldron Falls - Access & Campsite		28.0	42.0	1.6	left bank	QF 065 196	
	4150	27.6	42.4				5.3
Callum Creek		26.8	43.2		left bank	QF 077 196	
	4000	26.3	43.7				11.7
Heath Creek		23.4	46.6		left bank	QF 088 167	
Edge of Map 82 G/16-82 G/9		20.8	49.2				
Olin Creek		18.2	51.8		left bank	QF 094 125	
Olin Creek or North Fork Bridge		17.3	52.7	10.7	right bank, above bridge	QF 101 123	
	3900	14.4	55.6				8.0
Cabin Creek		12.7	57.3			QF 104 085	
	3800	11.1	58.9				9.2
	3700	5.4	64.6				4.2
North Fork Picnic & Reservoir Access Site just below #510 Bridge		0.0	70.0	18.2	right bank, about 200 m below the bridge	QF 124 990	

Gradient

Gradients vary from as little as 3.3 m/km to over 11 m/km. This river well reflects that it is the interaction of bedrock and gradient, not just gradient alone that determines the difficulty of rapids. Maycroft Rapids and Waldron Falls are not on the highest gradient reach.

River Volume and Flow Rate

I've paddled these runs at various levels, and have had some fine runs with water levels in the 25 to 60 cms range. The June moonsoon when combined with late snow melts have taken the river to over 290 cms at Waldron's Corner. Flow rates at the gauge are reported as approximately 3 km/hr at 30 cms to over 8 km/hr at 150 cms.

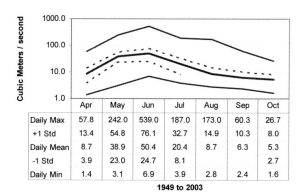

Oldman River near Waldron's Corner

	Apr	May	Jun	Jul	Aug	Sep	Oct
Daily Max	57.8	242.0	539.0	187.0	173.0	60.3	26.7
+1 Std	13.4	54.8	76.1	32.7	14.9	10.3	8.0
Daily Mean	8.7	38.9	50.4	20.4	8.7	6.3	5.3
-1 Std	3.9	23.0	24.7	8.1			2.7
Daily Min	1.4	3.1	6.9	3.9	2.8	2.4	1.6

1949 to 2003

Maps

1 - 1:125,000: *Adventure Guide and Topographic Map of Southwest Alberta*, available from Southwest Alberta Business Development Centre
2 - 1:50,000 NTS: 82G/16 Maycroft and 82G/9 Blairmore

On this run I generally carry both the NTS sheets and the *Adventure Guide* map noted above.

Camping

Most paddlers on these runs "car camp" and stay at one of the many public campgrounds. A favorite some years ago with the Ceyana paddlers was the Dutch Creek campground (403.563.5395). Some years we were even able to paddle Dutch creek down to the Oldman. On another trip when the kids were younger we stayed at Beauvais Lake Provincial Park (403.627.2021) for all the amenities and park based activities. On yet another more recent trip we stayed at the Cottonwood Campground (403.382.4097) just below the Three Rivers Dam. Other campgrounds include the Oldman River Campground at the top of this reach, Racehorse Creek just off the Gap reach, and the rather barren sites at Highway #22 and Waldron Flats. These reaches are difficult enough that I know of no paddlers that "trip" on these reaches and canoe camp. Once below Camp Creek, virtually all the lands are deeded, are cattle pasture, and do not provide great wilderness campsites.

Trip Notes

This is a great Alberta whitewater stream! Over all of these reaches seams of bedrock are exposed often forming river wide ledges and complex rapids. In the Gap large boulders add to the excitement and scenic beauty. At numerous spots the river drops into low short canyons, and in the Gap between Racehorse creek and Oldman Falls the river breaks through the Livingstone range. Thunder Mountain to the south towers nearly 1000m above the river.

When in the Three Rivers region, it helps to remember that oldtimers and many of the local roads are based on reference to the presently named Oldman as the "North Fork", the Crowsnest River as the "West Fork" and the Castle River as the "South Fork" of the Oldman River.

When I returned to these reaches after the flood of 1995, an old friend warned us that the floods had scoured the ledges, had scoured new ledges were there were none before, and in some very few spots filled in rapids. This happened again in the floods of 2005. Rapids do come an go over the years due to floods and other erosional changes.

Oldman River Campground to the Gap: The run from the campground to the Livingstone River offers pretty steady excitement. The most complex drops (class III to III+) are in the short reach from just above the FTR bridge to the Livingstone River. From the Livingstone to the Gap the river eases off a bit, as the gradients suggests, though a number of gravel chutes and small ledges will keep you awake.

Some years ago we had memorable experience in the Gap. It was windy! We in fact had pulled off the river and had tied our canoes to the biggest logs we could find. A second party came along and in the modest gravel chute opposite our landing one open canoe was blown over, and the second uncontrollably blown downstream. Fortunately the wind was with the throw-bag tosses, and the upset canoe and paddlers were quickly rescued. And then the wind died down!

Gap to Highway #22: In the Gap the river turns from an easterly run to a northerly run, and finally turns east again in the lead-up to Oldman Falls. Good rapids (III to III+) with a combination of boulders and ledges will be found on the run-up to the Falls. Forewarning for the falls comes in the form of a mid-stream island, and a small sharp ridge just south of the river. The falls and the ridge share the same rock formation. The falls are usually accessed and portaged from the right (south) shore. At low flows you may be able to run, or sneak the "approach" ledges to the falls and slide your boat over the big ledge at the falls. At higher flows start your portage above these ledges. I've always thought of the Oldman Falls as a rather "an ugly drop" as there is a band of rock that runs across, breaks the falls and would trap a paddler or swimmer. Almost immediately below the falls there are two or three good ledges, and then about 1 km below the Falls comes Cave Rapids, a significant ledge. The river eases off for a couple of kilometers, and then a series of rapids occur including "Submarine" and "the Gorge" as the river works it way around the next ridge to join Camp Creek. Rosie's Roll a class III to III+ rapid occurs about ½ way between Camp and Bob Creeks. Again the river eases off a bit, but don't get sleepy, there is action on almost every corner. In 1999 just below the Powerline crossing we canoeists all slid our craft around one ledge, though one of our kayakers did run it without incident. This run finishes with a nice II+ rapid immediately above the takeout.

Waldron Falls, July 1999, at 24 cms

Highway #22 to Waldron Falls and Maycroft Rapids: I've scouted most of this nearly 2 kilometers but have never paddled them. TOO many ledges, ending in TOO big a ledge, and TOO short a paddle, these are my excuses for not having run these 2 km! I would encourage all paddlers to scout this run throughly before attempting, many of the ledges go Class III+, and depending on water levels Waldron Falls is rated between Class IV to V.

Waldron Falls to Oldman River Reservoir: This 28 km reach can be accessed at Olin Creek Bridge, approximately 10 km down. I used to think of these two reaches as the easier runs, but, after the '95 flood the ledges are bigger and more numerous than before. This run will keep the average intermediate paddler awake. Modern play boaters may find more flat water than they really like between the drops. Between the put-in below the falls, and Callum Creek there are a number of partial ledges, and at times one large, nearly stream wide ledge just above Callum Creek that has been rated as Class III+. In 2004 we found that this ledge had been pretty much bypassed by the floods of '03. Once past Callum Creek, the significant rapids are all rated Class II to III. Just above the reservoir the river flows through a small canyon and the meanders are quite convoluted. This canyon provides the last real excitement before the reservoir.

Other Reaches
Above the Oldman River Campground there are a couple of runs that have been paddled, and one more waterfall. The rapids from Shale creek to the campground have been reported as Class II to III+ and this run is just over 7 km.

The reservoir may be best left to the sailboarders! Below the dam is an artificial slalom site, that at some water levels can provide a pleasant afternoons diversion. In early July 1999 with the dam releasing 90+ cms we found that we were just flushed through this site. At 90 cms the wave train (Class II) just above Cottonwood Campground and below the bridge provided some good excitement for our new and young paddlers. There is a further short run below Cottonwood Campground to the next bridge with no significant rapids reported.

Other Local Activities or Destinations

This Three Rivers region provides a wealth of other activities and sites to visit. When we Ceyana Paddlers head down here for a number of days we just about always take some time to hike or visit. Bob Creek provides access to some very fine hiking along the ridges west of the Whaleback, and access to the Whaleback ridge itself. Just to the east is the Head Smashed In Buffalo Jump Interpretative center, a UNESCO World Heritage site. To the west is the Crowsnest Pass with historic Frank Slide and the Hillcrest mine. If you have the fly fishing bug, on a good day you will find at least one peer in each eddy on the 'Crow and lower Castle.

Maycroft Rapid in flood - early June 1972
(photo by Eric Solomonson)

Oldman River

Fort McLeod to Grand Forks

Why Go
Prairie vistas, easy, leisurely paddling, spectacular bluffs, the opportunity view hawks, eagles and other game are all reasons to paddle the lower Oldman River.

Duration of Tour(s)
* 258 km
* ½, 1 Day and up to 7 Day tours are all possible.

Boat launch below the Lethbridge weir, looking downstream to the "High Level" Bridge, Aug. '99

Classification
1. Rapids: Class I to II+ with at least one working weir, and one former weir
2. Skill of Paddlers: Novice River Paddlers at below average flows; Intermediate River, or Novice River with good leadership at average to above average flows.

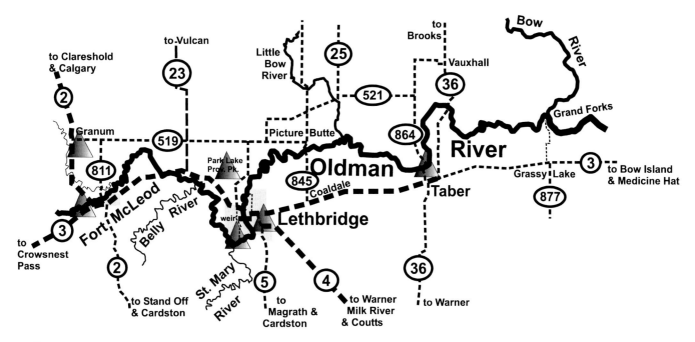

Start
At the former Highway #2 Campground just west of Fort McLeod, river right, just upstream of the highway #2 Bridge.

Finish
At the "Grand Forks" the confluence of the Oldman and Bow rivers, approximately 14 km north of Grassy Lake on Range Roads 133 and 132 (there is a "correction line along the way, jog east at it).

Intermediate Access and Distances

Location	Elevation meters	Km down	Km up	Km between	Access / Bank or Rapid / Class	MGRS datum NAD 1983 Zone 12 U	Gradient m/km
	945		-1				
Fort McLeod #2 Campground		258	0		right bank	UA 231 103	
Highway #2		258	0				
old weir/concrete slab?		255	3		Class I to II	UA 255 108	
	937	255	3				2.2
Highway # 811		254	5			UA 271 115	
start McLeod Island		253	5				
	930	247	11				0.8
Willow Creek		246	12		left bank	UA 296 153	
	922	243	15				2.3
	914	232	26				0.7
	907	228	30				1.9
Partial ledge		225	33		Class II to II+	UA 374 244	
Rnge Rd 250		224	34		right bank		
	899	220	38				1.0
CPR RR bridge		218	40				
	892	213	45				1.0
	884	210	48				2.8
Highway #3a Bridge		209	49	49	right bank	UA 472 175	
Highway #3 bridge		208	50				
	876	201	57				0.9
Belly river		200	58		right bank		
	869	197	62				1.6
Highway # 509		194	64	15		UA 559 127	
	860	192	66				1.9
	850	182	76				1.0
	840	174	84				1.3
St. Mary River		169	90		right bank		
start Popson Park		166	92		left bank		
	830	165	93				1.1
Popson Park - boat launch, key may be required		165	93		left bank	UA 659 002	
Weir - portage		158	100		right bank	UA 662 047	
Boat Launch		157	101		right bank		
Whoop Up Drive		157	101				
CPR RR bridge (High Level)		155	103	39		UA 656 077	
Highway #3 Bridge - access		154	104		right bank		
	820	153	105				0.8
Ryan Park - hand boat launch		147	111		right bank	UA 666 128	
	815	142	116				0.5
	808	137	121				1.4
	800	132	126				1.6
	792	125	133				1.1

Location	Elevation meters	Km down	Km up	Km between	Access / Bank or Rapid / Class	MGRS datum NAD 1983 Zone 12 U	Gradient m/km
	785	115	143				0.7
Highway #845		113	145				
Nolan's Bridge site / Rng Rd 201a		112	146	43	right bank	UA 840 243	
	777	109	149				1.3
	770	105	153				1.8
Little Bow River		99	159		left bank	UA 940 271	
Twnshp Rd 104a		91	167		right bank		
	762	91	167				0.6
	754	78	180				0.6
Highway # 864		69	189				
Taber Provincial Park		69	189	43	right bank	VA 159 186	
Woodpeck Island		68	190				
	747	65	193				0.5
	739	58	200				1.1
	732	49	209				0.8
Highway #36		45	213	24		VA 221 348	
	724	32	226				0.5
	716	23	235				0.9
Wolf Island		21	237				
	709	8	250				0.5
	701	2	256				1.3
Grand Forks / Bow Island		0	258	45	right bank	VA 502 313	

Gradient

From looking at the gradients noted above, one can understand why the paddle into Lethbridge is one of the most popular sub-reaches here – it displays some of the most consistent higher gradients. I calculate a mean gradient over this whole reach of just 1 m/km.

River Volume and Flow Rate

The Oldman River at Lethbridge is subject to a very wide range of flows. Buhrmann & Young (1980) reported optimal paddling on these reaches with 17 to 170 cms at the Ft. McLeod Station, or 56 to 227 cms at the Lethbridge station. Rood & Tymensen (2001) suggest that a minimal flow for paddling is approximately 25 cms. The Discharge - Velocity relationship for the Lethbridge station reports approximately 2 km/hr at 80 cms and 8 km/hr at 2200 cms.

Maps & Guides

1 - I think first choice for these runs should be the 1:250,000 sheets, and an up-to-date copy of the *Alberta Road Map*. If one is to paddle in the Lethbridge area often I would acquire the 1:50,000 sheet (82 H/10) as it has been updated.

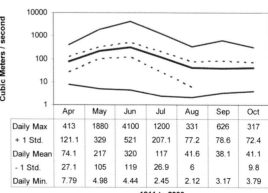

Oldman River at Lethbridge

	Apr	May	Jun	Jul	Aug	Sep	Oct
Daily Max	413	1880	4100	1200	331	626	317
+ 1 Std.	121.1	329	521	207.1	77.2	78.6	72.4
Daily Mean	74.1	217	320	117	41.6	38.1	41.1
- 1 Std.	27.1	105	119	26.9	6		9.8
Daily Min.	7.79	4.98	4.44	2.45	2.12	3.17	3.79

1911 to 2003

In 1980 Buhrmann & Young completed *Canoeing Chinook Country Rivers*. Even though this guide is now a quarter of a century old, I find it a most useful reference for any paddling I do in southern Alberta. Check your local library, other paddlers or used book store for copies.

Camping

Public campgrounds, on the river, and along this reach are a bit thin. The last time I was through Fort McLeod the campground at the Highway #2 bridge still looked like it needed redevelopment since the last flood. Bridgeview RV Resort (403.381.2357 - no tent sites!) in Lethbridge is close to the river, and Taber Municipal Park (403.223.0091) is right on the river. In many ways Henderson Lake Park Campground (403.328.5452) is a good alternative if staying in Lethbridge.

Random or wilderness camping along these reaches is possible on the many islands and beaches, especially after the high waters of early summer. The Oldman flows through parts of the oldest settled portions of Alberta and virtually all the lands along the river are privately held and permission should be sought for camping on the shoreline. In addition the south (right) bank between the Belly and St. Mary river confluences is reserve land held by the Blood tribe and again permission is required to access the banks.

Wildlife

As noted often in this guide, wildlife tends to concentrate in central and southern Alberta along the rivers and the wildlife viewing of the larger mammals, aquatic birds, and the other birds of the prairies should be good during spring and into mid-summer. For those like me from central Alberta or further north, most of this reach is prime rattlesnake country, be aware and wary. It is territory where one must keep close control on pet dogs and young kids! And do not step or reach into spots where the ground can not be seen. In my experience, and the experience of many of my paddling colleagues you are about as likely to spot a rattlesnake swimming in the river as find one coiled up on land. Rattlesnakes do tend to be shy and given a chance will disappear, often even before you are aware of their presence. They generally rattle only when startled, or when you get too close. Rattlesnakes are a protected species. Moreover, they do far more good in terms of rodent control than any risk they present to us humans.

Trip Notes

At lower to average water levels these are great reaches for novice paddlers. One caution of course is that this is windy country, if a chinook is not blowing, then on a hot day there is likely to be the classic"local" upstream breeze. These are runs where it is probably best to get your paddling in early, and then find a place to rest during the mid-afternoon heat, which will likely be windiest time most days.

Novice paddlers should scout the "concrete slab" just upstream of Fort McLeod – one result of recent floods is that all such man-made and natural structures have been scoured and the Class I rating may no longer "stand." Given the recent floods the one reported partial ledge, noted above, may no longer be the only ledge that shows. Paddlers must always be wary, rivers do change and change significantly (see my notes on the upper Oldman!).

Other Reaches

Much of the reach above Fort McLeod runs through the Piegan Reserve (#147) and access requires band permission. The run below Grand Forks is reviewed in the South Saskatchewan report.

Other Local Activities or Destinations

If you've read much of this guide you know I'm a sucker for museums. I have been to the Fort Whoop-Up restoration and recommend it, my Travel Alberta materials tell me that for 2006 they have just finished a major reconstruction of the Galt Museum and I look forward to that. And Lois will not let us pass through Lethbridge without a visit to the Nikka Yuko Japanese Garden, in Henderson Lake Park.

Rentals and Shuttles

High Level Canoes & Kayaks 403.327.4506

South Saskatchewan River

Grand Forks to Estuary, Saskatchewan

Why Go
This is the classic Alberta prairie river paddle. The reach though the Suffield reserve is the closest you can get to wilderness tripping in sout-eastern Alberta.

Duration of Tour
* 302 km
* 7- 11 days with half, full day, and shorter multi-day trips possible.

On Bow Island, looking north to confluence with Bow River

Classification
1. Rapids: Class 1 (at some water levels Rapid Narrows on the Suffield Reach may go Class 2)
2. Skill of Paddlers: Novice River Paddlers at average and lower flows, Intermediate river paddlers at above average flows.

Starts

To paddle the whole reach covered by this report one starts at Grand Forks. Grand Forks is 11 km north of Grassy Lake. Head straight north out of Grassy Lake, jog right at the correction line and follow the road down into the river valley. In 1999 it was quite possible to drive right onto Bow Island at the confluence of the Bow and Oldman rivers – The Grand Forks. Milage measurements were taken from the downstream end of Bow Island.

Other access points provide a variety of single and multi-day tours. Possibly the most popular reach is the run from Medicine Hat through the Suffield Military Reserve to Highway #41at Sandy Point.

Finish

The wrap-up for this whole reach is at the Estuary Ferry, in Saskatchewan, just north of the town of Estuary and on secondary highway #635. This ferry can be reached from Alberta Highway #41 from both the north (#562) and south (#545) sides of the South Saskatchewan.

Intermediate Access and Distances

Location	km down	km up	km between	Access/Bank or Rapid Class	MGRS Datum
					NAD 1983 Zone12 U
Grand Forks	302	0		right bank	VA 500 314
#879 Bridge north of Bow Island	283	19	19	either side	VA 658 279
River Valley Park, South of Redwater	217	85		left bank	WA 142 444
Echo Dale Park West of Medicine Hat	215	87	68	right bank	WA 159 444
Kiwanis River Park	209	93		right bank	WA 203 434
Police Point Park, in East Medicine Hat	204	98	11	left bank	WA 251 430
entering Suffield Base	151	151		left bank	WA 281 637
entering Suffield Base (sentry post)	122	180		right bank	WA291 830
leaving Suffield Base	102	200		right bank	WA 397 856
Rapid Narrows	99	203			WA 423 853
Leaving Suffield Base	69	233		left bank	WB 507 071
Sandy Point / Highway #41	44	258	160	right bank, upstream of bridge	WB 654 202
Confluence with Red Deer River	8	294		left bank	WB 776 417
Estuary Ferry, Saskatchewan	0	302	44	either shore, beware of ferry cables	WB 840 443

Gradient

This whole reach is of relatively low gradient, approximately 0.6 m per km.

River Volume and Flow Rate

Normal summer flows from approximately 150 cms to 600 cms should provide good paddling. Floods on the South Saskatchewan have exceeded 4000 cms! Current speed varies from 2 km per hr at 100 cms, to 6 km per hr at 2000 cms (at the Medicine Hat station).

Maps & Guide Books

1 - N.T.S. 1:250,000
72E Foremost, 72L Medicine Hat, & 72K Prelate
2 - N.T.S. 1:50,000
72E/13 Grassy Lake, 72E/14 Bow Island, 72L/3 Suffield, 72L/2 Medicine Hat, 72L/7 Watching Hill, 72L/8 Hilda, 72L/9 Middle Sand Hills, 72L/16 Bindloss, 72K/13 Leader
County or M.D. maps
M.D. of Cypress, County of 40 Mile, Special Areas Map
3 - **Guide Book**
Dickinson, D & Baresco, D (2003) *Prairie River*. Society of Grasslands Naturalists, Medicine Hat
- when I go back to this river, I will MOST certainly have a copy of this guide along (I own three!). This book includes 1:50,000 strip maps, and a wonderful wealth of interpretative material on the natural and cultural history along the river.

I would suggest that the above guidebook, the 1:250,000 sheets and an up-to-date *Alberta Road Map* should be all you need, unless you are planning on using some of the more obscure access trails not reported here.

South Saskatchewan River at Medicine Hat

	Apr	May	Jun	Jul	Aug	Sep	Oct
Daily Max	1300	2340	4200	2110	1110	1680	524
+ 1 Std.	263	509	926	547	260	215	177.4
Daily Mean	173	335	600	331	157	118	110
- 1 Std.	83	161	274	115	54	21	42.6
Daily Min.	13.1	14.8	33.4	24.5	13	11.8	10.4

1911 to 2003

Camping

The only public campgrounds on the river are at Echo Dale Park, upstream of Medicine Hat, and Sandy Point at the Highway #41 bridge, otherwise one is wilderness camping – or trespassing. Off river campgrounds are available in Medicine (Gas City), Empress and at Bow Island. In the Red Cliff / Medicine Hat urban area the land owners are likely to be fairly protective of their property and one should only camp with permission. On other parts of this river the banks above the high water mark are the property of farmers and ranchers, grazing associations, and for much of the middle reach, the Canadian Military! This run of the river does have a good many islands for wilderness camping, and after the big flows of the early summer, the banks below the high water mark are available to wilderness travellers.

Trip Notes

I have fond memories of my paddle on the reach from Medicine Hat to Estuary with the Canoe Alberta crew in 1972. Our crew had been separated for the week before, paddling on the Red Deer, the Bow, and the Oldman rivers, and we then reunited for the run down the South Saskatchewan. The week prior had been wet, but we "lucked out" for the Saskatchewan run and had modestly high, fast water, and lots of sun for our run down to Estuary. We were all paddling marathon racing canoes and made the run through to Sandy Point with just one overnight (I would NOT recommend this pace now!), and then one more day for the run to Estuary.

After all the flat water and afternoon upstream breezes, we were primed for "Rapid Narrows." It turned out to be just a "splash in the face!" Rapid Narrows would appear to be caused by a very broken ledge or boulder bar, and with the very low gradient proved to be no more than a few modest pressure waves. These waves can reach 1m or more in height. As I remember, and as others report (Dickinson & Baresco, 1996), the whole rapid can be avoided on the far right side, and it may be portaged on the right bank if necessary.

For us, the highlight of the trip was the wildlife. Collectively we paddled over 1600 miles in the summer of '72, but no other run stands out like the South Saskatchewan for wildlife. We decided that year that on the prairie rivers, ALL the wildlife must live along the river. We were blessed with multiple sightings of deer, antelope, hawks of all sort, fox, coyotes, herons and eagles.

Suffield Military base can throw a "wrench" in your trip plans. They do CLOSE the river at times for military exercises and you must call the base Operations Office (403-544-4310) to confirm accessibility. A year or two ago, I heard of a group of paddlers who failed to do so, and they were flown out by helicopter from Drowning Ford by the military police - and given a stern reprimand! This military reserve extends from approximately km 151 to km 233 on the left bank, and for much less on the right bank. I understand that at present it is well signed, and a sentry is posted at the point where the river enters the reserve on both banks if the river is closed.

Most of my friends who have paddled the South Saskatchewan report rattlesnake sightings, either during coulee walks (most often) or frequently swimming in the river! Rattlesnakes in Alberta are not particularly big, or particularly poisonous, though they can seriously harm pet dogs and small children. One must be careful where they reach with their hands and one should not put one's hands where one cannot see. Rattlesnakes prefer to avoid confrontation, thus the rattle. Give 'em berth, and you should not have a problem. Most adults are bitten when either trying to pick-up or kill rattlers. Avoid both! If bitten, victims should be immobilized, kept calm, cool, and evacuated as quickly as possible to a hospital. A restrictive bandage may be applied on the heart side of the bite to slow lymph drainage – but not so constrictive as to reduce blood flow to the extremity! Tourniquets and incisions are NOT required.

This is a deeply incised prairie river in places and the afternoon upstream breeze on some days can require "strong" paddling. Also due to the deep valley walls, summer thunderstorms can sweep in very quickly and surprise paddlers.

This can be a hot, dry run! Most recent reports on this river suggest that drinking water should be taken from home or from reliable sources. The South Saskatchewan river is subject to pollution from agricultural, industrial, and urban sources.

In '72 I remember that on our last day it was particularly hot and as often the case amongst young paddlers, a water fight broke out. After inflicting great soaking on our friends my partner and I took refuge in a side channel. Little did we realize that Allan Island (at the confluence with the Red Deer) is almost 3 km long. At one point we thought we might have wandered into an irrigation ditch and were going to end our trip in the middle of an alfalfa field! A water fight can cool paddlers, but in this modern age, lots of fluids, sun-screen and sun-protective hats and clothing are required.

Other Local Activities or Destinations
Medicine Hat is the major urban centre close to these reaches and provides all the modern amenities. Of particular interest to paddlers may be the nature centre in Police Point Park. And if you are in this area for long, one should spend some time in the Cypress Hills to the SE of Medicine Hat. This "glacial refuge" is well worth a visit of two or three days, including a trip into the Saskatchewan side and Fort Walsh.

Highwood River

Ings Creek to the
Town of High River

Why Go
Whitewater and Alberta's foothills scenery!

Duration of Tour(s)
* 50 km
* 2 days, but better done as a series of day, or even ½ day trips

Classification
1. Rapids: Class I to III+
2. Skill of Paddlers: Skilled River Paddlers

Roping a canoe down to the river at start, Fall 2005
photo by T. Jacklin

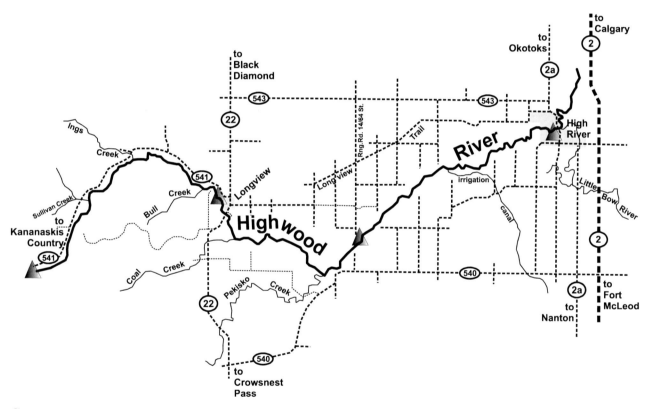

Start
The primary start for this run is off of Highway #541 approximately 600 m south of the Ings Creek Bridge. As you may note from the picture above, this does require sliding or roping one's canoe down a rather steep embankment!

Finish
The best finish for the overall run is in the George Lane Memorial Park (& campground) right in High River.

Intermediate Access and Distances

Location	Elevation meters	Km down	Km up	Km between	Access / Bank or Rapid / Class	MGRS datum *NAD 1927* Zone 11U	Gradient m/km
	1234		-0.2				
start		49.7	0.0			PG 881 038	
Ings Creek		49	0.7		left bank		
	1219	46.8	2.9				4.8
	1204	43.2	6.5				4.2
	1189	41	8.7				6.8
Hwy. # 22		38.1	11.6	11.6	left bank, downstream	PG 961 002	
	1173	36.2	13.5				3.3
Bull Creek		35.9	13.8		right bank		
	1158	32.8	16.9				4.4
	1143	30.5	19.2				6.5
	1128	26.5	23.2				3.8
Pekisko Creek		26.2	23.5		right bank		
	1113	22.9	26.8				4.2
Archie & Janet Hogg Park		22.7	27.0	15.4	left bank	QF 061 981	
	1097	18.3	31.4				3.5
	1082	14.1	35.6				3.6
						NAD 1983	
Irrigation Headworks	1074	12.4	37.3		right bank	TB 880 045	4.7
	1067	9.9	39.8				
	1059	9.4	40.3				
	1052	5.7	44.0				
	1044	3.6	46.1				
	1036	2.5	47.2				3.8
George Lane Memorial Park		0.6	49.1		right bank	TB 961 071	
Highway # 2a bridge in High River		0	49.7	22.7	left bank	TB 966 073	

Gradient

The gradients above are generally representative of the river and the toughest (most fun) section is from Ings Creek to above Longview. You should note that I have averaged the gradients for the section from below the irrigation headworks down to High River. Individual calculations give one interval a gradient of 16 m/km, and I don't remember anything that exciting. I strongly suspect an error and the 3.8 km/m average better reflects my memory or paddling the reach and reading of the map.

River Volume and Flow Rate

These reaches are best paddled with flows between 15 and 60 cms. Flow rates at Diebel's ranch range from approximately 4 km/hr at 28 cms to 9 km/hr at 140 cms.

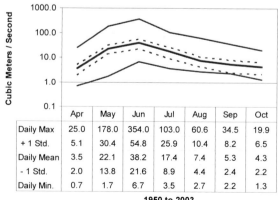

Highwood River at Diebels Ranch

	Apr	May	Jun	Jul	Aug	Sep	Oct
Daily Max	25.0	178.0	354.0	103.0	60.6	34.5	19.9
+ 1 Std.	5.1	30.4	54.8	25.9	10.4	8.2	6.5
Daily Mean	3.5	22.1	38.2	17.4	7.4	5.3	4.3
- 1 Std.	2.0	13.8	21.6	8.9	4.4	2.4	2.2
Daily Min.	0.7	1.7	6.7	3.5	2.7	2.2	1.3

1950 to 2003

Maps
1 - NTS 1:50,000

82 J/09 - Turner Valley   82 J/08 - Stimson Creek

82 I/12 - High River

Camping
Public campgrounds are available along the upper Highwood, 22 km W of Longview at the Green Ford Provincial Recreation Area (1.866.366.2267); in Longview at the Tales & Trails Campground (403.850.0256); downstream of Longview at Archie & Janet Hogg Park (403.558.2092) and in High River at the George Lane Memorial Park (403.652.5315).

Trip Notes
I'll confess I've not made the run from Ing Creek to Longview, and the run below Longview just once, in 1999. Reports from fellow paddlers and Smith (1995) suggest that the Ings Creek reach is a good whitewater run for skilled open canoe paddlers, and intermediate closed boat paddlers with numerous ledges, partial ledges and tight corners. Smith reports numerous good surfing spots on the first part of this run.

From below Longview to the Irrigation headworks, the river has sections of modest ledges, and then flatter stretches as the gradients above indicate. The flat stretches tend to be depositional and can actually be more dangerous because of the logjams and sweepers. Below the irrigation headworks the river flows steadily, is braided and the outside banks of the bends are good locations for sweepers, and a bad location for paddlers .

Other Reaches
Smith (1995) is the best source for information on the reaches above Ings Creek. These reaches are mostly advanced whitewater with many rapids rated Class III to IV, and a few as V at high water! Immediately below High River there is a pretty calm flat stretch, followed by the Highway #547 to Highway #552 run.

Other Local Activities or Destinations
The times I've been in the High River area I've been blessed with good weather for paddling. But if you are not so lucky check out to the Bar U Ranch National Historic Site, which is 8 km south of Longview on Highway #22, and approximately ½ km west of Highway #22 at the Highway #540 intersection.

Rentals
Aquabatics
  403.288.9283
Mountain Equipment Co-op
  403.269.2420
Undercurrents
  403.262.4327
U of C Outdoor Program Centre
  403.220.5038

Broken ledges below Ings Creek, Fall, 2005
photo by T. Jacklin

Highwood River

Highway #547 to Highway #552

Island Rapid, left channel, July, 2006 at 28 cms

Why Go
This is a fine spring to early summer paddle that offers some good intermediate whitewater, all within a ½ hour drive of south Calgary.

Duration of Tour(s)
* 17 km
* ½ to a full day paddle, if you play every hole and rapid.

Classification
1. Rapids: Class I to III
2. Skill of Paddlers: Intermediate River Paddler, or Novice River Paddlers with good leadership. At modest flows this is a good teaching stream.

Start
The start for this run is just north of secondary Highway #547, and just east of the Highway bridge over the Highwood, off the end of Range Road # 285

Finish
The finish is just off Highway #552, on the east bank and upstream of the bridge.

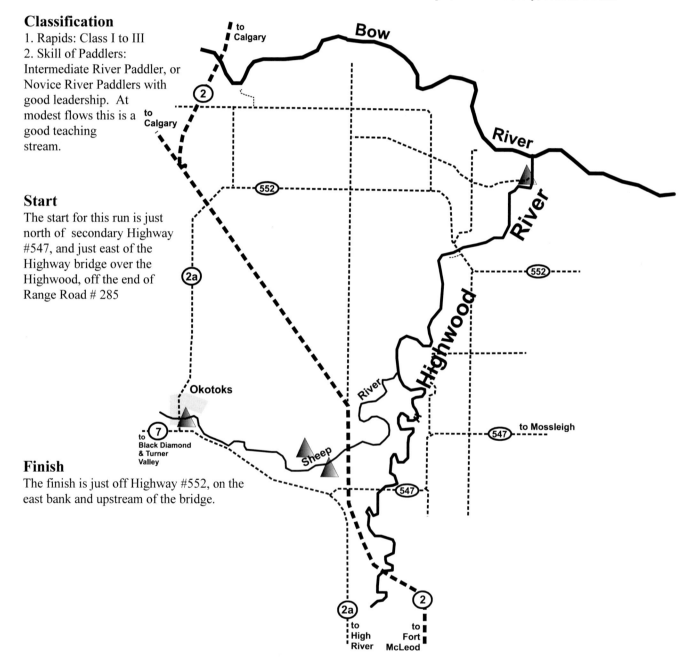

Intermediate Access and Distances

Location	Elevation meters	Km down	Km up	Km between	Access / Bank or Rapid / Class	MGRS datum NAD 1983 Zone 12U	Gradient m/km
Range Road 285, North of #547		17.0	0.0		Right bank	TB 980 201	
	1013	16.9	0.1				
	1006	14.4	2.6				2.8
	998	11.5	5.5				2.8
Island Rapid		10.6	6.4		Class II to III	TB 994 228	
	991	9.4	7.6				3.3
	983	7.7	9.3				4.7
Sheep River		7.2	9.8	9.8	left bank	TB 985 247	
	975	4.5	12.5				2.5
	968	1.9	15.1				2.7
above Hwy #552		0.0	17.0	7.2	Right bank for access	UB 010 294	

Gradient

The gradients noted above pretty much reflect the difficulty of the river with the greatest difficulty, best whitewater, in the vicinity of Island Rapid. I do suspect that the contour lines are out a bit, and the greatest gradient is associated with Island Rapid.

River Volume and Flow Rate

Good paddling is to be had on this reach of the Highwood with flows from about 25 cms through to about 90 cms.

Maps

1 - NTS 1:50,000

       82I 12 - High River

       82I 13 - Dalmead

Camping

There are a variety of campsites available. Once of the nicest is Nature's Hideway down towards the mouth of the river. There are also pleasant campgrounds along the Sheep River in, and below Okotoks that could be used as a "base" for paddling in this area.

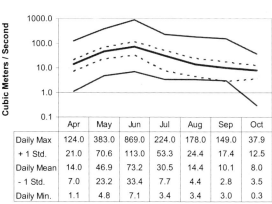

Highwood River near mouth

	Apr	May	Jun	Jul	Aug	Sep	Oct
Daily Max	124.0	383.0	869.0	224.0	178.0	149.0	37.9
+ 1 Std.	21.0	70.6	113.0	53.3	24.4	17.4	12.5
Daily Mean	14.0	46.9	73.2	30.5	14.4	10.1	8.0
- 1 Std.	7.0	23.2	33.4	7.7	4.4	2.8	3.5
Daily Min.	1.1	4.8	7.1	3.4	3.4	3.0	0.3

1970 to 2003

This reach of river is well within the acreage "'burbs" of Calgary and random, or wilderness, camping is not a realistic activity.

      Nature's Hideway 403.938.8185

      River Bend Campground 403.938.2017

      Okotoks Lions Sheep River Campground 403.938.4282

Trip Notes

I've paddled this reach twice from the Hwy #547 start, and on the lower half once more when running down the Sheep from Okotoks through to Nature's Hideway Campground. From just above Highway #547 the river downgrades to the confluence with the Sheep River. On this part nearly every corner has a modest bit of whitewater, and most can be scouted from the canoe, or eddy above. Both on my first run with the Bow Waters Canoe Club, and my second run in '06 stopping to scout Island Rapid proved to be a prudent decision. The river had changed between runs with much erosion and scouring, and at Island rapid the river had mostly shifted to the left hand channel, and it had become a much longer and more significant rapid. In '06 we saw it with only 28-30 cms, and I suspect it could be fearsome at 100 cms.

The river eases off a bit below the confluence with the Sheep, though there are still riffles and rocks to watch for, and still eddies in which to play and practice skills. The last ledge of the run to Highway #552 is about 150 m above the bridge and can usually be run on river right - see picture below.

Other Reaches

I have never paddled above Highway #547 and my observation of the stream from passing over it, driving alongside, and review of the top sheets has it as a meandering reach from High River down to Highway #547.

Below Highway #552 is a pleasant paddle with some modest riffles through to the Bow River, though the last access before the Bow is either through Nature's Hideway Campground, or off the end of the Township Road 214a (also called 256 Ave. S.E.). Possibly the most spectacular part of this run is the paddle past the historic St. Joseph's Dunbar Industrial School. Lois and I had to stop and take about 2 dozen pictures of the remains of the barns, some of which then were beginning to fall into the river, I suspect more have gone now. The run right through to the Bow confluence is 6.4 km, with a further 6 km down to McKinnon Flats, on the north bank of the Bow River.

In this area there is also a pleasant run with considerable modest (Class 1 to II+) whitewater on the Sheep from Okotoks through to the Highwood and then takeout at Highway #552. This run is 15.7 km. When I last paddled this reach there was considerable driftwood, debris and logjams in the first few kilometers below Okotoks.

Other Local Activities or Destinations

If I'm ever stuck in the Calgary area on a day too wet and cold for pleasant paddling I head to the Glenbow Museum in downtown Calgary. And if I am with younger ones, then the choice is either Calgary Zoo, or Heritage Park Historic Village on Glenmore Reservoir.

Rentals and Shuttles

Rentals:
Aquabatics
 403.288.9283
Mountain Equipment Co-op
 403.269.2420
Rocky Mountain Paddling Centre
 403.202.8490
Undercurrents
 403.262.4327
U of C Outdoor Program Centre
 403.220.5038

Shuttles:
Louise Shotton Shuttle Service
 403.282.5071
Bow River Shuttles
 403.278.9165
Calgary Bow River Shuttle Service
 403 510.0138

Hwy # 552 Bridge Access, early July, 2006

Sheep River

Sandy McNabb Campground to Turner Valley

Why Go
A fine foothills whitewater stream!

Duration of Tour(s)
* 24.5 km
* 1 day

Classification
1. Rapids: Class 1 to III+
2. Skill of Paddlers: Skilled River Paddlers, or Intermediate River Paddlers with good leadership (strong rescue skills!).

Start
The start for this run is west from Turner Valley on secondary highway #546 to Sandy McNabb Campground, through the campground and down to the day use area by the river.

At Sandy McNabb, mid-June, 2000, at 10 cms

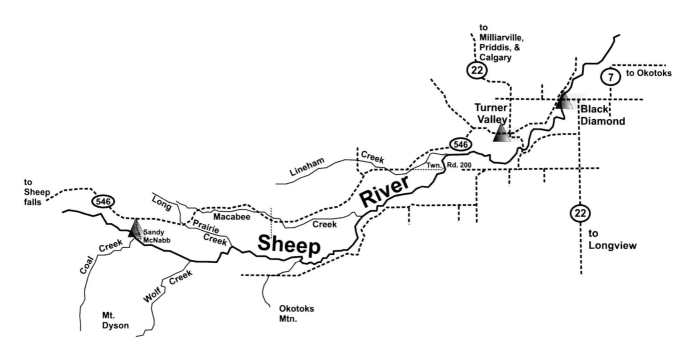

Finish
When I made this run in June 2000 we paddled right through to the old refinery (Decalta Drive) bridge in Turner Valley. In 2000 access down to the river on Township Road# 200 was possible on the left/west bank and this would save considerable (5 km) of flat water paddling.

Intermediate Access and Distances

Location	Elevation meters	Km down	Km up	Km between	Access / Bank or Rapid / Class	MGRS datum NAD 1927 Zone 11U	Gradient m/km
	1372		-1.8				
Sandy McNabb Campground		24.5	0.0		left bank	PG 750 112	
	1341	23.1	1.4				9.7
Wolf Creek		22.0	2.5		right bank		
	1326	21.9	2.6				12.5
	1311	19.6	4.9				6.5
Long Prairie Creek		19.2	5.3		left bank		
	1295	18.5	6.0				14.5
	1280	16.7	7.8				8.3
	1265	13.6	10.9				4.8
Macabee Creek		10.5	14.0		left bank		
	1250	9.9	14.6				4.1
	1234	7.6	16.9				7.0
Twn.Rd.200		5.3	19.2	19.2	left bank	PG 892 153	
Lineham Creek		4.5	20.0		left bank		
	1219	4.2	20.3				4.4
	1204	1.4	23.1				5.4
Decalta Dr. SE		0.0	24.5	5.3	left bank	PG 927 163	

Gradient
As always the above gradients are a bit suspect given how incised the Sheep River is, but the numbers do highly correlate with the difficult (read multiple ledge) sections.

River Volume and Flow Rate
I would expect that the best (fun, not scary) paddling on this run will be had with flows from approximately 8 cms through to 30 cms.

Maps
1 - NTS 1:50,000
         82 J/10 - Mount Rae
         82 J/9 - Turner Valley

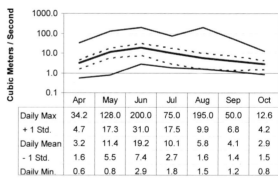

Sheep River near Black Diamond

	Apr	May	Jun	Jul	Aug	Sep	Oct
Daily Max	34.2	128.0	200.0	75.0	195.0	50.0	12.6
+ 1 Std.	4.7	17.3	31.0	17.5	9.9	6.8	4.2
Daily Mean	3.2	11.4	19.2	10.1	5.8	4.1	2.9
- 1 Std.	1.6	5.5	7.4	2.7	1.6	1.4	1.5
Daily Min.	0.6	0.8	2.9	1.8	1.5	1.2	0.8

1909 to 2003

Camping
Camping is available on the river at Sandy McNabb (403.949.3132), in Turner Valley off of the river at Hell's Half Acre Campground (403.933.5130), and in Black Diamond next to the river at the Foothill Lions Centennial Park (403.933.5785). This is primarily a whitewater stream; I'm pretty sure I'd rather run this reach "sans" camp gear. Random camping is not allowed in Kananaskis Country, the first quarter of the trip. The remainder of the trip is through ranch and acreage country and in my experience permission to camp is both required and hard to get in such areas.

Trip Notes

I believe the pictures below give the best sense of this run: ledges, lots of ledges. At 10 cms in June, 2000, the river was not particularly powerful and we had time to make decisions. I am not sure I would want to be on this river at the upper end of recommended paddling flows: there may be a more room to maneuver, but everything would come at you very quickly. Given how narrow much of the first part of this run is, paddlers must maintain a sharp eye for sweepers that may bridge the whole stream. Most of the excitement is in the first third of this trip, and the lower two-thirds of the trip is a very pleasant foothills paddle.

Other Reaches

Skilled River paddlers regularly paddle the Sheep above Sandy McNabb, the water is very challenging! I would recommend those interested in these upper reaches review:

Archer, S. (2000) *Sheep River: paddling outside of time.* in Thomas, A.(ed.), **Paddle Quest:Canada's best canoe routes.** and,

Smith, S. (1995) **Canadian Rockies Whitewater: a river guide for canoeists, kayakers and rafters (Southern Rockies).** I believe that floods have scoured the ledges since S. Smith made his survey for this river, and the river is more difficult than Smith reports.

Rentals

Aquabatics 403.288.9283
Mountain Equipment Co-op 403.269.2420
Rocky Mountain Paddling Centre 403.202.8490
Undercurrents 403.262.4327
U of C Outdoor Program Centre 403.220.5038

Elbow River

Canyon Creek to Bragg Creek

Why Go
Great spring and early summer whitewater!

Duration of Tour(s)
*20.7 km
* 1 long day, but better paddled as a series of ½ day or shorter runs.

Just below Canyon Creek, 2005
photo by T. Jacklin

Classification
1. Rapids: Class I to III+ (even IV- at higher flows on the Canyon Creek stretch)
2. Skill of Paddlers: Skilled River Paddler below Canyon Creek, Intermediate River Paddlers below Paddy's Flats

Start
Canyon Creek is just over half way from Paddy's Flats campground to Elbow Falls. Canyon Creek is signed on Highway #66, and there is a picnic site and boat launch area.

Finish
The last finish for this reach is at the bridge on Balsam Avenue in Bragg Creek. Access has been best on the north shore, downstream side of the bridge.

to
Cochrane
& Calgary

to Calgary

8

22

Sarcee (Tsuu T'ina)
Indian Reserve
#145

River

Redwood Meadows

Bragg   Creek

Bragg Creek

Moose
Mtn.

Prov.
Park

Elbow

Ranger   Creek

66

Gooseberry

to Priddis
& Calgary

22

Canyon
Creek

Paddy's
Flats

762

to
Millarville

Beaver
Flat

Elbow
Falls

Silvester   Creek

66

to
Little Elbow
Rec. Area

Intermediate Access and Distances

Location	Elevation	Km down	Km up	Km between	Access / Bank or Rapid / Class	MGRS datum	Gradient m/km
	meters					NAD 1983 Zone 11U	
	1463		-1.2				
Canyon Creek Launch / picnic site		20.7	0.0		left bank, rapids up to Class IV- below	PS 581 373	
Canyon Creek		20.5	0.2		left bank	PS 583 373	
	1433	18.5	2.2				8.8
Paddy's Flat Campground		17.9	2.8		left bank		
	1402	14.5	6.2				7.8
River Cove Group site		13.8	6.9				
Allen Bill Pond		12.9	7.8	7.8	left bank		
Highway #66 bridge		12.7	8.0			PS 628 415	
McLean Creek		11.4	9.3		right bank		
	1372	9.7	11.0				6.3
	1341	6.3	14.4				9.1
start Bragg Creek Prov. Park		2.9	17.8		right bank		
	1311	1.7	19.0				6.5
Bragg Creek - west road access		1.4	19.3	11.5	right bank	PS 703 465	
Bragg Creek, Balsam Ave. bridge		0.0	20.7		left bank	PS 709 474	
	1280		22.5				8.9

Gradient

This reach does start with some pretty good gradient, and some big ledges! I am a skeptical of the middle gradient (9.1 m/km) interval noted above. There are some interesting ledges between Bragg Creek Provincial Park and the Bragg Creek town bridge. If nothing else, this run does bear out that the difficulty of rapids is a combination of gradient and geology.

River Volume and Flow Rate

Good paddling can be had on this run with between 15 and 30 cms.

Maps

1 - My first choice map for this reach is the Gem Trek Publisher's: *Bragg Creek and Elbow Falls* sheet at 1:50,000 (NAD 1983). It covers this whole run.

2 - NTS 1:50,000 82 J/15 (NAD 1927)

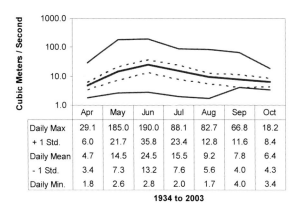

Elbow River at Bragg Creek

	Apr	May	Jun	Jul	Aug	Sep	Oct
Daily Max	29.1	185.0	190.0	88.1	82.7	66.8	18.2
+ 1 Std.	6.0	21.7	35.8	23.4	12.8	11.6	8.4
Daily Mean	4.7	14.5	24.5	15.5	9.2	7.8	6.4
- 1 Std.	3.4	7.3	13.2	7.6	5.6	4.0	4.3
Daily Min.	1.8	2.6	2.8	2.0	1.7	4.0	3.4

1934 to 2003

Camping

Numerous public campgrounds are available along and near this run. Little Elbow and Beaver Flats are upstream, Paddy's Flat and Gooseberry are along this reach, and McLean Provincial Recreation Area (4X4 country) is just to the south of the river. All of these campgrounds are managed by the same operator and can be reached at: 403.949.3133. Given that much of this run is in Kananaskis Country, and the remainder runs through small private holdings, wilderness or random camping is not recommended.

Wildlife

The Elbow valley is popular with Calgarians, especially on weekends, but you may still catch a glimpse of the common foothills wildlife: moose, deer, and coyotes. I've spotted mink on these reaches, and my old friend Bruce once reported seeing otter just downstream of Bragg Creek. Bird life may include kingfishers, dippers, and osprey.

Trip Notes

I was first introduced to these reaches in the mid '70s when some of the early whitewater races in the province were hosted along here. I can remember my first run below Canyon Creek in a down river C-2, and the big ledge on the second left corner below Canyon Creek may have been the biggest ledge I had ever run up to that point. My eyes were wide open the rest of that run – I'm still not sure how we made it over. The slalom events were hosted on the long bend immediately below Canyon Creek and I can remember racing there for at least two or three years in a row.

Other Reaches

Immediately above the Canyon Creek run, there is a very demanding run from below Elbow Falls. This reach includes rapids that have been rated as high as Class IV+. In fact, this reach claimed the life of a semi experienced paddler in recent years. Above Elbow Falls, Calgary area whitewater paddlers regularly make the run from Cobble Flats to Beaver Flats through a stretch they refer to as Rainbow Canyon.

Below Bragg Creek the Elbow continues to flow quickly, but the channel is often choked with logjams and sweepers. In addition, the run into Calgary flows through the Tsuu T'ina Reserve (#145) and permission must be acquired from the Band office before attempting the run.

Other Local Activities or Destinations

So you drove all the way from......... (Edmonton), and it is pouring buckets, the river is rising quickly, and is full of debris but you are not yet prepared to pack up camp and head home. Me... I'd head into Calgary to either the Glenbow Museum, or if my daughter Anna is along, we'll be off to the zoo! Both are world class facilities.

Rentals

Aquabatics
 403.288.9283
Mountain Equipment Co-op
 403.269.2420
Undercurrents
 403.262.4327
U of C Outdoor Program Centre
 403.220.5038

Ledge and soon to be swimmer on the Elbow River, Canyon Creek Run
photo by T.Jacklin

Kananaskis River

Widow Maker to Seebe

Why Go
The first section, Widow Maker to Canoe Meadows provides the finest human enhanced whitewater in Alberta. With the cooperation of Trans Alta Utilities, it offers nearly year round paddling with a predictable release schedule. Below Canoe Meadows is a fine introductory river paddling reach that flows through some spectacular scenery.

Duration of Tour(s)
* 9.8 km
* ½ day or less – this is a river to "play"!

Classification
1. Rapids: Class I to III+
2. Skill of Paddlers:
- Above Canoe Meadows & Race site - Skilled River Paddlers in open canoes, Intermediate River paddlers in closed boats
- Below Canoe Meadows & Race site - Intermediate River Paddlers, or Novice River Paddlers with good leadership

Start
The Widow Maker day use area, parking lot and access to the river is approximately 1 kilometer south of the Barrier Lake Information Center on Highway #40, with access at the Highway #68 junction.

Finish
The finish noted in this report is the river access site just off the Seebe road (Highway #1X) before it crosses the Bow River.

the former "Santa Claws", August, 2005, at 31 cms
photo by T. Jacklin

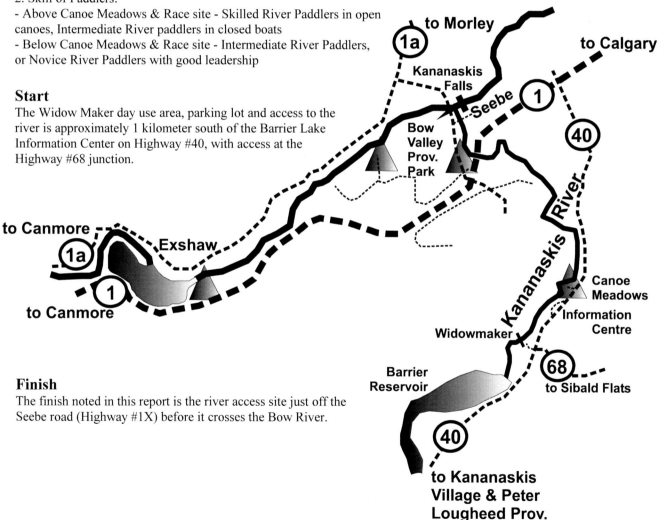

Intermediate Access and Distances

Location	Elevation	Km down	Km up	Km between	Access / Bank or Rapid / Class	MGRS datum	Gradient m/km
	meters					NAD 1983 Zone 11U	
	1360		-1.0				
Widowmaker / launch		9.8	0.0		right bank / Widowmaker Class III	PS 379 563	
					numerous Class II - III+		
Canoe Meadows - upper access		8.1	1.7	1.7	right bank	PS 389 576	
					slalom race site Class II - III+		
Canoe Meadows - lower access		7.5	2.3	0.6	right bank	PS 391 579	
	1320		3.7				8.5
Seebe / river access	≈ 1300	0	9.8	7.5	right bank	PS 356 622	3.3

Gradient

The above calculated gradients fairly represent what one finds on the river. One must remember that this river has been greatly enhanced and the river is a challenge, especially for those in open canoes.

River Volume and Flow Rate

Best paddling on these reaches are to be had with flows between 15 and 35 cms. Up-to-date flows, and scheduled release information can be found at:
http://transalta.com/transalta/river.nsf/.vwRiverWeb/River+Flow By+Schedule?Opendocument

Kananaskis River below Barrier Dam

	Apr	May	Jun	Jul	Aug	Sep	Oct
Daily Max	25.9	65.1	107.0	55.9	32.0	30.8	22.9
+ 1 Std.	16.2	19.6	32.9	21.7	15.8	13.5	12.9
Daily Mean	11.7	14.8	21.7	14.3	11.6	10.3	10.1
- 1 Std.	7.2	10.0	10.5	6.9	7.4	7.1	7.3
Daily Min.	0.0	0.1	0.3	0.3	0.3	0.2	0.3

1975 to 2003

Maps

1 - Gem Trek Pub. (1998) *Canmore and Kananaskis Village* at 1:50,000 is my first choice for this area.
2 - NTS 1:50,000   82 O/3 - Canmore

Camping

Paddling groups are able to book directly into the Canoe Meadows site, otherwise good camping is available in Bow Valley Provincial Park. All campgrounds can be booked through Bow Valley Campgrounds (403.673.2163). Further information is available on-line at: www.bowvalleycampgrounds.com. Note that group reservations open on February 1, others on April 1.

Trip Notes

Upgrades to this river by the Alberta Whitewater Association at the slalom race site began in the mid-1980s. The floods of 1995 & 2005, and the increased utilization have lead to further rehabilitation and enhancements in 1997, 2003 and 2006. The 2003 enhancements, organized by the *Lower Kananaskis River Users Association*, included the moving and placement of over 650 tons of rock, and extended the enhanced features upstream from Canoe Meadows almost up to the Widowmaker.

At the Widowmaker one has the option of running or not running the "Widowmaker" a solid rock ledge that has been rated Class III. Below the Widowmaker the river provides a series of frequent enhanced eddies, mid-stream obstacles and waves all the way down to "Santa Claws". Santa Claws is a large enhanced chute and surfing wave approximately behind the Barrier Information Centre. Tony from Undercurrents reports that the name has changed, it was Santa Clause, but the work of 2006 has lead local paddlers to refer to it as "Claws", as the feature is significantly more threatening. Mark, from Rocky Mountain Paddling Centre, and one of the design team for the new river features, suggests that first time on the river paddlers should stop to scout Santa Claws before running it. There are additional features just downstream, and a swim in and below Santa Claws can get ugly! Mark also reports that paddlers should be aware that on the run down from the Widowmaker, Pointe Break, another wave feature is earning a reputation for tipping the unaware. I think what Mark is trying to say is; "If you don't know what is over the next 'horizon line,' **get out and have a look!"**

The "Green Tongue" another large enhanced chute, is located on the upstream side of Canoe Meadows, and it marks the start of the slalom race site. The race site is now over 300 m of enhanced eddies, mid-stream obstacles, and surfing waves. Paddlers new to the site are encouraged to start at the bottom and work their way up through the site by surfing and eddy hopping. Once you have a "feel" for the river (the water is fast!) take the hike through Canoe Meadows and make the run down from the "Green Tongue".

Below Canoe Meadows the gradient slackens, and the river is a pleasant run for intermediate paddlers or even novice paddlers with good leadership. These days, most new paddlers in the Calgary area have at least part of their paddling education on these reaches of the Kananaskis.

Other Reaches

Back in 1972 the Kananaskis was one of the first rivers we paddled for Canoe Alberta. We ran the river in late May, from the Fortress Ski Hill road right through to Barrier Dam. It was generally a good paddle, but our summer of paddling nearly ended on a sweeper and log jam. Two of our team broached a sweeper, and were stuck upside down and under the water for far longer than we wanted. Fortunately both swimmers washed out!

I understand that in the spring some Calgary area paddlers do still paddle this section of the "Kan." A quick 'n dirty estimate of distances for the middle Kananaskis provides the following:
- Fortress Ski Hill Road Bridge to Galatea Creek Trail Bridge 11.5 km
- to Ribbon Creek road bridge 10 km (21.5)
- to near Mtn. Lorette ponds 6 km (27.5) - last chance to exit before heading down to Barrier reservoir.
- to head of Barrier reservoir 4 km (31.5)
- to Barrier Dam 6 km (37.5)
This is a run with at least one Class III drop, and one long stretch of bouncy, pushy whitewater in the vicinity of the Galatea Creek trail bridge. Much of the river is heavily braided and one must be on the constant lookout for logjams, sweepers and obstructed channels.

lower Slalom Course at Canoe Meadows, August, 2005, at 31 cms
photo by T. Jacklin

Banff & Yoho Park Lakes

Lake Louise, Moraine & Emerald Lakes

Why Go
These three lakes in Banff and Yoho parks all offer spectacular mountain scenery, on relatively sheltered lakes, and each has a canoe and boat rental facility for those without their own craft.

Looking southwest down Lake Louise to Mount Victoria

Duration of Tour(s)
Each of these lakes offers a pleasant escape for an hour or two and up to a ½ day paddle and picnic.

Lake Louise is approximately 2 km long, 530 m wide, and a shoreline paddle will be 4.3 km.
  - My Calgary friends suggest adding the 3 km hike to the Tea House on the Plain of the Six Glaciers!
Moraine Lake is approximately 1.5 km long, 400 m wide, and a shoreline paddle will be 3.3 km.
Emerald Lake is approximately 1.5 km long, 1.2 km wide, and a shoreline paddle will be 4.6 km.

Classification
Novice Flatwater Pddlers, these are flat water paddles with the risk of mountain winds.

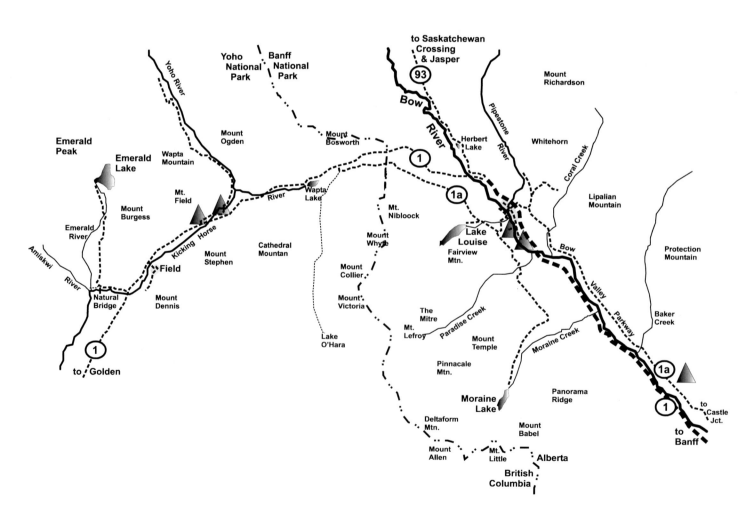

Start(s)

Lake Louise is reached by taking the Lake Louise Village exit from the Trans Canada Highway (Highway # 1). Once on Lake Louise Drive continue southwest through the village, under the railway, across the river and up the hill towards the Chateau Lake Louise. Stay right past the Moraine Lake road junction, and turn left off of the old highway, and stay on the Lake Louise drive. Just past Deer Lodge take a left into the public parking lot and park as close to "the Chateau" as possible. The Boat house and dock are on the NE corner of the lake.

Moraine Lake is reached by taking the left turn off Lake Louise Drive as note above, onto the Moraine Lake Road. It is approximately 12 km to Moraine Lake. The boat house is below the Moraine Lake Lodge on the NW side of the lake.

Emerald Lake is further west in Yoho National Park, and the Emerald Lake access road turns right off the Trans Canada Highway approximately 2.5 km west of the Field access, gas station and Alberta Information centre.

Maps

1 - My first choice map for paddling and hiking in the Lake Louise area is the: *Lake Louise & Yoho* map at 1:50,000 from Gem Trek Publishing. It is likely the only map you will need for this area, it spans from just west of Castle Junction, to well west and south of Field, and from south of Moraine Lake to well north of Herbert Lake on the Icefields Parkway.

Camping

Public campgrounds are available at: Protection Mountain east of Lake Louise on the Bow Valley Parkway, in Lake Louise and in Yoho Park near Field. Banff / Lake Louise area campgrounds (1.877.737.3783), Yoho Park information (250-343-6783 - no reservations taken) Parks Canada on-line reservations: www.pccamping.ca/parkscanada/

Emerald Lake boathouse

Wildlife

If you spend enough time in this area you will see all the big game, and much of the smaller wildlife too. You are in Bear country – both black and grizzly bear may be spotted. One of my favorite birding activities in this area, summer and winter, is to quietly wander along the creeks and look for the slate grey dippers. This little bird feeds by walking along the bottom of fast flowing streams and catching invertebrates to feed on.

Rentals

Emerald Lake Boat House:
  250.343.6000
Moraine Lake Lodge Canoe Rentals:
  403.522.3733
Fairmont Chateau Lake Louise Boathouse:
  403.522.3511

Moraine Lake & dock

Banff Park Lakes

Vermillion Lakes

Why Go
A pleasant, flat water paddle with wonderful mountain vistas and often good wildlife viewing.

Duration of Tour(s)
* 5.0 km to the far end
* This is a pleasant afternoon's paddle, or an early morning or evening adventure for wildlife viewing.

Looking across Vermillion Lakes to Banff, and Mount Rundle
photo from the Curtiss Lund collection

Classification
Lake trip: This is the classic Novice Flatwater Paddlers first trip in the Banff area. Stay home, visit the museums if the weather is windy and ugly!

Start
The start is at or near the Bow Avenue Canoe/Boat rental concession on the Bow River, on the river side of the Banff town site.

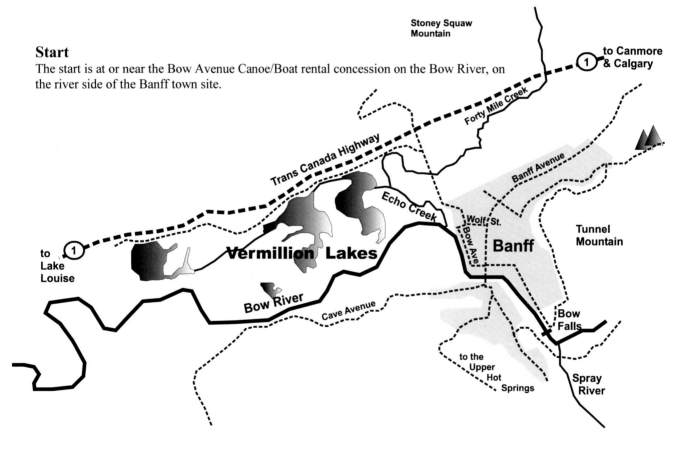

Finish
This is an "out-and-back" with the finish back at the Bow Avenue Boat House.

Intermediate Access and Distances

Location	Km up	MGRS datum NAD 1983 Zone 11U
Bow River Boat House	0.0	NS 994 704
mouth Echo Creek	0.3	NS 993 705
conflunce 40 Mile Creek	1.0	NS 986 710
North Shore Vermillion Lake 1	1.6	NS 982 711
North Shore Vermillion Lake 2	2.5	NS 974 708
NW Shore Vermillion Lake 3	5.0	NS 955 702

Maps

1 - first choice would be *Banff: Up-Close* from Gem Trek Publishing at 1:35,000
2 - NTS: 1:50,000 *82-O/4 Banff*

Camping

Car Camping: For a base of operations in the immediate Banff Townsite, Tunnel Mountain Campgrounds are the closest, those looking for a little bit more of a wilderness experience usually choose to stay at one of the Two Jack Lake campgrounds , for reservations at either 1.877.737.3783.
Parks Canada on-line reservations: www.pccamping.ca/parkscanada/

Trip Notes

From the Boat House work your way upstream to the mouth of Echo Creek, then wind your way up to the First Vermillion Lake. Once on the lakes it is probably best to work your way around the edges, avoiding the worst of the shallows and reeds. This will also give you your best wildlife viewing. This paddle is best in th early morning or early evening when you are least likely to experience wind, and most likely to see wildlife.

Access can usually be found at the most northerly portions of each of the three Vermillion Lakes from the Vermillion Lakes Scenic Drive.

Rentals

Blue Canoe - Bow River Canoe Docks (403.760.5465)
Canoe Season: May 15th to October 15th

Between the Lakes, July, 2005
photo by P. Haskin

Banff Park Lakes

Lake Minnewanka

Why Go
Great mountain scenery, wilderness camping, and mountain day hikes without a long slog around the lake!

Duration of Tour
* 20.8 km along the north shore from the public boat launch to the east end.
* From a few hours for a partial tour, to three or more days, depending on the side hikes and exploring into the Ghost Lakes and Devils Gap that one may want to do.

Classification
Lake trip: Novice paddlers should have considerable experience on flat water, and under windy conditions with waves before undertaking this trip. Lake Minnewanka pretty much parallels the prevailing wind, and can be a wind tunnel at times. Be prepared to be "wind bound" and to then paddle very early or very late in the day to make up for lost time.

Looking east towards Mount Costigan

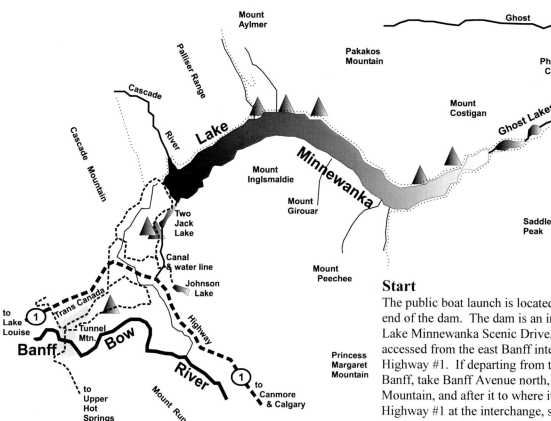

Finish
This is an "out-and-back", the finish is the boat launch at Lake Minnewanka.

Start
The public boat launch is located near the north end of the dam. The dam is an integral part of the Lake Minnewanka Scenic Drive, which is accessed from the east Banff interchange off of Highway #1. If departing from the town of Banff, take Banff Avenue north, towards Cascade Mountain, and after it to where it passes under Highway #1 at the interchange, stay left and continue up to the Dam. The left branch of the Lake Minnewanka Drive, at the first intersection, is the shortest route up to the dam. The right fork will take you past the Two Jack Lake campgrounds, and the access road to Johnson Lake. In summary, Lake Minnewanka is a ten minute drive north and east from downtown Banff.

Intermediate Access and Distances

Campground #	Name	Approximate km from Start	UMG datum 1927
Lm8	Aylmer Pass Trail Junction	6.0 km	PG 097 815
Lm9	Aylmer Canyon	7.4 km	PG 109 819
Lm 11	Mt. Inglismaldie	8.5 km	PG 122 819
Lm 20	Mt. Costigan	16.6 km	PG 186 783
Lm 22	The Narrows	18.8 km	PG 203 792

Maps

1 - *Banff -Mtn. Assiniboine* from Gem Trek Publishing at 1:100,000 for all BUT the most easterly 3 km of the lake, and all of the Ghost Lakes area. This map is more up-to-date for trails and campsites than the NTS sheets below.
2 - NTS: 1:50,000 *82-O/3 Canmore* and *82-O/6 Lake Minnewanka* – these two sheets provide good coverage, especially if you are considering the easterly portion of the lake, or side hikes.

Camping

Car Camping: for pre/post trip accommodation is available very close by at the Two Jack Main Campground and Two Jack Lakeside Campground. Lakeside is very popular. In the summer arrive early and expect to wait for an opening, or to be put on a wait-list. Additional car-camping is available at Tunnel Mtn. Campground's two villages and RV park, all are just east of the Banff town site on the Tunnel Mtn. road. For reservations at all: 1.877.737.3783
Parks Canada on-line reservations: www.pccamping.ca/parkscanada/

Wilderness Camping: Banff Park maintains five campsites along or near the north shore of Lake Minnewanka. Wilderness camping permits are required and are available from the Trail Office at the Parks Information Center (403.762.1550) on Banff Avenue, in Banff.

Trip Notes

These notes have been provided by my long time paddling partner Ted Bentley, who has paddled on Lake Minnewanka numerous times. Ted has used both canoes and touring kayaks for his tripping on the lake.

Lake Minnewanka is about 5 miles from Banff, and is the biggest lake in the park. Lake Minnewanka was extended and raised in the 1920's by a dam which feeds water to the Cascade power generation plant that is by the highway just east of Banff.

The paddling challenge on this lake is that there are frequent and strong winds which can go either direction. One Saturday, we paddled east at 15 km/hr because of a strong tail wind. We were near surfing but not quite and the waves were no real problem for 18' boats with lots of gear. I have also been on the lake with a strong following wind pushing me west. The winds are not really predictable. Going into the wind can be a very cold and wet experience and hypothermia can be a real concern.

There are 5 campsites by the lake Every campsite has a terrific view, and great geology to look at if you are into thrust faults, synclines and anticlines. Seeing the campsite from the water can be a trick. Careful map reading is needed or else hug the shore. It is very easy to paddle past because the campsites are not easy to see from the lake, they were designed for hikers!

Water at the camps is usually from the lake. The water is good tasting and clear, but who needs a bug. Bring your water filter or iodine treatment kit. Yes there are taps but often no water in them and it is a short hike to nearby outwash streams, which may be dry any way.

Apparently there is good fishing in the lake, there sure have been a lot of fishermen out trying during our trips. During our trips we have been able to see deer, bighorn sheep, and a fair variety of birds. Bird life on the water was also fun to watch and hear: Loons with their calls, grebes and ducks.

Alymer Pass, Alymer Mountain, & Alymer Lookout hikes all start from the Alymer Pass Trail Junction campsite. *Scrambles in the Canadian Rockies* by A. Kane, gives a good description. I have gone to the lookout three times. One Sunday, after 12 km of paddling, we did the hike in one hour 20 minutes to the lookout, it is just an uphill walk. The lookout was a fire watch tower for 60 years and thus is set to have very wide sweeping views. You can see most of the way to Calgary and all the way to Sunshine. The historic irony here is that a prescribed burn of the forest slopes near the lookout was carried out around 1990 consuming many of the trees the tower had been protecting for the last 1/2 century. The peak hike is tougher, takes all day, and early in the summer may require crampons or snow shoes. *(As of 2005 this trail is closed in berry season, late July through October, to reduce human and bear conflicts.)*

Other hikes or scrambles are possible at most of the numerous out-wash streams from the ravines between the mountains. These can be wet, slippery scrambles which you can take on or avoid as your taste dictates.

This is the only lake in the park that allows motor boats. There are quite a few fishermen out during the day but they all go home before sunset and do not come back until about 10 a.m. except for 1 or 2 dedicated ones who are out by 7 a.m.

There is a tour boat that takes tourists up and down the lake. Runs about every hour. I am probably now in about 3 million home videos because the tour boats have stopped beside us so often for the passengers to record us for posterity. I have become an official, scenic, local native.

Ted

Bow River

Lake Louise to Banff

Why Go
Mountain Scenery, and fun paddling on fast flowing, clear running water.

Lower portion of Louise Rapid

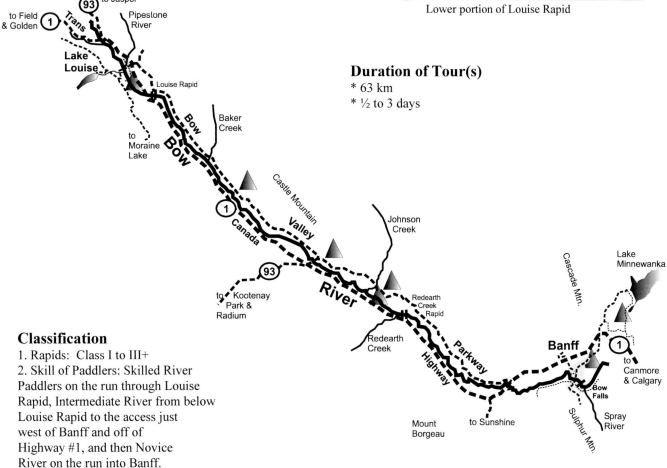

Duration of Tour(s)
* 63 km
* ½ to 3 days

Classification
1. Rapids: Class I to III+
2. Skill of Paddlers: Skilled River Paddlers on the run through Louise Rapid, Intermediate River from below Louise Rapid to the access just west of Banff and off of Highway #1, and then Novice River on the run into Banff.

Start
The start for this run is the bridge to Lake Louise Campground. Take the main access road into the Village of Lake Louise from the Trans Canada Highway (#1), straight through at the 4-way stop, under the railway overpass, and turn left onto Fairview road. The bridge to the campground is about 0.8 km east.

Finish
The primary finish proposed for this run is at the boat concession on the river, off Bow Avenue in the heart of the Banff Town site. Take Wolf Street west off Banff Avenue, or Gopher and Lynx Avenues to Bow Avenue and the boat concession.

Intermediate Access and Distances

Location	Elevation meters	Km down	Km up	Km between	Access / Bank or Rapid / Class	MGRS datum NAD 1983 Zone 11U	Gradient m/km
Lake Louise Campground Bridge		63.2	0.0			NS 574 964	
Highway #1 / Louise Rapid		60.9	2.3		Class II to III+ portage or line along right bank	NS 586 948	
	1520	60.1	3.1				5.0
Recommended Access below Louise Rapid		59.8	3.4	3.4	right bank	NS 596 944	
Highway #1 viewpoint		55.9	7.3		right bank	NS 618 919	
	1480	50.0	13.2				4.0
Taylor Creek		45.5	17.7		right bank	NS 681 845	
	1440	38.5	24.7				3.5
Castle Mtn. Jct./Bridge		36.5	26.7	23.3	left bank below bridge	NS 749 799	
Johnson Creek / Campsite		29.7	33.5			NS 800 772	
Redearth Creek Rapid		26.2	37.0		Class II+ to III+ portage on right bank	NS 828 755	
	1400	24.7	38.5				2.9
access above #1 bridge		9.8	53.4			NS 932 690	
Bow Ave. Boat House & Concession		0.0	63.2	36.5	left bank, Bow Falls is not far below the Banff Avenue Bridge!	NS 995 703	

Gradient

This is a classic mountain reach, starts steep at over 5 m/km, and then gradually tapers into a flat reach of much less than 2 m/km through the wetlands upstream of Banff town site – and then, all of a sudden the river falls off the edge of the earth at Bow Falls! I've tried to calculate the gradient of the wetlands reach, but I cannot find a map with any contour line crossing between the 1400 m line, and Bow Falls.

River Volume and Flow Rate

These reaches are best run with the Banff station reporting about 75 to 150 cms. At the Banff station river velocity is approximately 2 km/hr with 30 cms of water, and 7.5 km/hr at 300 cms.

Bow River at Banff

	Apr	May	Jun	Jul	Aug	Sep	Oct
Daily Max	98.3	306	377	314	174	129	76.5
+ 1 Std.	13.56	72.2	156.9	133.7	79.4	46.64	28.08
Daily Mean	10.5	50.9	126	107	66.4	39.1	23.6
- 1 Std.	7.44	29.6	95.1	80.3	53.4	31.56	19.12
Daily Min.	4.9	6.85	24.2	34	29	17.9	9.46

1910 to 2003

Maps

1 - My first choice for a map for these reaches is the Gem Trek Publishing ***Banff & Mt. Assinboine*** sheet at 1:100,000. This sheet covers all of this reach report.

2 - NTS 1:250,000   NTS 1:50,000
    82 N Golden   82 N/8 Lake Louise
    82 O Calgary   82 O/5 Castle Mountain
                          82 O/4 Banff

Banff Park has a very informative on-line (http://www.pc.gc.ca/pn-np/ab/banff/activ/activ28c_e.pdf) brochure for this run and the Bow Falls to Canmore run.

Camping

There is a wide variety of public campgrounds through the Bow Valley to support day paddling: Lake Louise (1.877.737.3783), Protection Mountain (403.522.3833 info' only), Castle Mountain, and Two Jack Lake (1.877.737.3783). Parks Canada on-line reservations: www.pccamping.ca/parkscanada/

There is only one "on river" wilderness campsite, and it is at the mouth of Johnson Creek (Park # Bo1C). These reaches are all in Banff National Park and "random camping" is NOT allowed. One must book their site in advance for Johnson Creek at either of the Park offices in Banff (403.762.1550) or Lake Louise (403-522-1264). The Banff Park brochure does stress that the Bow river is polluted and paddlers should filter their water, or carry water into this campsite.

Wildlife

This is a national park, you will see wildlife! You may see more wildlife than you want. Some years ago my teenage daughter thought she would rather read than paddle and opted to stay with the van at Castle Junction, the finish of our run for that day. She stayed in the van all right, a big grizzly bear showed up and kept her inside the vehicle for much of the day. Not much reading got done!

According to the above mentioned park notes, the Bow River hosts one of the highest concentrations of harlequin ducks in North America. Male harlequin ducks are very colorful, but you must be on the river early in the season to view them. They do "their work" and then soon head back to the coast leaving the females to raise the brood. As always with waterfowl on the river, do your best to avoid "herding" them down the river; this can tire out young ducklings and result in their drowning. It is best either to pull over and hope the ducks take refugee in a side channel or go to shore, or try to sneak by them on the far side of the river. Once you pull a little ahead of a mother duck and her brood she will usually head to shore, or head back upstream out of harm's way.

Trip Notes

The first part of this run is challenging for open canoeists, Class II+ right from the campsite bridge through to the bottom of Louise Rapid (III- to III+). Even when we used to put in right under the Highway #1 Bridge east of Lake Louise many of our trip participants would opt to portage to the bottom of the rapid. Others of us would run the rapid with the canoes empty (no load, no kids, no dogs and lots of flotation!). The picture at the start of this report shows that Louise rapid can be a fun run for the skilled and properly equipped. I have also fished out some very cold, wet and scared paddlers after a long, rough swim through this rapid.

Most paddlers, and the Banff Park information brochure, recommend starting this run below the Louise Rapid. Access to the river is some 750 m east of the Highway #1 Bridge, and north down an old road to a side channel. If the water is high you can float your boat the last 100 m or so on this channel into the main stream.

The first few kilometers below Louise Rapid are fast, bouncy, with tight corners and the river requires precise maneuvering skills. Boulders, sweepers and logjams are present. Keep a sharp eye looking downstream at all times and, if in doubt, SCOUT! The lower two-thirds of this run are easier, but log jams, sweepers and fast, bouncy gravel bar chutes do occur.

From Castle Mountain Junction, there are 9 km of modestly fast, winding river to Redearth Creek Rapids, a Class III- to III+ rapid at most water levels. As noted above one can portage on the right bank, but there is no formal trail. And if unfamiliar with this rapid, do NOT slide into them without scouting. The waves are larger the further you get into the rapid with the largest wave train at the bottom. This rapid is well known for swamping poorly skilled and ill equipped paddlers. For the next dozen kilometers or so below Redearth Creek rapid the river is fast, winding and with many logjams, sweepers and side channels. Care must be exercised, and generally if in doubt stay tight to the inside of corners, in the slower water and try to pick either the largest channel, or the channel that is flowing back to more of the river.

Other Reaches
Above Lake Louise is serious whitewater and interested paddlers should refer to Smith (1995) *Canadian Rockies Whitewater: Southern Rockies.* Banff to Canmore is the next report!

Other Local Activities or Destinations
There is much to do in Banff. On cold, ugly paddling days my family is most likely to opt to warm-up in the Upper Hot Springs, then visit the Wildlife Museum just north of the Banff Avenue Bridge, and finish the trip to town with a shopping spree in the Banff Avenue candy store.

A C-1 paddler at the 1983 National Whitewater Slalom Championships,
held on the Bow River, upstream of Lake Louise.

Bow River

Banff to Canmore

Start below Bow Falls and the Spray River

Why Go
To view Bow Falls from the safety of below, and contemplate the stunt men in Marilyn Monroe's film, *River of No Return,* running the falls! One paddles this reach for the scenery, the wildlife (best run around to see elk), the fast flowing water and easy paddling (well most of the time!).

Duration of Tour(s)
* 27.5 km
* ½ to 1 day tours are available

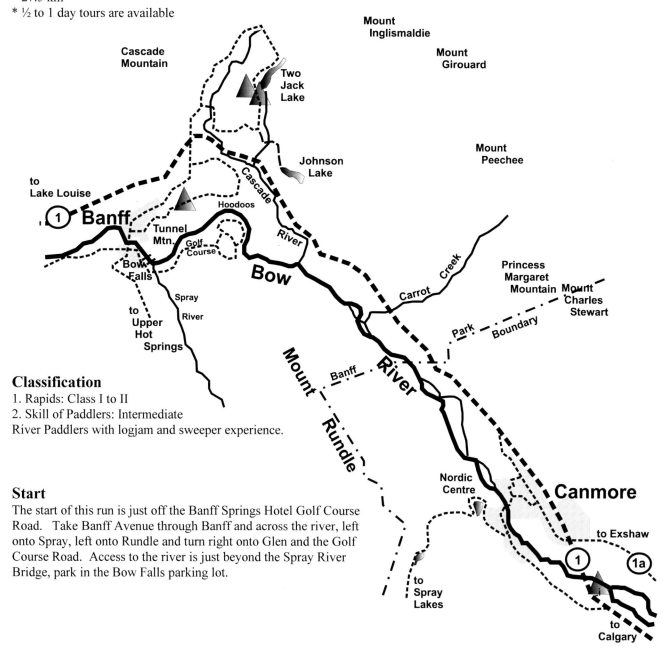

Classification
1. Rapids: Class I to II
2. Skill of Paddlers: Intermediate
River Paddlers with logjam and sweeper experience.

Start
The start of this run is just off the Banff Springs Hotel Golf Course Road. Take Banff Avenue through Banff and across the river, left onto Spray, left onto Rundle and turn right onto Glen and the Golf Course Road. Access to the river is just beyond the Spray River Bridge, park in the Bow Falls parking lot.

Finish

The most popular finish for this run is the Canmore town bridge. A raft and canoe landing is just downstream of the bridge on the right bank, and there is a small parking lot. To reach this access from Highway #1, take Highway #1a / Bow Valley Trail into Canmore, then turn onto Railway Avenue, and then onto 101 St. Turn south/left onto 8th Avenue, which will lead you through to the town bridge, just past downtown Canmore.

I have taken this report through to the Bow River Provincial Recreation Area campground which is just downstream of the Highway #1 bridge east, south and downstream of Canmore. Access to the river can be had at the bridge, or through the campground.

Intermediate Access and Distances

Location	Elevation meters	Km down	Km up	Km between	Access / Bank or Rapid / Class	MGRS datum NAD 1983 Zone 11U	Gradient m/km
Spray River / Start		27.5	0.0		right bank	PS 007 692	
Golf Course Rd. Access		22.4	5.1	5.1	right bank	PS 042 706	
	1360	20.6	6.9				
Cascade River		19.0	8.5			PS 063 694	
Carrot Creek		15.2	12.3			PS 087 671	
Park Boundary		12.5	15.0	10.0	left bank	PS 109 657	
	1320	9.6	17.9				3.6
Old Railway Bridge		5.6	21.9			PS 141 612	
Canmore Town Bridge		4.9	22.6	7.6	right bank	PS 144 606	
Highway #1 Bridge		0.4	27.1			PS 174 581	
Bow River Prov. Rec. Area		0.0	27.5	5.0	right bank	PS 178 579	

Gradient

Gradients for this reach are a bit of mystery. Bow Falls and the long flat reach above, and the long flat reach below Highway #1 east of Canmore complicate calculations. I was a bit surprised to see that the one average gradient possible to calculate is as high as 3.6 m/km. But this section is know as fast, winding and often full of logjams and sweepers.

River Volume and Flow Rate

Optimal flows for paddling this reach is with the Banff station reporting approximately 50 to 160 cms. Velocities at the Banff station vary from 2 km/hr at 30 cms to 7 km/hr at 300 cms!

Maps

1 - First choice map would be the Gem Trek Publishing *Banff & Mt. Assiniboine* map at 1:100,000.
2 - NTS 1:50,000
   82O/3 Canmore

Bow River at Banff

	Apr	May	Jun	Jul	Aug	Sep	Oct
Daily Max	98.3	306	377	314	174	129	76.5
+ 1 Std.	13.56	72.2	156.9	133.7	79.4	46.64	28.08
Daily Mean	10.5	50.9	126	107	66.4	39.1	23.6
- 1 Std.	7.44	29.6	95.1	80.3	53.4	31.56	19.12
Daily Min.	4.9	6.85	24.2	34	29	17.9	9.46

1910 to 2003

Camping

This is a run commonly done as a day trip; about one half of it is in the National Park and no wilderness camping is allowed and much of the other half is within the Town of Canmore. Good car camping sites for staging this run are the Two Jack Lake campgrounds (1.877.737.3783) in Banff Park, or the Bow River Provincial Recreation Area campground (403.673.2163) at the end of this run. Parks Canada on-line reservations: www.pccamping.ca/parkscanada/

Wildlife

Much wildlife can be seen along this run, with a good possibility of elk as you float by the Banff Springs Golf Course, and then rocky mountain sheep in the vicinity of the hoodoos a little further along.

Trip Notes

This is a very scenic run, and with no really significant rapids, it attracts many novice paddlers without the skills to negotiate the logjams and sweepers. This run, like the run above Banff, is also supported by a Banff Park web page of river information at: http://www.pc.gc.ca/pn-np/ab/banff/activ/activ28c_e.pdf.

Throughout this guide I do try to deliver the message that logjams and sweepers generally strike greater fear into me than virtually all Class II to III rapids. This run has had some significant incidents with novice paddlers being swept into sweepers.

In particular it should be noted that the stretch just above the hoodoos, has some tight corners with sweepers and strainers. Just below the Golf Course road access the river splits into two channels. For most of the last decade the left channel has been choked with a channel wide logjam. At times Parks has signed this channel as unnavigable, and their present literature suggests it is still choked (as of 2006). Again from the Cascade River through to the town of Canmore the river is braided, and prone to sweepers on the outside of most bends, with logjams (strainers) at the upstream end of most bars and islands.

At the Banff Park Boundary (which may be signed on the right bank) there is a 200 m trail on the left bank to a parking area near the Park Gates. If planning on using this access, it is best to check it out first, and flag it.

Other Reaches

The upstream reach is included within this guide. Below this reach, and just below the Bow River campground the river disappears under, and flows through a extensive series of logjams, requiring some extensive portaging and is generally not run.

Other Local Activities or Destinations

This part of the Bow Valley is well developed and for outdoors folks, there are extensive hiking and mountain biking trails in the area. Again, a cold day in the Bow Valley has driven me more than once to the pleasures of the Upper Hot Springs in Banff, followed by a trip to a fine restaurant and the Banff Avenue Candy store.

Rentals

Canmore
Gear Up Mountain Sports Rentals 403.678.1636

Bow River

Dead Man's Flats to Seebe

Why Go
This run like those upstream offers great mountain scenery and is a little easier, with a number of short sub-reaches.

Duration of Tour(s)
* 21 km
* ½ to 1 day

Classification
1. Rapids: Class 1 - gravel bar riffles mostly
2. Skill of Paddlers: Intermediate River (or Novice River with good leadership who know the log jams)

Osprey on nest near Dead Man's Flats

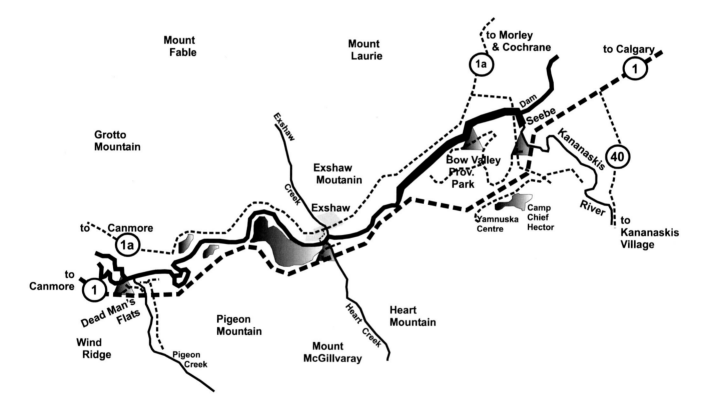

Start
The proposed start for this run is in Dead Man's Flats at the Three Sisters Campground.

Finish
The finish for this reach is at the boat launch on the reservoir just above the Seebe / Kananaskis Falls dam on the Kananaskis River bay, just south of the bridge over the Bow.

Intermediate Access and Distances

Location	Elevation meters	Km down	Km up	Km between	Access / Bank or Rapid / Class	MGRS datum NAD 1983 Zone 11U	Gradient m/km
Three Sisters Campground		21.0	0		right bank	PS 211 557	
Pigeon Creek		20.4	0.6		right bank		
Lac des Arcs Campground		10.0	11	11.0	right bank	PS 284 572	
Exshaw Access		9.5	11.5		left bank	PS 287 576	
Bow Valley P.P. Whitefish Day Use Area		4.5	16.5	5.5	right bank	PS 322 601	
Seebe - takeout		0.0	21	4.5	left bank on Kananaskis reach	PS 356 622	

Gradient
This is a relatively flat reach and due to the dam, no worthwhile average gradient can be determined. The river does ease off and become a reservoir at the upstream end of Bow Valley Provincial Park, and the fastest water of the trip is the stretch just below Exshaw Creek.

River Volume and Flow Rate
Given the low gradient of this reach, it can be paddled with lower flows, certainly down to the 40 cms range. When flows rise much above 150 cms at the Banff station this reach should be avoided by paddlers.

Maps
1 - Map of choice is the Gem Trek Publishing *Canmore and Kananaskis Village* sheet at 1:50,000, this sheet covers this whole report
2 - NTS 1:50,000
        83O/3 Canmore

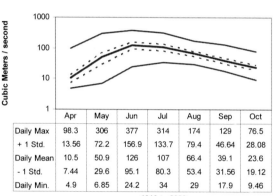

Bow River at Banff

	Apr	May	Jun	Jul	Aug	Sep	Oct
Daily Max	98.3	306	377	314	174	129	76.5
+ 1 Std.	13.56	72.2	156.9	133.7	79.4	46.64	28.08
Daily Mean	10.5	50.9	126	107	66.4	39.1	23.6
- 1 Std.	7.44	29.6	95.1	80.3	53.4	31.56	19.12
Daily Min.	4.9	6.85	24.2	34	29	17.9	9.46

1910 to 2003

Camping
This reach has three public campgrounds along the river: Three Sisters at Dead Man's Flats, Lac des Arcs, and Bow Valley Provincial Park (for all three call 403.673.2163). This is not a reach for wilderness camping!

Wildlife
Highlights of my runs on these reaches have been the osprey and great blue herons.

Trip Notes
These reaches of the Bow are basically leisurely paddles: BUT, the end of Lac des Arcs can present powerful winds, and below Exshaw there is a stretch of braided channels with ever present sweepers and logjams. Side channels can be blocked and very dangerous, even this placid reach has drowned unwary paddlers – so BE wary! BE skilled!

Other Reaches
Immediately upstream of Dead Man's Flats is an infamous logjam that has blocked the river for a number of years. Below this reach are two dams, portages, and a long series of major rapids (class II to V+) below the second dam (Horseshoe Falls). Also once below Horseshoe dam the river flows through the Stoney Indian Reserve and permission must be sought to paddle through the reserve. For whitewater paddlers this permission has been given in the past, especially to folks camped at the Stoney Indian Park.

Bow River

Ghost Dam to Cochrane

Why Go
This reach is paddled by those who want to play the eddies down to the Gas Plant rapid and then exit below, or those wanting to camp on Wildcat Island, or those looking for a fun and pleasant paddle through foothills scenery.

Duration of Tour(s)
* 22 km
* ½ to 2 days

Classification
1. Rapids: to Class II+
2. Skill of Paddlers: Intermediate River, or Novice River with good leadership

below Ghost Dam, mid-May '99

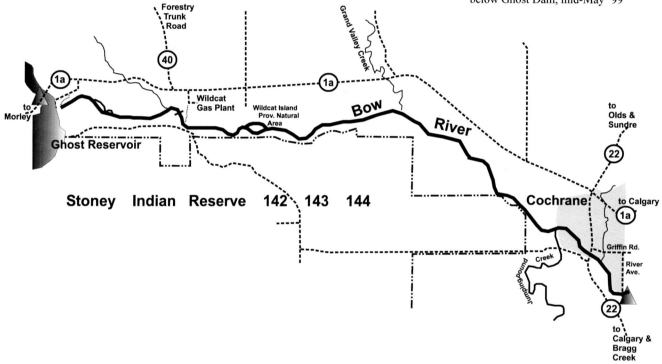

Start
The start for this run is just below the Ghost Dam. The road down was damaged during the floods of 2005. The road is presently closed and as I update this report in August 2009, the road repairs are NOT under consideration and are not likely to occur! This means it is about a 400 m hike down to the river from the top of the bank.

Finish
The proposed finish for this run is at the River Avenue Bridge right in Cochrane.

Intermediate Access and Distances

Location	Elevation meters	Km down	Km up	Km between	Access / Bank or Rapid / Class	MGRS datum NAD 1983 Zone 11U	Gradient m/km
below Ghost Dam		20.1	0		left bank		
	1143	18.1	2				
Gas Plant Rapid		16.6	3.5		Class I-II, diagonal ledge	PS 636 766	
Gas Plant Rd Access		16.1	4	4	left bank, hike in/out	PS 639 762	
Wildcat Island		14.3	5.8	1.8		PS 656 763	
Railway Bridge		6.1	14			PS 727 751	
	1128	5.9	14.2				1.2
Jumpingpound Creek		3.6	16.5		right bank	PS 746 737	
Highway #22		2.2	17.9			PS 756 731	
River Avenue		0.0	20.1	14.3	left bank, just below the bridge	PS 770 721	
	1113	-1.5	21.6				2.0

Gradient
Average Gradient on this run varies between 1.2 m/km and 2 m/km.

River Volume and Flow Rate
Best paddling on this reach will be had with flows of approximately 75 to 200 cms at the Calgary station. Because this reach is immediately below a major hydroelectric dam, do expect flows to fluctuate considerably, especially in the morning and evening as Calgarians power-up their homes.

As I review this report in August 2009, I find that the Cochrane station, on the Alberta Environment web site, is still not reporting on the standard graph or table, and other stations are one dam above or below this reach. To the right is the data from the old Ghost Dam station. The Calgary station does tend to report higher flows at each data point, as one might expect for a station further downstream.

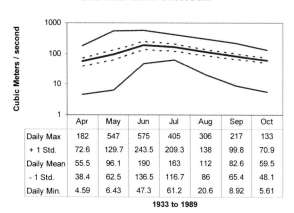

Bow River below Ghost Dam

	Apr	May	Jun	Jul	Aug	Sep	Oct
Daily Max	182	547	575	405	306	217	133
+ 1 Std.	72.6	129.7	243.5	209.3	138	99.8	70.9
Daily Mean	55.5	96.1	190	163	112	82.6	59.5
- 1 Std.	38.4	62.5	136.5	116.7	86	65.4	48.1
Daily Min.	4.59	6.43	47.3	61.2	20.6	8.92	5.61

1933 to 1989

Maps
1 - First choice map for this reach would be the ARCA Alberta River Guide *The Middle Bow River: Ghost Dam to Carseland* along with one's ever present *Alberta Road Map*.

2 -   NTS 1:250,000   NTS 1:50,000
        82 O Calgary   82 O/1 Calgary
                               82 O/2 Jumping Pound Creek

Camping
Public campgrounds are available just off the river at both the start and finish of this run. At the start you have your choice on either side of Highway #1a on the Ghost Reservoir (403.851.0766) just above the dam, and in Cochrane at Bow Riversedge Campground (403.932.4675) just up River Avenue from the Bridge. Wilderness camping is available on Wildcat Island. Wildcat Island is a Provincial Natural Area, and does tend to get well used, so please plan on not using the local forest to fuel a camp fire; take a stove instead! If I lived in Calgary, I can certainly envision a late afternoon escape to Wildcat Island and then a pleasant early morning paddle down to Cochrane.

Wildlife

Deer, coyotes and beaver are the most likely mammals to be spotted, along with a wide variety of bird life.

Trip Notes

In the past, for Calgarians, this was the classic "training" run. One took their lessons with the Bow Waters or Calgary Canoe Club, or the Rocky Mountain Paddling Centre and after a river and eddy turn intro' at the "Bowness eddies" one's first canoe trip was likely to be this reach. White water paddlers most often just paddle the first 4 km as this part of the run does have the best selection and concentration of eddies and river features for practice. But the whole run is very scenic as the river begins the transition from the foothills to the prairies.

The most significant rapid is the Gas Plant rapid. This rapid is a partial diagonal ledge extending out from the left bank.

Other Reaches

Upstream of this reach is the 12 km long Ghost Reservoir, a body of water best left to the sailing "set," though I must admit that the reservoir did make a good site for a sea kayak instructors course I once took. The run below through Calgary is next in this guide.

Other Local Activities or Destinations

On a cold, ugly day, or if Trans Alta "turns the river off" – there is much to do in the Cochrane and Calgary region. I would suggest checking out the Historic Cochrane Ranch in Cochrane, or taking in the Calgary Zoo (one of the world's best), or I'm most likely to head to the Glenbow Museum in downtown Calgary.

Rentals and Shuttles

Rentals:

       Aquabatics: 403.288.9283
       Mountain Equipment Co-op: 403.269.2420
       Rocky Mountain Paddling Centre: 403.202.8490
       Sports Rent: 403.292.0077
       Undercurrents: 403.262.4327
       U of C Outdoor Program Centre: 403.220.5038

Shuttles:

       Louise Shotton Shuttle Service: 403.282.5071
       Bow River Shuttles: 403.278.9165
       Calgary Bow River Shuttle Service: 403.510.0138

Cochrane's Riversedge campground with River Avenue bridge in the
background, May '99

Bow River

Bowness Park to Fish Creek Park

Why Go
Paddling the Bow may be the best way to see Calgary; it is a fun paddle with some interesting spots to play, or practise!

Duration of Tour(s)
* 40 km
* ½ to 1 day

Classification
1. Rapids: Class I plus 1 weir to portage *(this will change)*
2. Skill of Paddlers: Intermediate River, or Novice River with knowledgeable leadership

CRCA Sea Kayak School in the Bowness eddies, Aug. '04

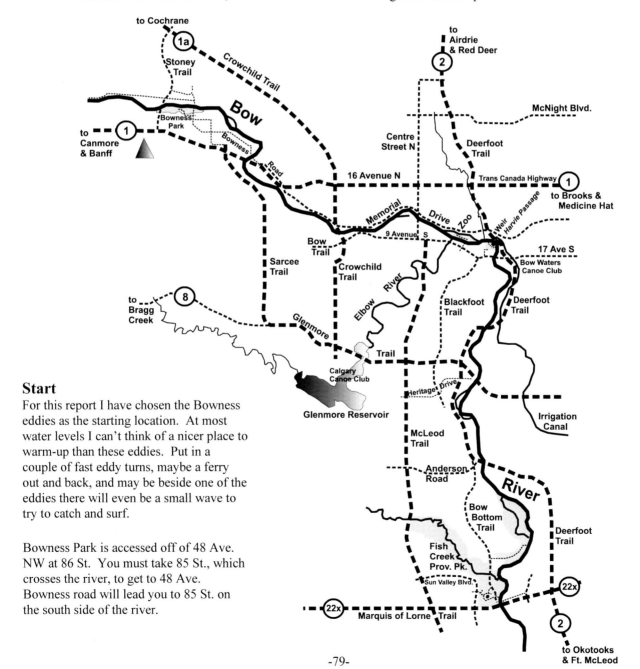

Start
For this report I have chosen the Bowness eddies as the starting location. At most water levels I can't think of a nicer place to warm-up than these eddies. Put in a couple of fast eddy turns, maybe a ferry out and back, and may be beside one of the eddies there will even be a small wave to try to catch and surf.

Bowness Park is accessed off of 48 Ave. NW at 86 St. You must take 85 St., which crosses the river, to get to 48 Ave. Bowness road will lead you to 85 St. on the south side of the river.

Finish

I have also chosen a major park to finish this run – at the Fish Creek Provincial Park boat launch just upstream of the Marquis of Lorne Trail Bridge. The best access is by following Bow Bottom Trail through to the boat launch. Access from the west via Sikome Lake may be closed by gates. For those living east of the Bow, the McKenzie Meadows Drive access, on the east (left) bank, under the Marquis of Lorne Trail is an easy alternative and adds very little to the run.

Intermediate Access and Distances

Location	Elevation meters	Km down	Km up	Km between	Access / Bank or Rapid / Class	MGRS datum NAD 1983 Zone 11U *	Gradient m/km
	1074		-4				
Bowness Park		41	0		right bank	PS 945 644	
	1067	40	1				1.4
16 Avenue N / Sholdice Park		35	6		left bank	PS 978 622	
	1059	35	6				1.6
Edworthy Park		33	8	8	right bank	PS 994 607	
	1052	31	10				1.7
Crowchild Trail		29	12				
14 Street SW		28	13				
	1044	27	14				2.0
below 10 St. Bridge		27	14		right bank	QS 044 595	
Princess Island		26	15			QS 048 599	
Centre Street Bridge		25	16				
Zoo / Centenary Park		23	18	10	left bank, on St. Georges Island	QS 076 591	
	1036	23	18				1.9
CPR Railway Bridge		22	19				
portage start (will change)		22	19		right bank	QS 090 589	
Pearce Estate Park		21	20		right bank, from 17 Ave. & 17a St. SE		
17AveS / Cushing Bridge		20	21				
Inglewood Bird Sanctuary		19	22		right bank	QS 101 571	
	1029	19	22				1.7
Ogden Road / Bonnybrook		17	24		right bank	QS 095 554	
	1021	14	27				1.9
Glenmore Trail / Graves		13	28	10	right bank, from Heritage Drive	QS 088 525	
	1006	5	36				1.5
						Zone 12U	
Fish Creek Bankside		4	38		right bank	TB 896 447	
Fish Creek - confluence		1	40		right bank		
Fish Creek - Boat Launch		0	41	13	right bank	QS 102 426	
	991		42				2.5

*note Fish Creek Bankside is just into MGRS zone 12U and the boat launch is back in zone 11U

Gradient

Gradients are pretty consistent on this run, and I suspect much of the last average gradient noted above is actually used up in the riffle immediately below Marquis of Lorne Trail, and downstream from the Fish Creek Park finish suggested here.

River Volume and Flow Rate

This reach is a fine, fun paddle with anything from about 80 cms up to 250 cms.

Maps

1 - First choice masp for the run would be the ARCA River Guide *The Middle Bow River: Ghost Dam to Carseland* and an *Alberta Road Map.*

2 - NTS 1:250,000   1:50,000
     82 O Calgary   82 O/1 Calgary
     82 J Kananaskis Lakes   82 J/16 Priddis
     82 I Gleichen   82 I/13 Dalmead

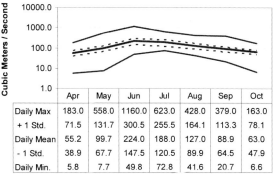

Bow River in Calgary

	Apr	May	Jun	Jul	Aug	Sep	Oct
Daily Max	183.0	558.0	1160.0	623.0	428.0	379.0	163.0
+ 1 Std.	71.5	131.7	300.5	255.5	164.1	113.3	78.1
Daily Mean	55.2	99.7	224.0	188.0	127.0	88.9	63.0
- 1 Std.	38.9	67.7	147.5	120.5	89.9	64.5	47.9
Daily Min.	5.8	7.7	49.8	72.8	41.6	20.7	6.6

1911 to 2003

Camping

Not much for camping on this reach. Back in the "good old days" there was a city campground on St. George's Island but it is no more. For "out-of-towners" looking for a "base of operations" the Calgary West KOA (403.288.0411) is reasonably close to the start, and Nature's Hideway (403.938.8185) on the Highwood River is not too far from the finish of this run.

Wildlife

I suspect that for many people one highlight on this run maybe watching the pelicans feeding at the bottom of the portage around the weir. Bird life will constitute the majority of wildlife that most folks are likely to see on this run. Masterman (1999) reports that over a year, Calgary is home to, or a temporary shelter at least, to more than 200 species of birds. He also notes that all of the common mammals of Western Canada may be seen withing the municipal limits of Calgary. A couple of interesting recent arrivals to Calgary that some Albertans may not be familiar with are the large eastern gray (mostly black actually) squirrels, and raccoons.

Trip Notes

One could squeeze another 3 km out of this run by starting up the Bears Paw Dam road, but I like the parking, washrooms, access and eddies at Bowness Park for starting this run. This run is relatively fast, and probably should not be the "first" run for novice river paddlers, unless under the guidance of skilled leaders/instructors. If you are the "self taught" kind of paddler, tackle the middle Red Deer reaches and get your eddy turns, ferrying and river reading skills "in hand" before taking on this run.

This run is fast at most water levels, and can be very powerful and dangerous at high flows (over 250 cms or so). Over the whole reach the river breaks up into multiple channels around the many islands and gravel bars, and one must remain vigilant to stay in the best "flow." Bridge piers and mid-stream boulders are the most common hazards. The north most pier of 10th St Bridge has claimed a boat or two in it's time. Sweepers and log jams are relatively rare (due to Bearspaw Dam), but they do occur.

The biggest danger on this run is the Western Irrigation District weir just below the Zoo. Once you spot the CPR Railway bridge below St. Georges Island, get to river right (the south bank). The portage commences in less than 100 m and is accessed from the small side channel. It is a great portage trail, flat, and smooth. Check out the photos at the end of this report. Once below the weir the paddling is again pretty straightforward paddling all the way to Fish Creek Provincial Park.

As I review this report in August 2009 the redevelopment of the weir as a paddler friendly whitewater site, to become the "Harvie Passage" is well underway. This redevelopment will result in two channels being developed over and past the weir, one for most boaters (the south or right channel), and one for the "play" boaters, this second channel will be more challenging. Expected completion is for the spring of 2011. and updated information is available at: http://www.harviepassage.ca/. As of August 2009 the portage around the weir has been extended due to the construction. Before a trip to, from, or past this site do check the web for updated access and portage information.

Other Reaches

River Avenue in Cochrane to Bearspaw Dam is approximately 21 kilometers. Given my laborious grunt down this reach in the 1971 Banff to Calgary canoe race (over two days) I've not been inclined to retrace those strokes, but on a pleasant summer afternoon with a modest tail wind – it could be a grand paddle. Bearspaw Dam is portaged on the left or north bank. Calgary to Carseland is the next report, and a great run.

Other Local Activities or Destinations

When stranded in Calgary due to poor paddling conditions, I usually head for either the Glenbow Museum, or the Zoo! Just finished the run down to Fish Creek Park on a hot summer's day, don't miss the chance for a dip in Sikome Lake in the park.

Rentals and Shuttles

Rentals:
Aquabatics 403.288.9283
Mountain Equipment Co-op 403.269.2420
Rocky Mountain Paddling Centre 403.202.8490
Sports Rent 403.292.0077
Undercurrents 403.262.4327
U of C outdoor Program Centre 403.220.5038

Shuttles:
Louise Shotton Shuttle Service 403.282.5071
Bow River Shuttles 403.278.9165
Calgary Bow River Shuttle Service 403.510.0138

Fish Creek Provincial Park boat launch
June 1999

approach to CPR bridge above weir,
June 1999

WID weir in Calgary just below Nose Creek
June 1999

warning sign at Carseland Weir, June
1999

Bow River

Calgary to Carseland

Why Go
This is a scenic prairie paddle on a modestly fast flowing stream.

Duration of Tour(s)
* 52 km
* ½ to 2 days

Looking north across the Bow at the Highwood Confluence, Aug. '97

Classification
1. Rapids: Class I to II
2. Skill of Paddlers: Intermediate River, or Novice River with good leadership.

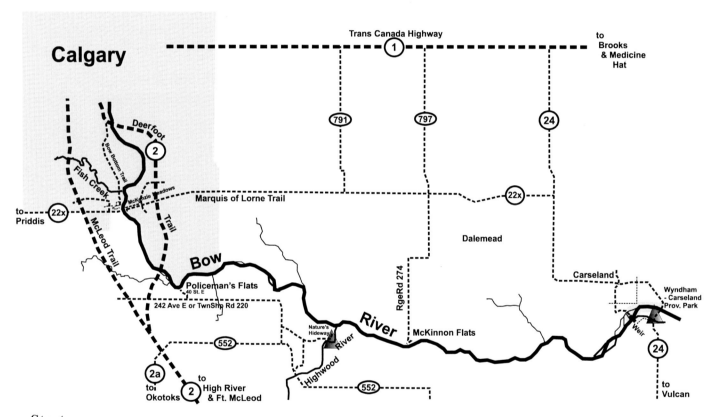

Start
This report and run starts at the Fish Creek Provincial Park boat launch just 300 m upstream of the Marquis of Lorne Trail Bridge. The best access to this start is by following Bow Bottom Trail through to the boat launch. River access from the east is also possible from under the bridge for the Marquis of Lorne Trail, via McKenzie Meadows Drive.

Finish
Finish for this run is at the west end of Wyndham-Carseland Provincial Park, on Johnson's Island, on the north bank of the river. This point is reach by going south from the town of Carseland on Range Road 260. This road turns east and then drops down into the river valley and crosses onto Johnson's Island.

Intermediate Access and Distances

Location	Elevation meters	Km down	Km up	Km between	Access / Bank or Rapid / Class	MGRS datum NAD 1983 Zone 11U	Gradient m/km
	1006		-5				
Marquis of Lorne Trail		52	0			QS 103 423	
	991	51	1				2.5
						Zone 12 U	
	983	47	6				1.8
Policeman's Flats		44	8	8	right bank	TB 923 364	
	975	42	11				1.6
	968	39	13				2.5
	960	35	17				2.1
	953	30	22				1.4
Highwood River		28	24	16	right bank	UB 042 332	
	945	26	26				2.0
	937	23	30				2.4
McKinnon Flats		22	30	6	left bank	UB 097 315	
	930	18	34				1.6
	922	14	38				1.9
	914	5	47				0.9
	907	2	51				2.1
Johnson's Island		0	52	22	left channel	UB 272 334	
Carseland Weir						UB 280 330	

Gradient

This reach of the river flows pretty consistently to below McKinnon Flats. I'm suspect of the last contour line and average gradient as the river at most water levels does slow down above the weir, and branches out into a number of channels before Johnson's Island and the weir itself.

River Volume and Flow Rate

Rivers change over time, and especially rivers like the Bow that do not carry as much water as they did nearly 100 years ago when records were first kept. Thus normal ranges are now less than the chart to the right might suggest. This means that in this day and age, the best paddling is to be had on this reach with flows ranging from about 80 cms through to about 200 cms.

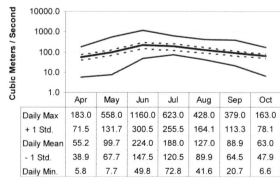

Bow River in Calgary

	Apr	May	Jun	Jul	Aug	Sep	Oct
Daily Max	183.0	558.0	1160.0	623.0	428.0	379.0	163.0
+ 1 Std.	71.5	131.7	300.5	255.5	164.1	113.3	78.1
Daily Mean	55.2	99.7	224.0	188.0	127.0	88.9	63.0
- 1 Std.	38.9	67.7	147.5	120.5	89.9	64.5	47.9
Daily Min.	5.8	7.7	49.8	72.8	41.6	20.7	6.6

1911 to 2003

Maps

1 - First choice maps for the run would be the ARCA River Guide *The Middle Bow River: Ghost Dam to Carseland* and an *Alberta Road Map.*

2 - NTS   1:250,000   1:50,000
            82 J Kananaskis Lakes   82 J/16 Priddis
            82 I Gleichen   82 I/13 Dalmead (90% of this reach is on the 1:50,000 Dalmead sheet!)
                                                    82 I/14 Gleichen

Camping

Public campgrounds are available at the end of this run in Wyndham-Carseland Provincial Park (403.934.3523), but below the weir. Nature's Hideway (403.938.8185) is about 1 km up the Highwood River, and could easily be lined up to.

Wilderness camping is practical all along this reach on any of the many islands, or below the high water mark once past the early summer high flows. Virtually of the land along this river is privately owned and permission should be sought if camping along the banks.

Wildlife

As you might guess from the "drift boat" picture below, this reach is a "fishing" reach. This reach of the Bow is world famous for rainbow trout, and is one of the few streams in Alberta that truly supports a sport fishing guiding industry. There are Bow River specific regulations for this fishery and anyone interested in fishing this reach must be familiar with the provincial regulations – seek guidance at the local fishing shop and in the annual provincial Fishing Guide.

Drift Boat on the Bow River, Aug. '97

If there are fish, there will be "fish eating krysters" as my old friend and paddling guide the late "Mister Kievitt" would say. Yes, bald eagles, pelicans, osprey and kingfishers can be spotted on this run. And given the open hills along much of the run, Red Tail and Swainson's hawks are likely to be seen soaring and hunting on any sunny day with a breeze. Besides the feathered and hairless fishermen on this run, with a little luck you might catch a glimpse of a mink, but more likely a beaver.

Trip Notes

This is a classic Calgary paddle. With a few river skills and some trained leadership, just about any paddler can tackle this run. If you're "self guided" and working your way up the river difficulty ladder, make sure you've paddled the middle and lower Red Deer, and the Bow through Calgary before trying an overnight down to Carseland. And if relatively new to all of this, when you set up your shuttle at Carseland, go over and have a look at the weir, and take a very good look at the channels into the take out on Johnson's Island. You do NOT want to miss the take out! Look at the pictures at the end of the previous report!

When I paddled the run down to McKinnon Flats a few years ago I was surprised at how much fast water, and how many bouncy, splashy small rapids there were. It was a great paddle on an early, hot August Sunday. As always with such runs keep a sharp eye out for those boulders that hide just under the surface, and sweepers or logjams (relatively infrequent) and take care around the bridge piers.

Given that the waters of the Bow usually come from the bottom of the reservoirs it does remain cold for a long way out of the mountains and past Calgary. The mouth of the Highwood River is a favorite lunch, or afternoon rest stop for the run down to McKinnon Flats. On hot days it can be hard to keep the younger, and even the older paddlers out of the water.

Other Reaches

See the previous report for the reach through Calgary. From Carseland to the Grand Forks, the confluence with the Oldman and formation of the South Saskatchewan river there is another 250 kilometers of paddling. Besides the Carseland weir to portage, there is Bassano Dam. One must consult the flow reports for any paddling below Bassano Dam. In dry years, during irrigation season, more than one paddler has found insufficient water below Bassano dam to float their boat! All of this lower run is easy paddling, with rapids to only Class I.

Other Local Activities or Destinations

A visit to the Bar U National Historic site west of High River can be a great way spend a non-paddling day. And my daughter (an editor for this guide), will always suggest a trip to the Calgary Zoo!

Rentals and Shuttles

Rentals:
Aquabatics 403.288.9283
Mountain Equipment Co-op 403.269.2420
Rocky Mountain Paddling Centre 403.202.8490
Sports Rent 403.292.0077
Undercurrents 403.262.4327
U of C Outdoor Program Centre 403.220.5038

Shuttles:
Louise Shotton Shuttle Service 403.282.5071
Bow River Shuttles 403.278.9165
Calgary Bow River Shuttle Service 403 510.0138

looking up the Bow River from the Highwood River confluence, Aug. '97

Kootenay River

McLeod Meadows Campground to Canal Flats

Why Go
Old Alberta paddlers who have been north to the Nahanni, often refer to this run as the "weekend Nahanni". Like its bigger cousin, it has it all: spectacular mountain scenery, whitewater that is the limit for open canoe tripping, waterfalls, tufa springs and often great wildlife.

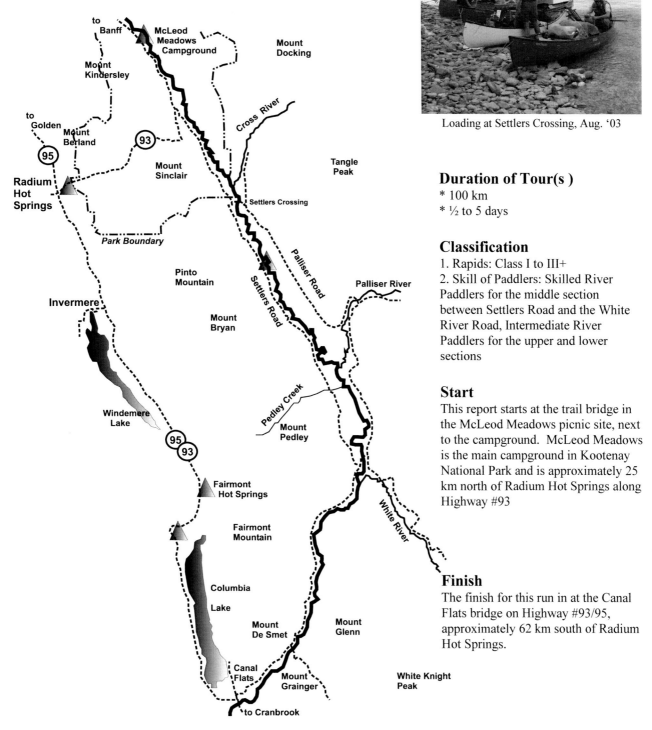

Loading at Settlers Crossing, Aug. '03

Duration of Tour(s)
* 100 km
* ½ to 5 days

Classification
1. Rapids: Class I to III+
2. Skill of Paddlers: Skilled River Paddlers for the middle section between Settlers Road and the White River Road, Intermediate River Paddlers for the upper and lower sections

Start
This report starts at the trail bridge in the McLeod Meadows picnic site, next to the campground. McLeod Meadows is the main campground in Kootenay National Park and is approximately 25 km north of Radium Hot Springs along Highway #93

Finish
The finish for this run in at the Canal Flats bridge on Highway #93/95, approximately 62 km south of Radium Hot Springs.

Intermediate Access and Distances

Location	Elevation meters	Km down	Km up	Km between	Access / Bank or Rapid / Class	MGRS datum NAD 1983 Zone 11U	Gradient m/km
	1160		-9				
McLeod Meadows / Trail Bridge		100	0		right bank	NS 762 222	
	1080	88	12				3.8
Cross River		81	19			NS 841 093	
Settlers Crossing / Bridge Rapid		78	22	22	Access 100m above bridge on left bank at the Nipka Lodge Campground, Class II - III	NS 846 076	
Ledge Rapid		77	24		Class II - III	NS 851 062	
	1040	76	25				3.2
Boulder Rapid		74	26		Class III - III+	NS 857 047	
Horseshoe Rapids		70	31	9	Class II - III	NS 876 016	
	1000	66	34				4.1
	960	55	45				3.8
Palliser Rapids / River		50	50		Class II - III	NR 953 901	
another ledge		48	52		Class II - II+	NR 961 892	
Pedley Rapids / Falls		48	52		Class II- II+	NR 959 888	
	920	43	57				3.3
White River Rd. Bridge		35	65		poor access	NR 982 813	
access below bridge		33	67	36	right bank		
White River		32	68		left bank	NR 978 788	
Gibraltar Rock		29	72			NR 965 762	
	880	25	75				2.2
Logging Rd. Bridge		9	91			NR 913 616	
	840	9	91				2.5
Canal Flats / #93 Bridge		0	100	33		NR 856 557	
	800		110				2.1

Gradient

Gradients, rapids and difficulty correlate pretty well on this reach! 4.1 m/km is the highest average gradient computed and Boulder Rapid through Horseshoe Rapid certainly reflects this gradient.

Maps

1 - Gem Trek Publishing *Kootenay National Park* at 1:100,000 for the run down to Settlers Crossing; if you have this sheet you do not need 82 J/13 Mount Assinboine.

2 - NTS 1:50,000

      82 J/13 - Mount Assinboine   82 J/12 -Tangle Peak

      82 J/5 - Fairmont Hot Springs   82 J/4 - Canal Flats

River Volume

I've run Settlers Crossing to Canal Flats three times, either in May or later in August. The last run in 2003 was with the river dropping from about 120 to 100 cms over our three days on the reach; this proved to be a fine level and I would suggest that the best paddling (and camping) on this run will be with flows between about 80 and 200 cms. Rafters might prefer even higher flows but for an open canoe I suspect that the size of waves in some the rapids would guarantee swamping and a long cold swim for many paddlers. The Canal Flats station appears to be no longer available so you will need to use the Fort Steele station. The Fort Steele station reflects flows on the Kootenay better than the Kootenay Crossing station as the Vermillion River enters below the Kootenay Crossing and provides the "lion's share" of the volume in the river.

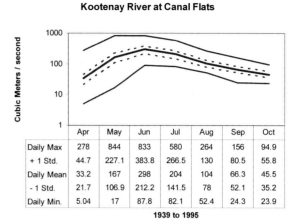

Kootenay River at Canal Flats

	Apr	May	Jun	Jul	Aug	Sep	Oct
Daily Max	278	844	833	580	264	156	94.9
+ 1 Std.	44.7	227.1	383.8	266.5	130	80.5	55.8
Daily Mean	33.2	167	298	204	104	66.3	45.5
- 1 Std.	21.7	106.9	212.2	141.5	78	52.1	35.2
Daily Min.	5.04	17	87.8	82.1	52.4	24.3	23.9

1939 to 1995

Camping

McLeod Meadows Campground in Kootenay National Park is on the river and provides a fine base to start this trip. Redstreak in Radium Hot Springs provides access to the National Park Hot Springs (www.pccamping.ca or dial toll free 1-877-737-3783 to make reservations).

This is primarily a canoe tripping stream for us open boat paddlers and one of the attractions is the great number of fine wilderness campsites. Of course you cannot random camp in the park, you must get beyond the park boundary the first day. The boundary of the park is marked by the Cross River on river left, and Settlers Crossing on river right.

Wildlife

This run starts in the National Park, but is largely through BC crown lands – the wildlife is widely distributed, not concentrated along the river as in the Alberta farmlands, but sightings do occur. As on similar mountain or foothills runs your chances of viewing wildlife are better if you are up and on the river very early, or float late, AND keep the noise down, especially on the quiet reaches. But then, who's looking for grizzly bears when trying to keep their boat dry in the middle of Boulder Rapid? You have a good chance of seeing any of the common Rocky Mountain fauna on this run.

Trip Notes

I've not paddled this run often enough. Calgary paddlers are known to refer to this reach as the "weekend Nahanni!" or "the affordable Nahanni!" The scenery, the paddling challenges, and the great camping all make this a first rate run!

For this report I've gone back often to Hooper's late '70s article *The Wild Upper Kootenay* that appeared in the *Foothills Wilderness Journal*. Hooper suggests that this run has forty-six Class I, seventeen Class II, and seven Class III rapids! I don't think he's far off and he and I both agree that Boulder Rapid can exceed the basic Class III status. The run in particular between Settlers Crossing and the White River Bridge is for **Skilled River** paddlers. The Kootenay is a mountain stream, in all seasons a good portion of the river is only a day or two from the glacier or snow pack from which it just melted. This is a fast river for the most part, swims tend to be long and cold – be prepared! Do **NOT** attempt this run until you have worked your way up to it. For Alberta paddlers you had better have a couple of tripping runs on the Nordegg to Rocky reach of the North Saskatchewan, **AND** be comfortable playing most of the most challenging rapids on the lower Kananaskis or upper Red Deer River, before tackling the Kootenay.

In the spring of 2003 my daughter suggested a family canoe-camping trip (we'd not had one for a number of years) and we agreed on the Kootenay in August with one other couple. As noted earlier we had modest flows with the river dropping from 120 cms to about 100 cms during our trip. Our four day trip was reduced to three due to forest fires in the Park – we were booted out of McLeod Meadows campground and not allowed to paddle the Park reach. We started at Settlers Crossing, and had no chance to warm-up – Bridge Rapid (Class II at most levels) is just 100 m below the start, Ledge and Boulder rapids are each only a few bends further along. We had an excellent couple of days of paddling and camping but once below the White River, the weather deteriorated. The logging road on river right, and lack of great campsites all combined to convince us to finish up a ½ day early and we paddled from lunch not far below Gibraltar Rock through to Canal Flats in a long afternoon. We had no swimmers in this trip, but Boulder Rapid was certainly a test for me, and for most of our crew. And we did stop to scout both halves of Horseshoe Rapid.

I've had a number of whitewater paddling colleagues make use of the BC Forest Service Campsite at Horseshoe Rapid as a base for play-boating the best of these rapids.

Some of the scenic highlights for this run are the tufa or travertine deposits along km 40 - 42 or so. Hooper notes these deposits on river right, we found a large deposit on river left. Hooper also notes that the Hoodoos between the White River Bridge and the White River are in large part due to uneven calcium cementing through the sediments. Pedley Falls and Gibraltar rock are noted in the table above and are "must stops" for anyone with a camera.

Other Reaches

In recent years I've paddled the Kootenay between Dolly Varden picnic site and McLeod Meadows campground (approx. 10 km) two or three times – it is a fast braided paddle with spectacular scenery. The first part of the Kootenay below the picnic site can have logjams and one time required a short portage, but once the Vermillion joins, the river opens right up with much more water and much faster water!

The Vermillion River above the confluence with the Kootenay River can be challenging for the open boat canoeist, particularly in the one Class III to III+ rapid in Hector Gorge. Above Vermillion crossing there are a number of serious short canyons, rapids and cataracts on the Vermillion! Smith (1995) includes the Vermillion river in his guide book.

Below Canal Flats the Kootenay slows down and spreads out. But beware, especially for the first few kilometers it is seriously braided and some channels can be completely blocked with logjams. As I prepared this guide during the summer of '06 we had one e-mail warning circulate about a nasty strainer not far below Canal Flats. Fort Steele is approximately 67 kilometers below Canal Flats, and one old (1974) BC Canoe Guide rates the river as Grade 2-3 for the run to Skookumchuk, Grade 2 to Wasa and Grade 1 to Ft. Steele – with rapids to Class II to III (with the most discussed rapid being right at Fort Steele).

Other Local Activities or Destinations

If it is too cold for paddling – maybe it is time to take the crew out to the Hot Springs at Radium – one of my favorites! Or if, like us, and you blew through the river too quickly, we had a fine day on the Columbia river between Invermere and Radium - a flat run - but great birding!

Pedley Falls, and last of the Pedley Rapid "wave train", Aug. '03

Shuttles

In 2003 we used Columbia Valley Taxi (250.342.5262) for our shuttle and vehicle storage. We unloaded our gear, left our vehicles in Invermere with the Taxi firm, road the taxi

back to Settlers Crossing, and then called the firm from a pay phone in Canal Flats on our arrival. They were most accommodating of our early arrival.

Palliser Rapid from river left, August '03

Red Deer River

Ya Ha Tinda (Bighorn Creek) to below Coal Camp (Range Road 63)

Why Go
The upper Red Deer River offers some of the finest, and most accessible whitewater in the province. The Ya Ha Tinda run offers fun paddling and mountain scenery.

Duration of Tour(s)
* 76.1 km
* up to 3 days with many great ½ and full day trips. On the upper Red Deer reaches allow lots of time to PLAY!

Yes that is the passenger's foot in the air – yes they did stay upright!
photo by M. Haskin - 03-May-17

Classification
1. Rapids: Class I to IV
2. Skill of Paddlers: Intermediate to Skilled River Paddlers, Novice River Paddlers under instruction. At modest flows this is a great training river; many a whitewater paddler in this province (including myself) cut their teeth on these reaches.

Start
All of these runs are usually accessed by heading west from Olds on Highway #27, then west from Sundre on Highway #584; approximately 8 km west of Sundre turn south on to the Red Deer River road, and watch for the signs to Mountainaire Lodge and the Shell Field Office.

The Bighorn Creek staging area and campsite (often monopolized by the horse set) is reached by taking the Ya Ha Tinda road west from the north side of the Forestry Trunk Road (now Secondary highway #734) bridge over the Red Deer River. Mountainaire Lodge is just a few dozen metres south of this bridge. When the road is wet or rough, it is almost an hour drive to Bighorn Creek.

Given the paddling skills of the group, many of the access points listed below provide an excellent starting point for a day's paddle, or a shorter training or play run.

Author in ledges above Cache Hill
photo by M. Haskin 03-May-18

Finish
The last run reported on here finishes where Range Road 63 meets the river. To access from Highway #584, take Range Road 63 south and where the Red Deer River Road first turns west, take the Range Road 63 road allowance some 400 m further south to the river. As of '09 this requires a bit of hike as the river has migrated 200 m or so from the road allowance.

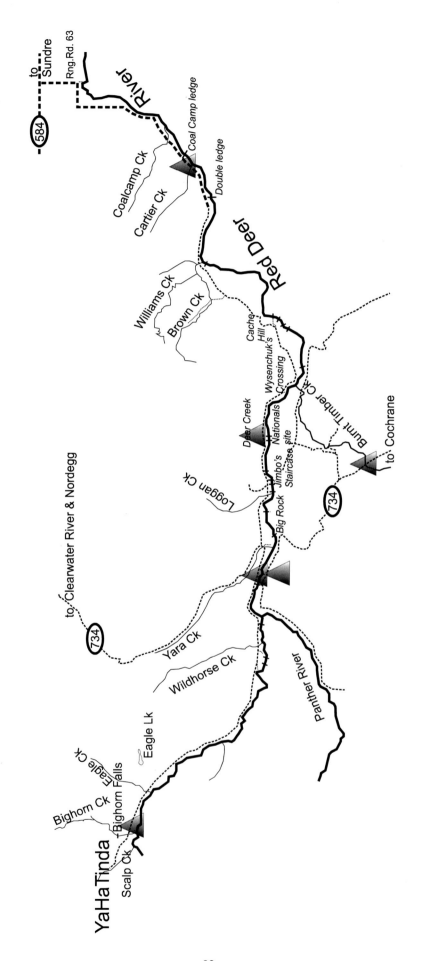

to
Sundre

Rng.Rd. 63

584

River

Coalcamp Ck

Cartier Ck

Coal Camp ledge

Double ledge

Red Deer

Williams Ck

Brown Ck

Cache Hill

Wysenchuk's Crossing

Burnt Timber Ck

Deer Creek

Nationals site

Jimbo's Staircase

to: Cochrane

Loggan Ck

Big Rock

734

to: Clearwater River & Nordegg

734

Yara Ck

Wildhorse Ck

Panther River

Eagle Lk

Eagle Ck

Bighorn Ck

Bighorn Falls

YaHaTinda

Scalp Ck

Intermediate Access and Distances

Location	Elevation meters	Km down	Km up	Km between	Access / Bank or Rapid / Class	MGRS datum NAD 1983 Zone 11U	Gradient m/km
	1600		-6.8				
Bighorn Creek		76.1	0.0		left bank	PT 010 318	
	1560	75.3	0.8				5.3
Eagle Creek		70.8	5.3		left bank		
	1524	67.0	9.1				4.3
	1494	60.4	15.7				4.5
Upper Access Wildhorse Creek Meadows		57.7	18.4	18.4	left bank	PT 123 241	
	1463	56.7	19.4				8.4
Lower Access Wildhorse Creek Meadows		55.7	20.4		left bank	PT 139 236	
Panther River Ledges		53.2	22.9		II - III		
Panther River		52.9	23.2		right	PT 162 239	
	1433	52.6	23.5				7.3
FTR Bridge / Mountainaire Lodge		49.9	26.2	7.8	either	PT 185 242	
access to Yara Creek Campground		49.0	27.1		left bank	PT 191 239	
Fisher Creek		48.2	27.9		right		
Yara Creek / west of runway access		46.9	29.2		left bank	PT 211 235	
	1402	46.5	29.6				5.1
Big Rock rapid		45.4	30.7		II - III	PT 226 235	
GasPlant access		44.1	32.0	5.8	left bank	PT 235 237	
Ledge		43.6	32.5		II - III		
Gooseberry Ledge		42.2	33.9		III - IV	PT 252 233	
Jimbo's Staircase		41.7	34.4		III - IV	PT 256 234	
	1372	41.3	34.8				5.8
"S" Bend		40.7	35.4		II - III	PT 265 239	
Pipeline Crossing - river access		39.3	36.8	4.8		PT 280 238	
National's Site ('72 & '76)		38.9	37.2		III - IV	PT 282 237	
	1341	37.0	39.1				7.2
Wysenchuk's Crossing		34.3	41.8	5.0	left bank	PT 319 226	
Burnt Timber Creek		33.5	42.6		right	PT 323 220	
Sauna Hole rapid		32.3	43.8		II+	PT 334 216	
Vam Creek		30.3	45.8		right	PT 353 216	
	1311	29.7	46.4				4.1
Ledge		29.3	46.8		II+	PT 361 222	
Ledge		28.6	47.5		II - III		
Upper Cache Hill Ledges		28.4	47.7		III - III+	PT 364 229	
	1300	27.6	48.5				5.2
Cache Hill Rapid		27.5	48.6		II - II+		
Cache Hill access		27.0	49.1	7.3	left bank	PT 371 240	
Lower Cache Hill ledge		26.9	49.2		II - III		
	1280	24.1	52.0				5.7
	1260	21.1	55.0				6.7

Location	Elevation meters	Km down	Km up	Km between	Access / Bank or Rapid / Class	MGRS datum NAD 1983 Zone 11U	Gradient m/km
Williams Creek Rapid		19.6	56.5		II+		
Williams Creek		19.1	57.0		left	PT 408 286	
	1240	16.7	59.4	4.5			
Access from Road		15.7	60.4		left	PT 438 283	
	1220	13.5	62.6	6.2			5.3
Double Ledge		12.9	63.2		left bank / III - IV	PT 461 286	
Cartier Creek		11.1	65.0		left	PT 475 295	
Cartier Creek Campground		10.6	65.5		left		
Coal Camp Ledge		9.8	66.3	3.1	II - III+	PT 485 303	
	1200	9.7	66.4				5.3
Funkhauser Rapid		7.4	68.7		II - II+		
	1180	5.1	71.0				4.3
						NAD 1927	
	1158	1.5	74.6				
Rnge Rd 63 access		0.0	76.1	9.8		PH 532 369	
	1143		78.0				4.4

Gradient

Gradients on these reaches vary by more than a factor of two, from a low of 4.1 m/km to a high of 8.4 m/km. But these gradients do not accurately predict the difficulty of the rapids. In fact some of the easiest reaches have the highest gradients, and thus the truism that rapid difficulty is a combination of gradient, flow and rock structure. If you look back to my previous guides for this reach you will see that gradient reports for these reaches vary. Over the years as the maps have changed from imperial to metric, the contour lines have moved. Thus the average gradients calculated using the new contours have varied.

River Volume and Flow Rate

The "below Burnt Timber Creek" station is the first choice for flows on these runs. The station is well below Burnt Timber Creek. It is actually at the bottom the upper Cache Hill ledges. Paddling season flows vary from a low of less than 10 cms to floods of nearly 400 cms. Best paddling occurs with the flows between about 25 cms and 100 cms. I generally discourage paddling these reaches when flows are much over 100 cms. If flows are high, and seem to be from melt of the high country snow pack, take a look at the Panther River, Burnt Timber Creek, or even the James River as alternatives.

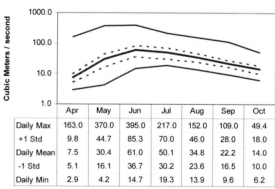

Red Deer River below Burnt Timber Creek

	Apr	May	Jun	Jul	Aug	Sep	Oct
Daily Max	163.0	370.0	395.0	217.0	152.0	109.0	49.4
+1 Std	9.8	44.7	85.3	70.0	46.0	28.0	18.0
Daily Mean	7.5	30.4	61.0	50.1	34.8	22.2	14.0
-1 Std	5.1	16.1	36.7	30.2	23.6	16.5	10.0
Daily Min	2.9	4.2	14.7	19.3	13.9	9.6	6.2

1973 to 2003

Maps

1 NTS 1:250,000 - 82 O - Calgary
   NTS 1:50,000
        82 0/10 Fallen Timber Creek   82 O/11 Burnt Timber Creek
        82 O/12 Barrier Mountain   82 O/15 Sundre.
2 - and an up-to-date Alberta Highways map

Camping

Provincial Forest Service Sites (reservations through Mountainaire Lodge 403.637.2229)
- Wildhorse Creek Group Campsite, west of the Forestry Trunk Road
- Red Deer River North /Yara Creek, near the FTR crossing
- Red Deer River South - south of Mountainaire Lodge - 1.5 km
- Fisher Creek Group Campsite - south of Mountainaire Lodge - 2 km
- Deer Creek Group Campsite, east of the FTR, near the National's Site Rapid
- Cartier Creek Recreational Area - near Coal Camp, and group campsite available

Unorganized - no facilities and rough road access
- Bighorn Creek (very popular with the "horse set")
- Wildhorse Creek Meadows
- Gooseberry Flats
- Wysenchuck's Crossing
- Cache Hill

Wilderness

Many good campsites exist along the river, but the biggest problem is their proximity to the road, possibly the best reaches to avoid the road are below Bighorn Creek, below Wysenchuk's crossing, and below Cache Hill.

Wildlife

The upper Red Deer valley is home to virtually all of the species of the eastern slopes, including grizzly bears and cougars. Spotting large wildlife from the river is often difficult, and the heavy recreational use of the valley does tend to force large game into the more secluded side valleys. In recent years deer populations have been good, and are often spotted from the canoe, or far more often, on the Friday evening drive in for a weekend of paddling. The river valley supports a wide variety of bird life, and paddlers will often spot osprey, kingfishers, dippers and the occasional eagle.

Trip Notes

This has been Alberta's pre-eminent white water stream. In the past no other river in the province attracted the usage that the Red Deer did. In recent years the enhancements, the predictable water and convenience have drawn many former Red Deer paddlers to the "Kan". But the Red Deer is near both population centers, it has excellent access, reliable water all season, great camping, and challenges for everyone. Yet, its moderate volume is generally not threatening. Here is a river which leaders and commercial outfitters can safely take relative novices on, a river with a teaching or practice site on every second corner, and yet enough "solid" water challenges to keep the most experienced paddlers interested. This is a river for everyone -- and unfortunately on some summer weekends, everyone comes: rafters, fishermen, hotdoggers, novices, commercial tours, university groups, everyone! Some days it does seem a little crowded -- if possible plan your summer season trips for mid-week and avoid the crowds. If out on a crowded weekend, please share the "play spots." Take a couple of turns, and then move on.

White water paddling grew up in Alberta on this stretch of the Red Deer. Our early closed-boat paddlers learned their skills and explored the river for the rest of us in the summer of '71. In 1972 the Canadian White Water Nationals came west for the first time ever, and to the Red Deer. We still refer to the slalom site as the "Nationals Site." The national championships returned in 1976. In '72 the wildwater event was held on the lower Panther. By '76 the sport and Alberta paddlers were ready to race on the Red Deer, over the Gooseberry ledge, and down Jimbo's Staircase.

Jimbo's Staircase takes its name from our first home grown C-1 paddler. Jim swam at that top of the staircase, followed his C-1 down the staircase, and suffered no more than the necessity of repairing his boat's nose, and the ignominity of having the rapid named for him.

Popular Reaches , for whom and progression:
- *for novices:* (should have basic control strokes, and have been introduced to basic river maneuvers before heading downstream)
    - F.T.R. to Gas Plant - weaker paddler may have to portage "the Big Rock"
    - Cache Hill to above Double Ledge
    - Coal Camp to lower access - maybe too full of logjams post 2005 flooding
- *next runs, more difficult*:
    - below Double ledge to Coal Camp
    - Wysenchuk's Crossing to Cache Hill
    - Bighorn Creek to Forestry Trunk Road
- *most excitement -- better paddlers*:
    - Gas Plant to below Nationals Site

Other Reaches

In former times we were able to drive to the National Park boundary and this provided another great ½ day paddle. Scalp Creek washed out the bridge some years ago and we seem to have lost this run -- a mixed blessing. To the best of our knowledge we can find no documented reports of running the Red Deer from its headwaters to the Banff Park boundary. The 1974 guide, *Wild Rivers - Alberta*, suggested that at least the last 16 km of this run are navigable upstream of the boundary. A map survey would suggest that the stream should be run-able (except for a canyon or two, and couple or three water falls) from Douglas Lake, or Red Deer Lakes. Access is the problem; one may be able to portage in from Lake Louise, and hire a horse outfitter to carry in supplies. Would "Parks" allow it?

Downstream there is approximately 19 more km of fast, braided water into Sundre. This lower reach some years has been full of tight, tricky logjams! I have a report from July '09, that there was in fact a very "tight" section about ½ way down, but at the bottom there was no sign of the "debris catchers" that had been installed in the early '80s.

Other Local Activities or Destinations

Twice over the past 25 years I have spent a very nice week of holidays on the upper Red Deer River. Both times we camped in the Wildhorse creek meadows and paddled some days, biked and hiked on others. Our hikes have taken us up the ridges north of the Bighorn Creek, along the ridge between Yara and Wildhorse Creek north of the bridge, and into Bighorn Falls just upstream of the staging area, and then into the meadows above the falls. Bike trips have taken us into Banff Park on the old park fire road, and into Eagle Lake in James Pass. One year we hired an outfitter and a horse-drawn wagon to take us up the Panther so we could paddle back down. The river proved to be too low so we loaded up the kids and all, and we trundled on up the Panther for a "look see", a picnic lunch, and a few of us even followed along on our Mtn. Bikes. The river may have been too low for paddling but we soon learned that bikes do not float, nor do they peddle well, when the water depth is above the axles. In the summer of '09 I finally made it into Klein Lake some 5 km or so up the Panther river road and off to the south about 800 m. A very pleasant little hike on a rough track to a pretty lake.

Approaching the Sauna Hole, 2003-May-18
(as of '08 not the challenge it once was!)

Red Deer River

Dickson Dam (west of Innisfail)
to Joffre Bridge (Highway #11 east of Red Deer)

Why Go
Pleasant scenic paddling with a modest current and good
Goldeye fishing.

Duration of Tour(s)
* 96 km
* 3-4 days with many ½ and full day tours possible

Classification
1. Rapids: easy Class II
2. Skill of Paddlers: Novice River at normal flows.

approaching Joffre bridge

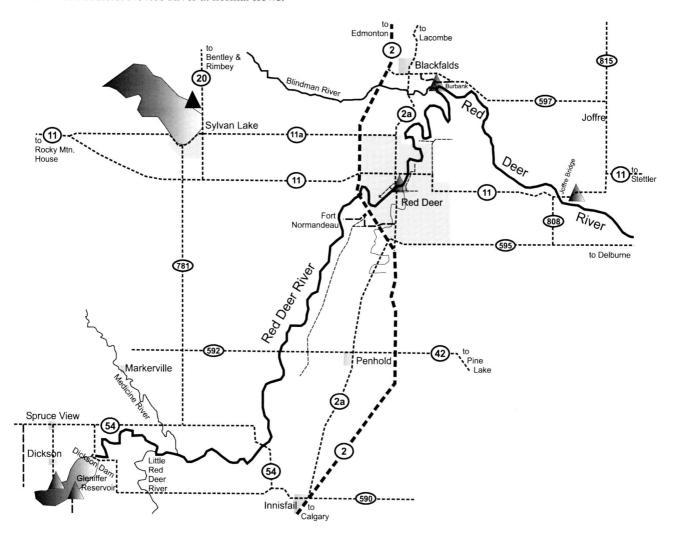

Start

Dickson Dam west of Innisfail is best accessed via Highway #54, and then Range Road 23 south to the Dam. To access the best launch site cross the dam, and drive down to the picnic area below the dam, on the lower part of the bend, and on the right, or south bank of the river.

Finish

Joffre Bridge is best accessed from the west, on Highway #11. The country maintains a boat launch on river right, below the bridge. But beware, they lock the gate every evening. I have reports of paddlers returning late to retrieve vehicles and being unable to access them.

Intermediate Access and Distances

Location	Elevation	km down	km up	km between	Access / Bank or Rapids / Class	MGRS Datum	Gradient m/km
	metres					NAD 27 Zone	
boat launch below Dickson Dam		96	0		right	PH 913 711	
	914	96	0				
Little Red Deer River	899	86	11		right	PH 964 719	0.7
Medicine River		82	14		left	PH 985 716	
	884	75	21				1.5
Water treatment plant		75	21		right	QH 048 714	
						NAD 83	
Highway 54		72	24	24	left, downstream	TC 953 730	
	876	67	29				1.0
Highway 592		62	34	10	right, upstream	TC 969 812	
	869	57	39				0.8
abandoned Railway Bridge		53	43			UC 008 881	
Fort Normandeau Park		46	50	16	right (east bank)	UC 034 939	
	861	46	50				0.7
Highway 2		45	51				
	853	41	55				1.8
Kiwanis Picnic Grounds		40	56		left	UC 063 940	
Great West Adv. Park boat launch, from Kerry Wood Dr.		39	57	7	left	UC 076 952	
Gaetz Avenue Bridge		39	57				
Lions Campground N / Waskasoo Cr. S		38	58		left	UC 086 957	
67 St. / Highway #11 Bridge		37	59				
	846	36	60				1.3
McKenzie Trail Park / Boat Launch		35	61	4	right	UC 097 979	
River Bend Park - Boat Launch		28	68		left	UC 109 998	
	838	28	68				1.0
	831	22	75				1.0
Blindman River / Burbank Park		19	78	17	left, below Blindman	UD 122 041	

Location	Elevation	km down	km up	km between	Access / Bank or Rapids / Class	MGRS Datum	Gradient m/km
	823	14	82				1.1
Canyon Ski Hill		8	88		right	UC 171 980	
	815	7	89				1.2
	808	1	95				1.1
Joffre Bridge / Highway #11		0	96	18	right, below old bridge piers	UC 230 941	

Gradient

Gradients on these reaches range from a low of .7 m / km to as much as 1.8 m/km. Certainly the most interesting water is on the run around the Red Deer Golf & Country Club through to the McKenzie Trails Park access.

River Volume and Flow Rate

Best paddling on these reaches is when the Red Deer station reports flows of between 50 and 200 cms. Floods on this reach have exceeded 1500 cms. Velocities at the Red Deer station range from less than 2 km / hr at 50 cms, 4+ km / hr at 200 cms and 8 km / hr at 900 cms.

Red Deer River at Red Deer

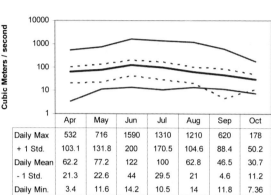

	Apr	May	Jun	Jul	Aug	Sep	Oct
Daily Max	532	716	1590	1310	1210	620	178
+ 1 Std.	103.1	131.8	200	170.5	104.6	88.4	50.2
Daily Mean	62.2	77.2	122	100	62.8	46.5	30.7
- 1 Std.	21.3	22.6	44	29.5	21	4.6	11.2
Daily Min.	3.4	11.6	14.2	10.5	14	11.8	7.36

1912 to 2003

Maps

1 - The ARCA *Middle Red Deer Map* is a must for the reach, and actually covers the river from the Dickson Dam through to Drumheller. The ARCA map and an up-to-date *Alberta Road Map* is all you really need.

2 - NTS 1:250,000   NTS 1:50,000

     83 A - Red Deer   83B/1 - Markerville

     83 B - Rocky Mtn. House   83A/4 - Innisfail

                                 83A/5 - Red Deer

Camping

Organized campsites are available at a number of locations around Gleniffer Reservoir, on the river at the Lions Campground (403.342.8183) in Red Deer, the Lacombe Country Campground (403.885.5335) at Burbank, and near the river at Riverview Campground (403.347.7663) east and just up the hill from the Joffre Bridge (Highway #11).

Wilderness camping is somewhat limited in the middle sections of this reach, but the river does offer a number of islands that can be used for camping when the river is not too high (>100 cms), on the Dickson Dam to Penhold reach, and on the reach between Burbank and Joffre.

Wildlife

Given that much of this reach is in or near an urban area, with much of the river bank dominated by acreages one can still view a surprising volume of wildlife – and some of the reaches still have a modest sense of wildness about them. Moose are common, even on the edges of Red Deer and both mule and whitetail deer can be found all along these reaches of the river. Great horned owls, great blue herons and osprey represent some of the more spectacular bird life that one is likely to see, and it would be a rare summer trip that does not witness the soaring, and hear the cry of the red tail hawk. The reach between Dickson Dam and Penhold, and the reach between Burbank and Joffre Bridge offer the greatest sense of wilderness.

Trip Notes

This is my home river! My first day trip on a river was from the Penhold Bridge back "into town" with my swimming instructor peers from the public pool. The "mighty" Conquest rapid (riffle really) just upstream of the Taylor Drive bridge in Red Deer was the site of my first near swamping of a canoe, during spring break-up, and later my first swim out of a kayak.

When I first contemplated a "southern Alberta" guide I had my father drive Lois and I out to Dickson Dam for the run down to Penhold. I had never paddled the reach from the Dam down to the Little Red. We had a very pleasant day's paddle with the river running in the lower end of the normal range.

Over the years I have taken many Ceyana friends on the Burbank to Joffre run, through the canyon. In my first paddling years with the Red Deer Canoe & Kayak Club we considered the run from Red Deer to Joffre, about 6 hours, and as the "season opener" each May. But now with the lower flows the run is a bit longer. With the drive down from Edmonton and with pavement from Burbank to Joffre on the north side of the river, we have opted for the shorter run; it usually takes us about 3 to 4 hours of what is probably the most spectacular scenery included in this reach report.

Access to the river has improved within the City of Red Deer and there are many short evening paddles available. And in fact, once high flows are over for the summer most paddlers can have a very pleasant evenings paddle working upstream from any one of the parking areas and then drifting back as the evening fades. In my first years training as a marathon racer, many an evening after work my partner Rick and I would park at the "burger joint" (Hannigans) at the Gaetz Avenue Bridge and paddle up to above the golf club, before turning around and sprinting for "home," a burger and a coke.

As mentioned above, some of the most "interesting" water on this reach is within the Red Deer City limits. Both the first stretch below Dickson Dam, and the run below Burbank can also offer some modest excitement. Below Dickson Dam to near Innisfail offers some good opportunities for log jams & sweepers, and modest riffles. Below Burbank there are some low grade rapids that can be pushy, even bouncy in modestly high water. In fact many years ago, I swamped a canoe in the riffle at the top of the Canyon, a couple of kilometres below Burbank. Last time through, there seemed slim chance of that happening again, except maybe at very high waters.

Other Reaches

Upstream of this report is Gleniffer Reservoir, a body of water pretty much taken over by the jet skis and water skiing crowd for much of the summer. Downstream from Joffre to the Content Bridge (Highway #21) is a pleasant paddle of some 50 km through the aspen parkland and rolling vistas of the river valley.

Red Deer to Drumheller is a paddle of just over 200 km and most groups take 5 to 6 days to complete this run. Kerry Wood (1967) in his book *A Corner of Canada* reports of a Red Deer to Drumheller canoe race during the 1930s. Sixteen canoes started from Red Deer, nine upset in the rapid below Burbank and the winners paddled all night completing the trip in just 25 hours.

Other Local Activities or Destinations

There is much to do along, and near these reaches of the Red Deer. Fort Normandeau from the Reil Rebellion (403.347.7550) and the Red Deer & District Museum (403.309.8405) offer opportunities to explore the human history of the area, while the Kerry Wood Nature Centre (403.346.2010) offers opportunities to explore the natural history. At the centre there is a wonderful loop trail around the oxbow lakes of the Gaetz Lake Sanctuary. Sylvan and Gull Lake both offer additional camping for the area, and some great sandy beaches.

Rentals and Shuttles

Red Deer:

    Valhalla Pure Outfitters (403.343.3658) rents canoes, kayaks and a canoe trailer.

Red Deer River

Content Bridge (Highway #21)
to Drumheller (Newcastle Park)

Why Go
This is a great scenic paddle that takes one through the transition from the aspen parkland, and into the prairies and badlands. The paddling at most water levels is well within the ability of anyone with a few hours of instruction.

Duration of Tour(s)
* 118 km
* 3 to 4 days, with a number of one and ½ day tours possible

at Dry Island Buffalo Jump

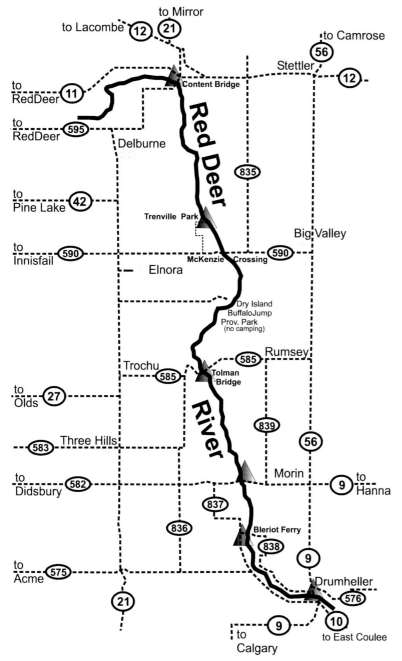

Classification
1. Rapids: Class I - II (Backbone Riffle)
2. Skill of Paddlers: This a fine run for Novice River Paddlers (canoe or kayak) with the basic boat handling skills for ensuring direction control, with some ability at ferrying and eddy turns. Like most incised prairie streams this river can generate a strong upstream breeze, and "strong" paddling can be required on many afternoons. This is a run for touring boats that move easily through the water.

Start
The start for this run is at the Content (Highway #21 Bridge) S.W. of Stettler, near the former Metis buffalo hunting village of Tail Creek. At Content Bridge there is both a public camground upstream of the bridge and a private campground just downstream of the bridge, both on the north bank. Both campgrounds provide useful access to the river.

Finish
Access in Drumheller has improved since my last guide: Newcastle Park on the west side of Drumheller, and south side of the river, is a great spot to end, or start a trip. From downtown Drumheller go west on either 3rd or 4th Avenues, these merge into Newcastle Trail, at 10th Street turn right (north), and then right (east) again onto the Newcastle Park access road.

Intermediate Access and Distances

Location	Elevation meters	km down	km up	km between	Access / Bank or Rapid Class	MGRS datum NAD 1983 Zone 12 U	Gradients m/km
Content Bridge Park		118	0		left - above bridge	UC 585 971	
	747	116	3				
	739	108	10				1.1
Backbone Riffle		102	16		class I - II	UC 613 838	
	724	91	27				0.6
Trenville Park		90	29	29	right	UC 631 720	
McKenzie Crossing		82	37	8	left - below bridge	UC 664 655	
	716	81	37				0.8
	709	70	48				0.8
Dry Island Buffalo Jump		68	50	14	right	UC 650 556	
	701	54	64				0.6
Tolman Bridge Campground		54	65	14	right - below campground	UC 609 448	
	693	47	71				1.1
Morin Bridge Campground		31	87	23	left - well above the bridge	UC 677 250	
Morin Bridge		30	89		right - below bridge	UC 683 239	
	686	25	93				0.3
Bleriot Ferry		20	98	11	right below ferry, beware of tow cable	UC 693 152	
Newcastle Park in Drumheller		0	118	20	right bank	UC 798 032	

Gradient

Stream Gradients on this run range from 1.1 m/km to a low of .3 m/km on the last reach just above Drumheller.

River Volume and Flow Rate

Best paddling on these reaches are with the Drumheller station reporting flows between 40 and 200 CMS. Some paddlers suggest this river can be run with as little as 20 cms, and record floods have exceeded 1100 cms. Flow velocity for the Drumheller station varies from approximately 3 km/hr at 100 cms to nearly 8 km/hr at 800 cms.

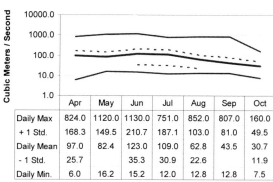

Red Deer River at Drumheller

	Apr	May	Jun	Jul	Aug	Sep	Oct
Daily Max	824.0	1120.0	1130.0	751.0	852.0	807.0	160.0
+ 1 Std.	168.3	149.5	210.7	187.1	103.0	81.0	49.5
Daily Mean	97.0	82.4	123.0	109.0	62.8	43.5	30.7
- 1 Std.	25.7		35.3	30.9	22.6		11.9
Daily Min.	6.0	16.2	15.2	12.0	12.8	12.8	7.5

1915 to 2003

Maps

1 - the ARCA *Middle Red Deer Map* is a must for this reach, and actually covers the river from the Dickson Dam west of Innisfail through to Drumheller. This map with an up-to-date *Alberta Road Map* is all you really need.

2 - NTS 1:250,00   NTS 1:50,000   82P/15 -Rumsey
83 A - Red Deer   83A/6 - Alix   82P/14 - Trochu
82 P - Drumheller   83A/3 - Delbourne   82P/10 - Munson
                     83A/2 - Big Valley 82P/7 - Drumheller

Camping

This is possibly the most popular canoe tripping river in the province. The great on-river and stream-side camping, the usually easy paddling conditions, and great scenery attracts a wide variety of paddlers. Unorganized or wilderness camping can be had below the high water mark along the banks or on many of the mid-stream islands.

Public and private campgrounds along this reach include:

Content Bridge Park 403.742.0777   Trenville Park 403.773.2273
MacKenzie Crossing Campground 403.740.4775 or 403.876.2524
TL Ranch (just above the Tolman Bridge) 403.442.2207   Tolman Bridge 403.823.1749
Morrin Bridge (Starland Recreation Area) 403.772.3793   Bleriot Ferry 403.823.1749

Paddlers must be aware that there is NO camping allowed within Dry Island Buffalo Jump Provincial Park.

Wildlife

This is a pleasant run that usually offers many opportunities for wildlife viewing. On a hot summer afternoon the cries of the red tail hawk will often be heard, and one is likely to follow a great blue heron down the river. In recent years both white pelicans and cormorants have returned to fish the river. Whitetail and mule deer may be spotted from the canoe, or at camp in the early morning or evening. This is a good run for spotting wildlife.

Some years ago a provincial wildlife biologist brought to my attention that groups of paddlers were unintentionally "herding" young ducks and goslings down the river. In their attempt to stay ahead of the paddlers the young birds can become exhausted, and may drown. Lead paddlers in a group need to be alert to avoid this problem. When families of young ducks or geese are spotted the group should either pull over and wait for a few minutes to allow the birds to gain shore or a side channel; or the group should get together, and then try to sprint past the birds on the far side of the river.

Trip Notes

As noted above this is a popular run. My first canoe trip was on part of this reach and I have returned many times over the past forty years to trip and race. Often with the Ceyana Canoe Club we chose to use the former McKenzie Crossing campground as a base, and then to day trip up stream and downstream. In these later years we generally opt for the shorter runs, and this allows time for long walks through the coulees and up the ridges. And like many paddlers I have opted for June or early July to make these trips, to take advantage of the higher waters. BUT I have also in recent years advised youth leaders to NOT tackle these runs when the river was very high. Even a flat river like the Red Deer IS dangerous at high flows. I was on the river in the early 'nineties with my scout troop and just above Trenville park we came across a Grumman canoe wrapped around a large rock in a very modest riffle – the only large rock we saw that day on the whole run from Content to Trenville. And on this run the river had been high enough to wash out Backbone Riffle, but not so high as to present any other problems.

Paddlers on the Bleriot Ferry run must also be well aware of the dangers of the ferry. It is best to pass the ferry on the far side of the river and one must never try to land on the upstream side of a ferry, as the current will pull (suck) your canoe under the ferry!

Other Reaches

I have chosen to not include the pleasant 49 km paddle from Joffre Bridge to Content bridge in this guide. The runs below Drumheller are fully reviewed in the next report.

Other Local Activities or Destinations

If you are camped at one of the bridges, planning to day trip on the river, and the rain gods are angry with you, load up and head down the highway to Drumheller and go to the Royal Tyrrell Museum. If the river is too high, or it is too windy, I would suggest driving to Dry Island Buffalo Jump Provincial Park, and go for a hike up to the Dry Island in the NE corner of the park, or out to the buffalo jump on the west side of the park.

Rentals and Shuttle Services

TL Ranch 403.442.2207
Taxi service in Drumheller seems to have deteriorated as of August 2009, and my one recent contact would only offer the possibility of shuttle service if an extra driver was available – check the yellow pages and give whoever is listed a try!

below Morrin Bridge

Red Deer River

Drumheller to Dinosaur Provincial Park

Why Go
Great Badlands scenery and gentle river paddling.

Duration of Tour(s)
* 145 km
* 4-6 days, with both half and full day trips available.

near East Coulee

Classification
1. Rapids: Class 1
2. Skill of Paddlers: This a fine run for Novice River Paddlers with good leadership. Like most incised prairie streams this river can generate a strong upstream breeze, and "strong" paddling can be required on many afternoons. This is a run for touring boats that move easily through the water.

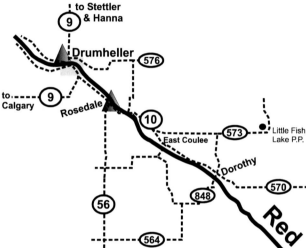

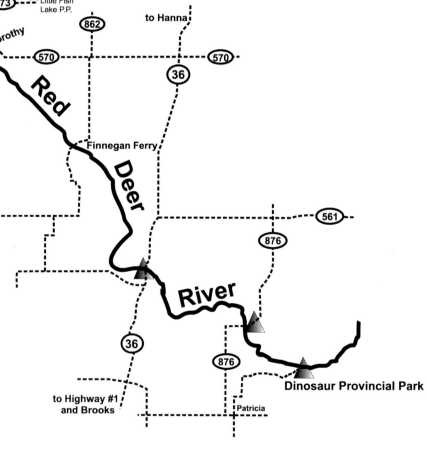

Start
This reach report assumes a start in New Castle Park in Drumheller and a finish in Dinosaur Provincial Park at the main campground. But, one may start or finish at any of the access points noted below. From downtown Drumheller, and north of the railway line, take 3rd Avenue west, it merges with and first becomes 2nd Ave, then Newcastle Trail. Turn north onto 10th Street and follow this into Newcastle Park.

Finish
Again, any of the access points for the run can be used to complete a trip. The final finish is in Dinosaur Provincial Park near the mouth of Little Sandhills creek, this is best accessed from the Day Use area.

Intermediate Access and Distances

Location	Elevation	km down	km up	km between	Access / Bank Rapids / Class	MGRS datum	Gradients m/km
	metres					**NAD 1983** Zone 12 U	
Newcastle Park, Drumheller		145	0		right bank	UC 798 032	
River Grove Park / #9 Bridge		144	1	1	left bank	UC 809 031	
	678	142	3				
Rosedale, bridge & Rosebud River		135	10	8	right bank	UB 866 978	
#10 Highway Bridge		131	14		be wary of old bridge piers still in the river		
Willow Creek		126	19		left bank	UB 930 927	
East Coulee / #569 Bridge		119	26	16	right bank, upstream of bridge	UB 968 877	
Dorothy / #848 Bridge		107	38	12	left bank, upstream of bridge	VB 071 819	
Crawling Creek		98	47		right bank	VB 121 758	
Homestead Creek		89	56		left bank	VB 183 703	
Finnegan Ferry		80	65	27	either, be wary of the tow cable	VB 240 643	
Galarneau Creek		75	71		left bank	VB 284 616	
Abandoned Railway Bridge		70	75			VB 308 589	
Bullpound Creek		68	77		left bank	VB 319 575	
Douglas Island & Creek		52	93		right bank	VB 329 449	
Emerson/#36 Bridge & Campground		42	103	38	right bank, upstream of bridge	VB 368 410	
Three Owl Island		36	109			VB 413 372	
Matzhiwin Creek		31	114		right bank	VB 426 324	
#876 Bridge / campground / Steveville		14	131	28	left bank, downstream of bridge	VB 568 320	
Coyote Island		12	133			VB 572 310	
Onetree Creek		5	140		right bank	VB 596 250	
	632	2	143				0.3
Dinosaur Prov. Pk. / Little Sandhill Creek		0	145	14	right bank	VB 636 238	

Gradient
This is a flat run that consistently drops approximately 0.3 m/km.

River Volume and Flow Rate
Best paddling on these reaches are with the Drumheller station reporting flows between 50 CMS and 150 cms. Some paddlers suggest this river can be run with as little as 20 cms, and record floods have exceeded 1100 cms. Flow velocity varies from approximately 3 km/hr at 100 cms to nearly 8 km/hr at 800 cms.

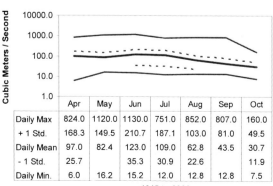

Red Deer River at Drumheller

	Apr	May	Jun	Jul	Aug	Sep	Oct
Daily Max	824.0	1120.0	1130.0	751.0	852.0	807.0	160.0
+ 1 Std.	168.3	149.5	210.7	187.1	103.0	81.0	49.5
Daily Mean	97.0	82.4	123.0	109.0	62.8	43.5	30.7
- 1 Std.	25.7		35.3	30.9	22.6		11.9
Daily Min.	6.0	16.2	15.2	12.0	12.8	12.8	7.5

1915 to 2003

Maps

1 - the ARCA *Lower Red Deer Map* is a must for this reach, and actually covers the river through to Estuary, Saskatchewan, on the South Saskatchewan. This map with an up-to-date Alberta Highways map is all you really need.

2 - NTS 1:250,00   NTS 1:50,000

82 P Drumheller	82 P/1 Finnegan	82 P/7 Drumheller	82 P/8 Dorothy
72 L Medicine Hat	72 M/4 Pollockville	72 L/13 Wardlow	

Camping

1 - An established campground is available in Drumheller at River Grove Park (403.823.6655). Other established sites on or near the river can be found: Pinters Campground (403.823.5810) in Rosedale, Emerson/ #36 Bridge (403.362.2772), Steveville / #876 Bridge, and Dinosaur Provincial Park (403.378.4342).

2 - Wilderness camping is possible all along this reach, below the high water mark, and on the many mid-stream islands. Firewood is a problem and paddlers should depend on stoves, fuel and briquets from home for all cooking. Water in large quantities (5-10 L / person / day) should be carried and for those on extended day trips, water filters or other treatment must be carried. Potable water adjacent to the river is hard to find.

Wildlife

As one might expect wildlife on this run varies with how close the river is to the communities and highways that are along the stream. Like the other prairie rivers in Alberta one can expect to find both mule and whitetail deer in the river valley, antelope towards the lower portion of this run, coyotes, foxes, skunks and badgers. Bird life can be very abundant and is most visible in the early portion of the summer. The large hawks, falcons and great blue herons frequent the river valley all summer. Snakes, including rattlesnakes, can be found on this reach, and children must be warned and taught basic preventative behaviors. Dogs are best kept on leash.

Trip Notes

This is one of the most popular canoe trips in the province. Except during floods this is a slow- moving stream with few hazards. At normal flows bridge piers, old bridge piers (i.e. Highway #10), sandbars, the occasional boulder, and side channels with a fallen tree are about the only in-river hazards that one must keep an eye open for. The sun, heat, upstream breezes, and thunderstorms are generally larger concerns than the river. This is a stream for novice paddlers. Take your time for side hikes, relaxed paddling, lots of just floating, and enjoy the ever changing scenery.

Other Reaches

The runs below Dinosaur Provincial Park down to the confluence with the South Saskatchewan, and onto (7km) Estuary Ferry in Saskatchewan (189 km in total), or just 38 km to the next good access at the Jenner Ferry, are well documented in the ARCA map to the *Lower Red Deer River*. The upstream runs from Red Deer to Drumheller are all in the ARCA map to the *Middle Red Deer River*. The runs closer to Red Deer have a little more current and the Badland reaches begin at about McKenzie Crossing (highway #590).

Other Local Activities or Destinations

If car camping and plagued with inclement weather, there is still much to do in this area. First priorities would be visits to the Royal Tyrrell Museum just west of Drumheller, and the Museum Field Station in Dinosaur Provincial Park. These two facilities provide a world class study of dinosaurs and the palaeontological history of the area. Other activities can include visits to the Atlas Coal Mine at East Coulee, the Hoodoos along Highway #10 near Willow Creek.

Rentals and Shuttle Services

Taxi service in Drumheller seems to have deteriorated as of August 2009, and my one recent contact would only offer the possibility of shuttle service if an extra driver was available – check the yellow pages and give whoever is listed a try!

Battle River

Fabyan to Riverdale Mini-Park
(Highway #14 to Highway #41)

Why Go
A pleasant spring paddle through the open vistas of a prairie glacial spillway.

Duration of Tour(s)
* 24.6 km
* 1 day

Classification
1. Rapids: Class 1
2. Skill of Paddlers: Novice River

Start
Start for this run is at the bottom of the old highways campground on the north side of river, just off of Highway #14, and east of Fabyan.

Finish
Finish for this trip is in the Riverdale Mini-Park on the east side of Highway #41 and south of the river. To access the river drive right through the campground and down to the river.

Battle River Valley, northwest of Wainwright, early May, 2006

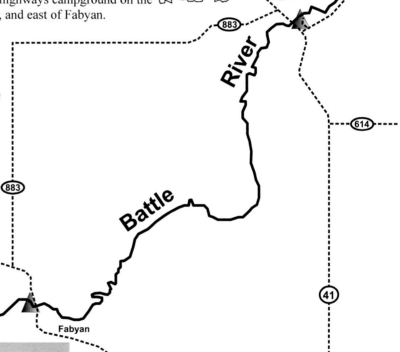

This picture to the left is of the one bit of fast water where the river snaked through an old slump block. Flow for this picture, early May, 2006, is at approximately 16 cms and dropping.

Intermediate Access and Distances

Location	Elevation meters	Km down	Km up	Km between	Access / Bank or Rapid / Class	MGRS datum NAD 1927 Zone 12U	Gradient m/km
Highway #14 Bridge / Fabyan Campground		24.6	0.0		left bank	VP 995 601	
	579	12.5	12.1				
Highway #41		0.4	24.2				
Riverdale Mini Park - river access		0.0	24.6	24.6	right bank	WP 103 719	
	572		32.6				0.3

Gradient
This is a "flat" run!

River Volume and Flow Rate
Good paddling should be had with flows between about 15 cms and 30 cms. As you can see from the hydro graph such flows can only be expected on the spring snow melt, or after the late June/early July monsoon.

Maps
1 - I think you could make this run safely on the Alberta Highways map Unless you know a landowner there really is no intermediate access.

2 - NTS 1:50,000
    73 D/15 Wainwright - this sheet covers all but the first kilometer or so.

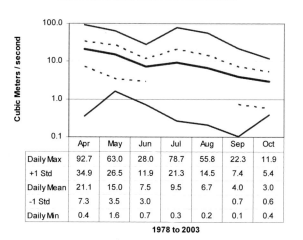

Battle River near Saskatchewan border

	Apr	May	Jun	Jul	Aug	Sep	Oct
Daily Max	92.7	63.0	28.0	78.7	55.8	22.3	11.9
+1 Std	34.9	26.5	11.9	21.3	14.5	7.4	5.4
Daily Mean	21.1	15.0	7.5	9.5	6.7	4.0	3.0
-1 Std	7.3	3.5	3.0			0.7	0.6
Daily Min	0.4	1.6	0.7	0.3	0.2	0.1	0.4

1978 to 2003

Camping
I can find no listing of an operator for the old highways campground at the start of this run. Riverdale Mini-Park (780.842.2996) at the finish appeared to be well maintained, and is associated with a golf course.

Wildlife
Herefords! This is ranch country! In our run this past spring we did see a number of whitetail and mule deer, and both great blue herons and bald eagles fishing along the river.

Trip Notes
This is a flat run, and most paddlers with minimal river skills should be able to safely navigate this reach at the recommended flows. The map does show a number of rapids. One includes the above mentioned S bend through a slump block and the others appear to be primarily gravel bars.

Other Reaches
I was appraised of this run after publishing my guide for central Alberta, I'm sorry to say it took me almost a decade to get out to paddle this reach. I'm hoping to come back in future years and use the Riverdale Mini-Park as a base and paddle the next reach or two below Highway #41. The reach above Fabyan does flow through C.F.B. Wainwright and I suspect that permission would be required to paddle through the base.

Other Local Activities or Destinations
We made this a day trip from Edmonton, and stopped at the Viking Ribstones on our way home. This proved to be an interesting and worthwhile side trip.

Astotin & Islet Lakes

Why Go
These two lakes, each less than an hour's drive east of Edmonton, generally offer sheltered paddling with great "birding" opportunities each spring.

Duration of Tour(s)
On **Astotin** Lake I have one GPS track for 9.4 km, and another for 4.4 km, and if one really tried and followed the outer perimeter I would expect a paddle of 11 to 12 km.

Islet is a smaller lake and a tour of the perimeter will provide a paddle of about 7 km.

Birding on Astotin Lake, May, 2004

Classification
1. Lake water - a little greater risk of winds on Astotin Lake.
2. Skill of Paddlers: Novice Flatwater

Start
Astotin Lake boat launch is at the north end of the Sandy Beach Recreation Area. From the main park road take the access in towards the golf course, then turn right onto the beach and campground access, continue on past the campground access, the beach parking lot, the concession building and up to the traffic circle. Go ½ way around the traffic circle and take the second exit, almost immediately turn left and follow the road back to a large parking lot and the boat launch. There are toilet facilities in the parking lot near the boat launch

Islet lake is accessed by heading east on Sherwood Park Freeway, which becomes Wye Road east of Sherwood Park. Continue on Wye Road past North Cooking Lake. Approximately 10.5 km beyond North Cooking Lake turn left onto Range Road 200 and follow this north and then back west to the Islet Lake staging area. It is well signed.

Maps
For **Astotin** Lake I like to carry the Elk Island National Park sheet at 1:35,000.

For **Islet** Lake pick up a copy of the Cooking Lake - Blackfoot Provincial Recreation Area trail brochures These are usually available at the big trail map and information display in the parking lot.

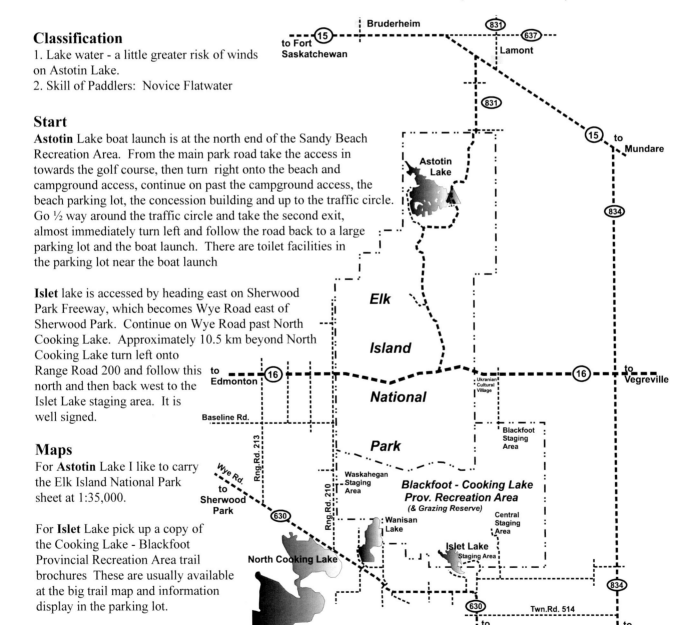

Camping

Sandy Beach Campground (780.992.2950) is adjacent to Astotin lake.

There is no camping allowed in the Cooking Lake - Blackfoot Provincial Recreation Area.

Wildlife

One goes to these lakes for the wildlife. **Astotin** has been an annual paddle for Lois and I for a number of years each June. Nowhere else in all our paddling do see such a variety and density of wildlife. On Astotin Lake there is a cormorant and heron rookery, and each year there seems to be more white pelicans feeding on the lake. On a trip in 2004 I photographed: red necked grebes, common terns, the above mention three birds, and on the drive in we passed through a great herd of bison.

Astotin Lake boat launch, May, 2004

Islet Lake may not have quite the density of wildlife that Astotin offers, but I have many memorable visits to this sheltered lake. One particular memory is of quietly watching a large family of beavers feeding in and on the willow patch I was using as a screen – they got within a few feet before being spooked by our presence. Islet Lake also has pelicans feeding upon it each spring.

Trip Notes

Astotin Lake is a skewed, tear-dropped shaped lake, nearly 3 km on the long axis and over 2.5 km at its widest. The south half of the lake has many islands and bays. The lake makes an excellent day trip. Because of the islands the south half is largely sheltered and a great place to initiate new paddlers. Astotin is a wonderful location for birding. For many years the late Bob Turner would lead a Ceyana Canoe Club trip each spring just for the birding. In recent years the Park has closed the lake to paddlers each fall (September to freeze-up) to reduce pressure on the migrating trumpeter swans. You may confirm this closure by calling the Park Warden's Office at 780.992.2950. There has also been discussion about closing the middle section of the parkway, which will mean that Astotin will only be accessible from the north, off Highway #15, and south just west of Lamont.

Islet Lake is a smallish lake, approximately 3 km long and nearly 1 km wide at its greatest. The lake has many little bays, one large island, and some smaller islets. The SW shore has a small acreage development. The east side is mostly within the Provincial Recreation Area. A walking/biking/ski trail follows the east shore. The staging area has good parking and a very nice picnic site with a wood-stove heated shelter. The lake is very sheltered, and a wonderful place for new paddlers to practise, and develop confidence in their new skills.

Other Local Activities or Destinations

Have you chosen to camp at Sandy Beach and had the weather turn, or a wind blow up? I would suggest while you wait for that change in the weather consider heading south down the park road and out east to the Ukrainian Cultural Heritage Village on the east edge of Elk Island National Park. Or maybe you and your crew would be up for a hike on one of the many trails in the park.

Rentals

    Mountain Equipment Co-op 780.488.6614
    Totem Outdoor Outfitters 780.432.1223

North Saskatchewan River

Ramparts Creek Campground to Preachers Point (Abraham Reservoir)

Why Go
Great mountain scenery, and very pleasant river paddling for Intermediate or better open canoeists.

Duration of Tour(s)
* 52 km
* 2 days – though I've just about always paddled this as two - "day" paddles from a local highway campsite.

Classification
1. Rapids: one Class V to VI, with a good portage trail, and then another good portage trail around the next rapid a III+, and then some Class II water above Whirlpool point.
2. Skill of Paddlers: Intermediate River

Start
This run starts at the west end of the Ramparts Creek Campground; you must drive in and around the campground to find the access in the SW corner.

Whirlpool Point, September 2003

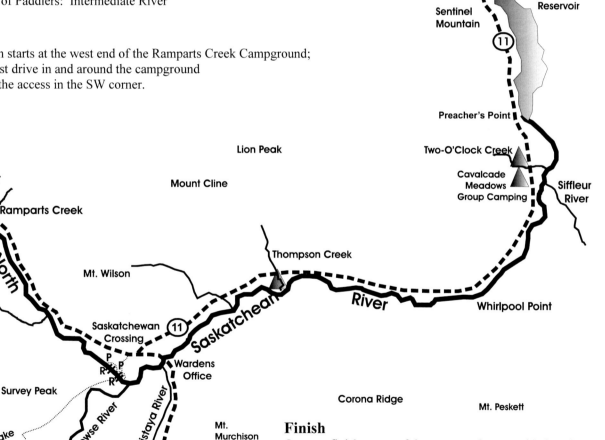

Finish
One can finish at any of the access points noted below, but Preacher's Point is the recommended take out, at the upstream end of Abraham Reservoir. This access is immediately adjacent to the David Thompson Highway, and is approximately 3 km east of the Two O'Clock Creek Campsite.

Intermediate Access, Distances, Key Points and Gradient

Location	Elevation meters	Km up	Km down	Km between	Access / Bank or Rapid / Class	MGRS datum NAD 1983 Zone 11U	Gradient m/km
	1440	-5.4					
Ramparts Creek Campground		0	52.4		left bank	NT 087 654	
Ramparts Creek		0.7	51.7		left bank		
Arctomy's Creek		7.2	45.2		right bank	NT 127 602	
Class V Portage Start		11.7	40.7		left bank,	NT 155 578	
Howse River confluence		13.9	38.5		right	NT 171 564	
	1402	15.5	36.9				1.8
Icefields Parkway / Saskatchewan Crossing		17	35.4	17.0	right bank	NT 192 578	
Thompson Creek		26.7	25.7		left bank	NT 262 620	
						NAD 1927	
Whirlpool Point		38.3	14.1		left bank	NH 363 761	
Siffleur Falls Trail Bridge		46.1	6.3		left bank	NH 408 663	
	1341	50.1	2.3				1.8
Preacher's Point		52.4	0.0	35.4	left bank	NH 396 711	

Gradient

The calculated gradient is consistent, but in reality the gradient does vary over this reach. Besides the big rapids upstream of the Glacier Lake Trail bridge, there is some fun water (easy Class II) above Whirlpool point.

River Volume and Flow Rate

Best paddling on these reaches are with the Whirlpool Point gauge reading between about 100 and 200 cms, though the river is often paddled at somewhat less than this. Flow rates range from just over 2 kmph at 25 cms, to approximately 7 kmph at 100 cms, to 8 kmph at 250 cms.

Maps

1 - NTS 1:50,000

     82 N 15 Mistaya Lake   82 N 16 Siffleur River
     82 C 1 Whiterabbit Creek 82 C 2 Cline River

At present there is not one good map. The old Banff Park sheet at 1:200,000 covers both runs, but it is short on details.

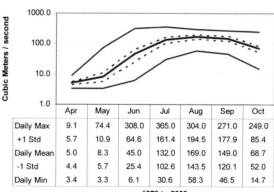

North Saskatchewan River at Whirlpool Point

	Apr	May	Jun	Jul	Aug	Sep	Oct
Daily Max	9.1	74.4	308.0	365.0	304.0	271.0	249.0
+1 Std	5.7	10.9	64.6	161.4	194.5	177.9	85.4
Daily Mean	5.0	8.3	45.0	132.0	169.0	149.0	68.7
-1 Std	4.4	5.7	25.4	102.6	143.5	120.1	52.0
Daily Min	3.4	3.3	6.1	30.6	58.3	46.5	14.7

1970 to 2003

Camping

As already noted most paddlers on these reaches stay at one of the highway campgrounds: Ramparts Creek in Banff Park, or Thompson Creek or Two O'Clock Creek (for both 403.721.2184) outside of Banff Park. I have most often stayed with the Ceyana Canoe Club at the group site, Cavalcade Meadows on the Kootenay Plains. Cavalcade Meadows (403.845.6855 [winter ph.#] or 403.721.2184) is a very large site with eight group sites, some good for up to 50 campers.

Wildlife

These reaches are largely within protected areas, and you have a good chance of seeing any of the large mammals, or birds of the Canadian Rockies. Encounters with black or grizzly bears are possible, so take all appropriate precautions. Until recently the big, half dead limber pine at Whirlpool point was considered the oldest trees in Alberta – it is still a spectacular tree.

Trip Notes

I have regularly lead Ceyana trips to these reaches, usually about every fourth or fifth Labor Day weekend. These reaches remain a popular destination because the upstream glacier provides dependable late summer paddling, and with good leadership the river can accommodate a wide range of paddling ability. The area also offers something for just about everyone: mountain bikers, hikers, climbers and serious whitewater hounds. It is a good area to take a diverse group.

The first picture to the right shows the approach to the first portage around the Class V to VI rapid. This rapid can be lethal. I am aware of at least two accidental deaths here: one during a British Army paddling exercise some years ago, and a solo kayaker in 2009.

approach to Class V to VI rapid

Approach this 500m portage carefully, stay close to the left bank. After the first portage there is 400 m of careful drifting down to the next portage, which is a little shorter. In 2003 we portaged most of the canoes and all the gear around the second rapid, and then three canoes challenged this lower rapid. Recent floods had scoured out the ledge and it was much more difficult than I remembered from our previous run here in the mid-90's. My adventurous companions discovered just how difficult the ledge is, as can be seen in the bottom right picture.

Access to the river at the Icefields Parkway bridge just south of Saskatchewan Crossing is available both upstream and downstream of the bridge. Both access points tend to involve some wading on a side channel to reach the main stream. Some years we have actually waded the canoes through the big culvert under Highway #93 to start the run downstream of the highway.

the Class V to VI rapid from below

The first part of the channel below the Icefields Parkway is braided and requires careful water reading to find the right channel, and like all braided reaches can present both logjam and sweeper hazards. Some 3 km above Whirlpool Point the river gathers itself together into one channel and presents some fun, easy Class II water. At very low water there can be some exposed, or partially submerged boulders to dodge. Whirlpool Point can be a very powerful eddy. I remember in '72 crossing right over a whirlpool that broke off from the eddy line. The whole canoe was sucked down about 10 cm, and my partner and I braced "for our lives!" We stayed dry!

swim in the lower rapid (Class III+), just above the
Glacier Lake Trail bridge

Other Reaches
Stuart Smith (1996) reports on the reaches upstream of Ramparts creek. These reaches present both some short easy sections, and some serious whitewater. Abraham Reservoir is the next reach, and due to the frequent strong winds (Windy Point is about half-way down the reservoir!) paddling the reservoir is not recommended.

Other Local Activities or Destinations
Over the years of camping at Cavalcade Meadows we've tackled many of the other options this area provides. We've made the hike into Siffleur Falls (about 4 km), up the ridge at Whirlpool Point, up the trail to Landslide lake, and on really wet days, we have made the drive into Banff for the Hotsprings, and the Banff Avenue candy store! Others in our club have mountain biked the old roads both upstream and downstream of the Siffleur River trail bridge on the south side of the North Saskatchewan. When our kids were younger we scrambled on the rocks and cliffs behind the campsite – one year we even drug along our climbing gear and "top roped" the kids on the longer pitches. Ross & Kyba (1995, 2004) *The David Thompson Highway: a hiking guide* is a wonderful resource for hiking options, and for much of the natural & cultural history of this area.

Below Highway #93, lunch break, with Mt. Cline in the background

North Saskatchewan River

Nordegg Bridge (Forestry Trunk Rd.)
to Rocky Mountain House

Why Go
This is the premier foothills whitewater, open canoe long-weekend camping run in the province. The rapids at the end are the closest, season-long, consistent whitewater available to Edmonton paddlers.

Duration of Tour(s)
* 106 km
* 3-4 days with overnight camping on the river, with a number of nice ½ to 1 day paddles

Classification
1. Rapids: Class I to III-
2. Skill of Paddlers: Intermediate River

Upstream view from Dutch Creek Campsite, 05-Sept-03

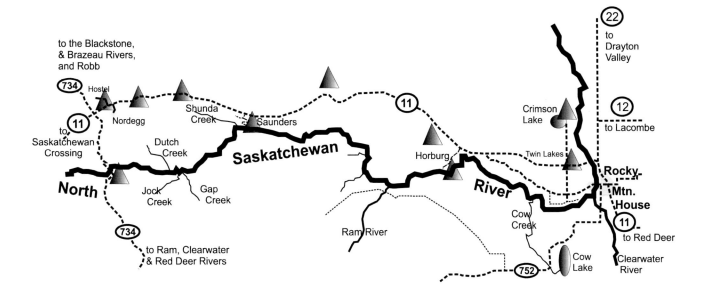

Start
This run starts at the Forestry Trunk Road (Highway #734) bridge approximately 11 km south of Nordegg. One can access the river on either side of the bridge. I prefer to put in at the old gravel pit on the north - upstream side of the bridge. This avoids exiting a rather strong eddy before one has warmed up.

Finish
One can finish at any of the access points noted below, but often the easiest shuttle is to paddle right into Rocky and finish under the old Highway #11a bridge.

Intermediate Access, Distances, Key Points and Gradient

Location	Elevation meters	Km down	Km up	Km between	Access / Bank or Rapid / Class	MGRS datum NAD 1927 Zone 11U	Gradient m/km
	1200		-5.5				
Nordegg Bridge / NW launch		106.0	0.0		left/upstream of bridge	NJ 628 054	
	1180	100.7	5.3				1.9
Dutch Creek		95.1	10.9		left	NJ 723 050	
	1160	93.5	12.5				2.8
	1140	86.0	20.0				2.7
Upper Saunders Rapid		80.0	26.0		Class II to II+	NJ 825 116	
Shunda Creek		79.1	26.9		left	NJ 830 121	
Saunders Ledge		78.6	27.4		stay tight right to avoid		
Saunders Access		78.0	28.0	28.0	left	NJ 842 121	
	1120	77.0	29.0				2.2
	1100	68.0	38.0				2.2
Sunset Creek		62.8	43.2		left	NJ 968 116	
	1080	59.8	46.2				2.4
Trout Creek		53.1	52.9		right	PJ 035 079	
	1067	51.3	54.7				1.5
	1052	48.2	57.8				4.8
former Phoenix Ferry site		45.3	60.7		right	PJ 071 041	
Ram River confluence		44.4	61.6		right	PJ 080 038	
	1036	40.4	65.6				2.1
Horburg Access		36.0	70.0	42.0	left - watch for side channel upstream	PJ 149 059	
	1021	34.5	71.5				2.5
approaching Devil's Elbow		30.7	75.3		Class 11+ to III- stay right to avoid	PJ 183 082	
	1006	26.4	79.6				1.9
	991	16.8	89.2				1.6
Cow Creek		15.1	90.9		right	PJ 300 023	
Fisher's Rapid		14.0	92.0		Class II+ - III-		
Blue Bridge Access / RR bridge		9.1	96.9	26.9	left	PJ 340 009	
Greer's Rapid		8.6	96.4		Class II		
Lower Fisher's Rapid		5.5	99.5		Class II		
	975	6.0	100.0				1.5
RMH Historic Site boat launch		5.0	101.0	4.1	left	PJ 375 015	
Brierly's Rapid		4.7	101.3		right channel Class II to II+		
Clearwater River		2.0	104.0		right	PJ 398 031	
	960	2.0	104.0				3.8 ?
Highway 11A / Bridge & Launch		0.0	106.0	5.0	right	PJ 403 045	

Gradients

Gradients on this reach vary a bit, with higher gradient stretches through the Gap to Saunders, and then again through the Devil's Elbow. I am suspect of the some of calculations above based on Garmin's Topo Canada (2004).

River Volume and Flow Rate

This reach of the North Saskatchewan is best paddled with the Rocky Mtn House station reporting flows of between 100 and 300 cms. Velocity at Rocky varies from approximately 3 kmph at 100 cms through to 8 kmph at 800 cms.

Other than floods the BIG concern with volume on this reach is the daily fluctuation due to the operations of the Bighorn Dam. Fluctuations of 50 to 150 cms in one day do occur and this can result in very large changes in the size of one's campsite beach overnight. A few years ago on the Saunders run, we came across a jet boat crew trying to drag their boat back to the river. Their boat had been stranded some 12-15 m horizontally, and 2 m vertically when the river receded. Paddlers have been known to have their untied boats wash away overnight.

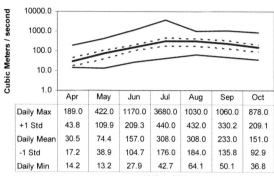

North Saskatchewan River at Rocky Moutain House

	Apr	May	Jun	Jul	Aug	Sep	Oct
Daily Max	189.0	422.0	1170.0	3680.0	1030.0	1060.0	878.0
+1 Std	43.8	109.9	209.3	440.0	432.0	330.2	209.1
Daily Mean	30.5	74.4	157.0	308.0	308.0	233.0	151.0
-1 Std	17.2	38.9	104.7	176.0	184.0	135.8	92.9
Daily Min	14.2	13.2	27.9	42.7	64.1	50.1	36.8

1913 to 2003

Maps

1 - In 2005 ARCA published the *Alberta River Guide: the North Saskatchewan River, Nordegg to Drayton Valley* – this should certainly be in your map case for this, and the next run. Combine this map with the *Alberta Highways Map* and you should not need anything else.

2 - NTS 1:50,000:

83 C 8 Nordegg	83 B 5 Saunders
83 B 6 Crimson Lake	83 B 7 Rocky Mountain House

Camping

This is one of Alberta's premier canoe camping trips. On some summer long weekends over 200 canoes have been counted on this reach. One of the joys of this reach is the wide variety of possible wilderness campsites, almost every bend has a site, though the first 40 minutes below Saunders, and the reach from Horburg to the Devil's Elbow are a little barren of large group camp sites.

Wilderness campsites such as the one at Dutch Creek, and the Devil's Elbow have begun to show our use and our provincial recreational canoe association has tried to mitigate this somewhat with the installation of back country (read plastic/no roof) dry pit toilets. If you get an early start on a long weekend, you should be able to find a secluded campsite, but do not plan on having the Devil's Elbow site to yourself Sunday evening!

As the map above shows there are also many established campgrounds along this reach. One can car-camp and do these reaches as day trips. The start (Almyer Staging Area), Saunders, Horburg and the Rocky Mountain House Historic Site (403.845.2412) all have public campgrounds. And if it gets ugly, the Shunda Creek Hostel in Nordegg (403.721.2140) is a wonderful facility, open to the public, and not very expensive.

One note of social caution: camping in the vicinity of the Nordegg bridge in Almyer Staging may result in a poor night's sleep. This area is popular with the "quad/dirt bike set." Two options are possible: get there early afternoon, and float downstream a few km to camp, or arrive early in the morning. Vehicle security is also a concern.

Wildlife

This can be a great run for wildlife, but to really see it, you must take the advice of that local, wily wildlife biologist Mel Kraft. Some years ago (Krafty) Mel told me the best way to see wildlife on this run is to stop early, have supper, and then drift through the early evening and hold off camping until nearly sunset. This run is home to all of the critters of Alberta's eastern slopes, so again, do practice all the good bear precautions.

Trip Notes

This is a great river, with good camping, a dependable flow, and rapids that always have a safe channel, but that also can provide excitement for just about any open canoeist, and a good many closed boat paddlers and rafters. As noted above I like to start on the north side launch and slip past the fast jet just above the bridge. Then it is an easy paddle down to the Gap. These days, in the late summer, the river maintains your interest as you try to find the fast water and the deepest channels. There are a couple of outside bends that do present sweepers, and at the higher waters of mid-summer, log jams can be a very significant hazard along here. Dutch Creek and the mid-stream boulder announce the start of the "Gap." Here the river breaks through the Brazeau range and out to the foothills. In the Gap there are three or four rapids depending on water levels. On the big bend to the north, there is a series of partial ledges extending out from the left shore, though the first ledge presents the only really challenge. There are some fast chutes, and some boulders to dodge, and one will earn a splash in the face in the Gap rapids.

From below the Gap through to Saunders rapid you will encounter another fast chute or two, and some wave trains. The Tufa mounds on the right bank, and the bend back to the NW announce the upper Saunders Rapid. Then Shunda Creek and the "S" bend below announce the approach to Saunders ledge. This ledge is no problem if you stay tight to the right, but many a paddler has learned that canoes do "swamp" in Saunders ledge – including these two chaps to the right. Saunders access is just downstream on the left.

Saunders Ledge, and yes, this crew did swim out!
05-Sept-04

From Saunders to Horburg there are no real rapids, just a few friendly sets of bouncy waves, and the occasional logjam and sweeper to stay alert for. If you have a novice group of paddlers this is the "first run of choice" as an introduction to the upper North Saskatchewan, and this reach has many good campsites in the middle section.

Often on the second day of a long weekend we plan lunch for the old Phoenix Ferry Crossing. The remains of the ferry may still be found on the right bank. My understanding is that this ferry primarily supported a logging camp on the north side, and logs once across the river were skidded up the bank to the mill and the railway. Remains of the skid way, and mill can be found on the north bank if you go for a hike.

Just below Phoenix, the Ram River comes in on the right, often through two channels. The run from the Ram down to Horburg often seems "flat" but there are a few small rapids that can wake you up. Horburg access requires that you stay alert for the side channel that goes into the staging area and campsite. Some years it can be a bit hard to spot, and the last flood seems to have taken out the sign that was once posted about a kilometre upstream – maybe it will be replaced!

From Horburg to the Devil's Elbow, there again are some easy Class II rapids, and really no good campsites. I've looked! Looked hard some years. The long shale bank on the right announces the approach to the Devil's Elbow, and then the houses high on the cliff to the north confirm your approach. In recent years there has been a very good series of rollers upstream of the actual Elbow, don't let these fool you – the best is yet to come.

Deep into the Devils Elbow, and no, this crew did not swim!
05-Sept-04

The Devil's Elbow is a long series of shale ledges that end in a large pool. Novice paddlers and the fearful can skirt all but a few waves by running down the right side. Others can go deep into the ledges, holes and waves, just like the paddlers on the previous page. Camping at the Devil's Elbow does allow one's group the opportunity to make numerous runs through, and probably practice their rescue skills too. It is good to have along a few float bags to replace your gear if this is your plan. Rescuers can speed up the process if they have a good on-river T rescue, and tow gear. I have seen some awfully long swims here by poorly prepared crews.

One advantage of staying at the Elbow the last evening of a long weekend is that your serious whitewater hounds just might get enough paddling in the evening before so that they do not slow you down on the run to the Brierley's by tempting fate at each of the many Class II to II+ rapids that occur between the "Elbow" and the Brierley's.

Rapids have come and gone over the years that I have been paddling this run between the Devil's Elbow and the Fisher's Rapid. Some years there are a couple of good riffles, and others nothing. Cow Creek announces the approach to Fisher's Rapid. The rapid is a kilometer or so downstream on the right hand bend, and through the full "S" bend. This is the one rapid where paddlers often have to cross over, from the inside of the first corner, to the inside of the second corner to avoid the worst of the waves and rollers. The 2005 flood made this somewhat easier, but for how long?

The Rocky Canoe Club has worked hard these past years at developing the access at the "Blue Bridge". It can be a steep access, and a bit of a difficult landing or launch for open canoes at higher waters, somewhat easier for modern play kayaks. On the run from the Blue Bridge to the Brierley's one is never really out of sight of either the last rapid, or the next. It is a grand few kilometers with lots of practice and play spots.

There is a bit of a flat stretch between the two part Lower Fisher's Rapid and the Brierley's. The National Historic Site river access is on the left, and the first rollers of Brierley's rapids can be seen just downstream and behind the midstream island/gravel bar from the boat launch. Novice paddlers can completely avoid the Brierley's by taking the left channel around the island. The greatest challenges are of course on the outside of the right channel. If you have members of your group who think they are up to the challenge, have your rescue crew ready at the bottom. At most water levels throw bag rescues can work well off of the shale shelf on the right side at the bottom of the rapid, but you should have a tow crew ready too.

Other Reaches
Upstream of the Nordegg bridge there is a very pleasant 25 km paddle from the Bighorn Dam down to the bridge, no rapids, but on some years there have been significant logjams and sweepers to deal with. The downstream run is the next report.

Other Local Activities or Destinations
One Canada Day weekend I was stuck with my scout troop at the Saunders Staging Area awaiting for the high water to recede. We filled in our non-river-paddling days by taking in the mine site tour at Nordegg, refining paddling skills on the Beaver Dam on Shunda Creek, just east of Nordegg, and hiking up the ridge at Windy Point. If we'd had to wait another day I was going to take them fishing on either the ponds on upper Shunda Creek, or the Harlick pond east of Nordegg. There are a good many other hikes in the area, and some great mountain biking around Nordegg.

Rentals and Shuttle Services
I have used the Rocky / Clearwater Cabs (403.845.4000) for a number of years for my shuttles back to Nordegg. Hela Adventures just west of Rocky, at the Horburg corner, (403.845.4325 or www.helaventures.com) will also provide shuttle service, canoe rental and outfitting.

North Saskatchewan River

Rocky Mountain House to Drayton Valley

Why go
Good wilderness camping is available along much of this reach, some modest whitewater and braided stream channels to keep folks on their toes, and the sense of history as this is the highest reach on the North Saskatchewan regularly traveled by canoe or York boat during the fur trade.

A Ceyana Canoe Club group just below Rocky

Duration of Tour(s)
* 133 km
* 2-3 days - This run makes for a pleasant, mid-summer, long weekend tour. There is a nice day run from Rocky to the mouth of the Baptiste River at km 40, and even a take-out is available off of the Buster Creek / Baptiste River road at km 25.5.

Classification
1. Rapids: Class I - II
2. Skill of Paddlers: Intermediate River Paddlers, and one paddler in each canoe must be wise in the ways of avoiding log jams and sweepers.

Start
The start for this run is under the Highway 11A bridge on the west side of the town of Rocky Mountain House. Riverside Park is on the east/right side of the river and the turn-off to the park is on the south side of the old highway, just east of the bridge.

Finish
The finish is the boat launch within the Willey West Campground. This county campground is below the Highway #39 bridge on the east or right bank of the river. Access to the campground is approximately 2 km east of and up the hill from the bridge along Highway #39. Recent floods have eroded away the original boat launch at Willey West, and there is a new launch downstream nearly 1 km below the bridge, and on the inside of the bend.

-120-

Intermediate Access, Distances, Key Points and Gradient

Location	Elevation meters	Km down	Km up	Km between	Access / Bank or Rapid / Class	MGRS datum NAD 1927 Zone 11U	Gradient m/km
	960	-1.5					
Riverside Park /#11A		0	134		right bank	PJ 403 046	
Riverview Campground		4	130		left bank		
Highway #11 bridge		4	130		right bank	PJ 392 083	
	945	6	127				1.9
	930	13	121				2.5
	914	19	115				2.4
Buster Creek		22	112		left bank		
Buster Creek Rd (Rge Rd 80a)		26	108		left bank	PJ 336 254	
	899	29	105				1.6
	884	37	96				1.8
access from Buster Creek Rd		39	95	39	left bank	PJ 304 368	
Baptiste River confluence		40	94		left bank		
	869	48	86				1.4
	853	57	77				1.9
Abraham's Gates		57	77			PJ 236 508	
	838	65	69				1.7
	823	72	62				2.2
Brazeau River		80	53		left bank	PJ 190 643	
	808	86	48				1.1
	792	92	42				2.4
Boggy Hall Access		94	40	55	left bank	PJ 193 761	
Blue Rapids		98	36			PJ 202 794	
	777	103	31				1.4
Rose Creek		110	24		right bank	PJ 310 804	
access west off Buck Creek		116	18		right bank	PJ 342 840	
	762	118	16				1.0
	747	128	6				1.5
Highway # 39/22 Bridge		133	1				
Willey West Campground		134	0	40	right bank	PJ 381 975	

Gradient

The average gradients between contour intervals is very consistent on this run, with a total variance from only 1 m/km to a maximum of 2.5 m/km, and most of calculated gradients are between 1.5 m/km and 2.2 m/km.

River Volume and Flow Rate

Good paddling occurs on this reach with flows in the 80-300 cms range.

At the Rocky Mountain House station, velocity varies from approximately 2.5 km/hr at 150 cms, to 6 km/hr at 400 cms and 8 km/hr at 800 cms.

On a Ceyana Canoe Club trip, Labor Day Weekend '96, we found the river to be at a very nice, modestly low level in Rocky at about 63 cms, but once we passed the Brazeau, which had been shut down at the dam and was barely contributing a trickle, we found that we really had to hunt for the deepest channel. This was an unusual occurrence for the North Saskatchewan.

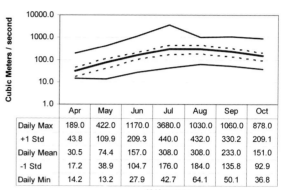

North Saskatchewan River at Rocky Moutain House

	Apr	May	Jun	Jul	Aug	Sep	Oct
Daily Max	189.0	422.0	1170.0	3680.0	1030.0	1060.0	878.0
+1 Std	43.8	109.9	209.3	440.0	432.0	330.2	209.1
Daily Mean	30.5	74.4	157.0	308.0	308.0	233.0	151.0
-1 Std	17.2	38.9	104.7	176.0	184.0	135.8	92.9
Daily Min	14.2	13.2	27.9	42.7	64.1	50.1	36.8

1913 to 2003

Maps

1 - First choice for on-river would be the ARCA (2002) *Alberta River Guide: the North Saskatchewan River - foothills region.*

2 - NTS 1:50,000:

83 B/7 Rocky Mountain House	83 B/10 Carlos
83 B/11 Baptiste River	83 B/14 Brazeau
83 G/3 Blue Rapids	83 G/2 Drayton Valley

3 - and an up-to-date *Alberta Highways Map.*

Camping

Public campgrounds are available at Riverview Campground (403.845.4422), just off of the river at the Highway #11 bridge, and at the finish at the Willey West Campground (780.542.5821). This run has a good many fine wilderness campsites, though they are not as frequent as on the upstream Nordegg to Rocky reach.

Trip Notes

This is a very fine run later in the summer for novice paddlers that have mastered the North Saskatchewan closer to Edmonton. Much of the run is braided, so paddlers must always be alert for logjams and sweepers. On our '96 run , not far above the Baptiste River we came across a short section where the river had cut a new channel across a meander bend. As is common in this situation, the entry to the new channel was nearly choked with logjams, and the river through the new channel was fast and overhung on the outside of the bends with many sweepers. In the entrance logjam was the remains of one canoe. Ten years later (2006) this is now the main channel and not a problem at all. This river changes a lot with each major flood, and paddlers must be especially wary for a season or three after a big flood.

The rapids on this run are usually formed as gravel bar lined chutes, or by the fast water on the outside of bends that may be running over bedrock shale ledges. There are some spots with larger boulders that have to be avoided. Generally an alert paddler, even a novice with basic control skills, has little trouble negotiating these problems at lower flows. Many paddlers are well below "Blue Rapids" before they realize it. **At late June / early July average flows or higher, this can be a powerful river that can quickly sweep the novice or unwary paddler into trouble on the many log jams and sweepers.**

Historical Notes

Paddlers should recognize the sense of history on this run. Voyagers and York Boat men regularly plied this run upstream and down for nearly ninety years in the fur trade era. Not only were there major fur houses just upstream of Rocky, but Boggy Hall, a minor fur post, existed for a short period, some 16 km below the Brazeau confluence.

Rentals and Shuttle Services

I have used the Rocky / Clearwater Cabs (403.845.4000) for a number of years for my shuttles back to Rocky. Hela Adventures just west of Rocky, at the Horburg corner, (403.845.4325 or www.helaventures.com) will also provide shuttle service, canoe rental and outfitting.

For our Ceyana Canoe Club, 2006 Labor Day weekend trip I contacted the various taxi companies in Drayton Valley, and received flat rate quotes for the shuttle back to Rocky Mtn. House from Willey West Campground ranging from $120 to $140.

      DJ's Cabs   780.542.7655

      Johnny's Taxi & Hotshot Service   780.542.5818

      Edmonton Canoe 780.470.5352   www.edmontoncanoe.com

Rapid near Boggy Hall – with a long telephoto to foreshorten
September, 2006

Willey West Campground - boat launch - September, 2006

-123-

North Saskatchewan River

Drayton Valley to Devon

Why Go

At most average to below average flows this reach above Devon provides good paddling for the Novice River Paddler. There is camping and overnight tripping, pleasant semi-wilderness and pastoral scenery, good fishing, wildlife and a variety of access points.

59th Edmonton Scouts on the run below Berrymore Bridge, Sept. '97

Duration of Tour(s)

* 130 km
* ½ day to 5 days with many combinations possible.

Classification

1. Rapids: Class I
2. Skill of Paddlers: Novice River

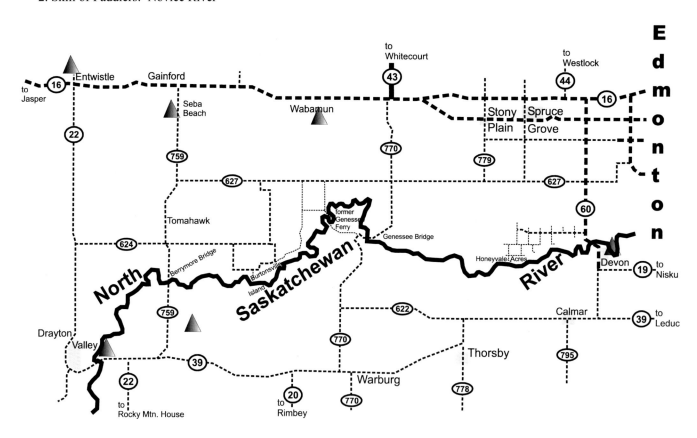

Start

Start at the Willey West Campground, the county campground just downstream of the Highway #39 bridge, on the east or right bank of the river. Access to the campground is approximately 2 km east of and up the hill for the bridge along Highway #39. Recent floods have required that the river access in the campground move, and it is now nearly 1 km below the Highway #39 bridge, and on the inside of the bend. You must enter the campground and about 2/3s of the way through the campground turn right (west) to reach the boat launch.

Finish

The finish is at the new Voyageurs Park in Devon just downstream of the Highway #60 Bridge on the west side of Devon, and on the east or right side of the river. Access to this park is via the north Devon access road, south of and just beyond the top of the hill from the river. This should put you on Athabasca Avenue, turn left/north onto Superior St, and then left/west onto Saskatchewan Avenue. This will take you back down the old highway hill to Voyageurs Park.

Intermediate Access and Distances

Location	Elevation meters	Km down	Km up	Km between	Access / Bank or Rapid / Class	MGRS datum NAD 1927 Zone 11U	Gradient m/km
Willey West Campground		130	0		right	PJ 381 975	
	732	121	9				
	716	110	20				1.4
#759 - Berrymore Bridge		104	26		left - above bridge	PK 494 094	
	701	102	29	29			1.8
Buck Lake Creek		98	32		right	PK 534 096	
Tomahawk Creek		90	40		left	PK 601 098	
	686	89	41				1.2
Rnge. Rd. 45 Burtonsville Island W		87	43	14	left - inside of bend	PK 625 096	
Burtonsville Island Canoe Camp site		83	47		left	PK 663 104	
	671	62	68				0.6
former Genesee Ferry site		61	69	26	left (and right)	PK 748 198 (L) PK747 197 (R)	
#770 Genesse Bridge		43	87	18	right -below bridge	PK 810 175	
	655	40	91				0.7
Strawberry Creek		24	106		right	PK 967 123	
	640	18	112				0.7
						NAD 1983	
Honeyvale Acres access		14	116	29	left	UE 060 139	
Devon below Highway # 60		0	130	14	right - below bridge	UE 170 170	

Gradient

This is a relatively flat river, with the highest gradient (1.8 m/km) on the run below Berrymore Bridge to below Burtonsville Island.

River Volume and Flow Rate

This is a river best paddled with the Edmonton station reporting between 150 and about 300 cms, much more and most of the river bank campsites disappear. Flow rates at Edmonton vary from 2 km/hr at 100 cms to over 8 km/hr at 2000 cms.

Maps

1 - At present I travel these reaches with the two 1:250,000 sheets listed below, an *Alberta Highways Map* and my GPS!

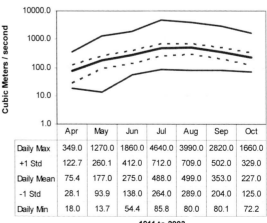

North Saskatchewan River at Edmonton

	Apr	May	Jun	Jul	Aug	Sep	Oct
Daily Max	349.0	1270.0	1860.0	4640.0	3990.0	2820.0	1660.0
+1 Std	122.7	260.1	412.0	712.0	709.0	502.0	329.0
Daily Mean	75.4	177.0	275.0	488.0	499.0	353.0	227.0
-1 Std	28.1	93.9	138.0	264.0	289.0	204.0	125.0
Daily Min	18.0	13.7	54.4	85.8	80.0	80.1	72.2

1911 to 2003

2 - NTS 1:250,000:   NTS 1:50,000:
     83 G Wabamun   83 G/2 Drayton Valley   83 G/6 Easyford
     83 H Edmonton   83 G/7 Tomahawk   83 G/8 Genessee
                                      83 H/5 Leduc

Camping

Public campgrounds are available on the river at both the start and just below the finish of this run. Willey West Campground (780.542.5821) is the starting point, just below the Highway #39 bridge, and the Devon Lion's River Valley Campground (780.987.4777) is just 3.8 kilometers downstream and has good river access. Saskatchewan Drive East will lead you down to this campground.

Wilderness camping is available on the banks below the highwater mark and on the many river islands. Because these riverside campsites disappear at high water, these reaches are best left for the early or late season paddling when other streams are too low.

Wildlife

On the run above Berrymore there are many high shale cliffs that are home to cliff swallows. Red tail hawks will commonly be seen in the summer soaring above sun heated hillsides. Given the good fish population of the river both osprey and bald eagles may be spotted. Moose, and both whitetail and mule deer, populate the whole river valley. Elk may be spotted upstream of Genesse, especially in the vicinity of Burtonsville Island. Over the years my scout group had one encounter with a black bear on Burtonsville Island, and one winter my college outdoor education class crossed fresh cougar tracks on Burtonsville Island. And I think every night I've ever camped in this river valley, I've been lulled to sleep by a coyote chorus.

Trip Notes

There are many trips possible within this report. Rarely do Edmonton paddlers do this whole reach in one go. Genesse Bridge to Devon is a popular weekend run. Our club often does Honeyvale to Devon as a fall day trip. For those looking for a bit more wilderness the Berrymore to Genessee reach is suitable. This river can be tackled by paddlers early in their career. With good flatwater skills and an introduction to river paddling under their belts most paddlers will successfully complete these reaches without incident. BUT as always, high water should be avoided.

My most exciting experience on this reach of the river occured one autumn when I had a college crew on the run below Berrymore. Just above Burtonsville Island, a large slump had put a strip of forest about 500 m long into the main river channel. My novice crew was just skilled enough to "slalom" through the upright trees and avoid the one or two small log jams that had formed. This run can have log jams and sweepers on just about any corner, or at the head of any bar or island. At the recommended lower flows of early or late season these hazards usually prove to not be very dangerous; of course at high water they are!

Other Reaches

Both the upstream and downstream reaches are included in this guidebook.

Other Local Activities or Destinations

If there is too much water in North Saskatchewan, consider the Pembina or Sturgeon Rivers, or head down to the Red Deer – but in most early summer monsoon seasons, all of these rivers can be too high for safe paddling at the same time. If you have come a long way away to paddle these rivers, consider the lake circuit in Lakelands Provincial Park near Lac la Biche. Or tour any of the multitude of visitor sites in Edmonton – my first choice for an out-of-town paddler would be Fort Edmonton, then the Royal Alberta Museum or Ukranian Village east of Elk Island National Park.

Rentals & Shuttles

Rentals: Shuttles:
Mountain Equipment Co-op 780.488.6614   Drayton Valley
Totem Outdoor Outfitters 780.432.1223   DJ's Cabs 780.542.7655
                                            Johnny's Taxi and Hotshot Service 780.542.5818
                                Devon
                                              Devon Taxi 780.908.9569
                                Edmonton
                                              Edmonton Canoe 780.470.5352 *www.edmontoncanoe.com*

North Saskatchewan River

Devon to Capilano Park, Edmonton

Why Go
These reaches are wonderful day trips, with great vistas of the river valley, the city skyline with easy novice river paddling at most water levels.

Duration of Tour(s)
* 50 km
* ½ to 2 days with many short variations possible

Provincial Archives of Alberta, photo A3007 circa 1937

Classification
1. Rapids: Class I
2. Skill of Paddlers: Novice River Paddlers at low flows, Intermediate River Paddlers at the upper recommended flow range.

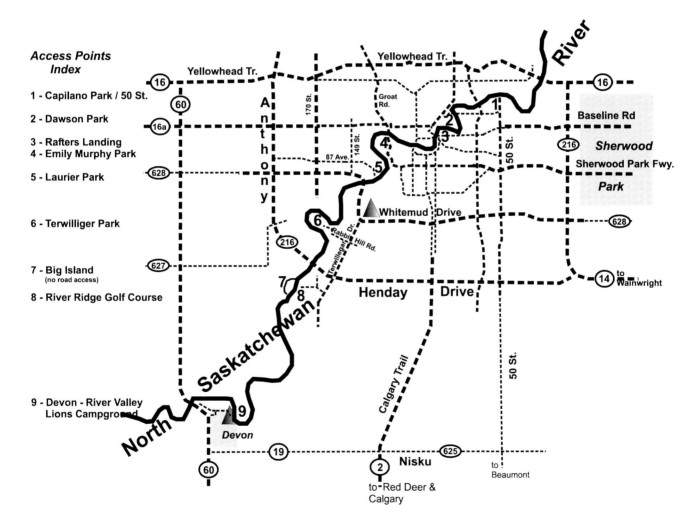

Access Points
Index

1 - Capilano Park / 50 St.

2 - Dawson Park

3 - Rafters Landing
4 - Emily Murphy Park

5 - Laurier Park

6 - Terwilliger Park

7 - Big Island
   (no road access)

8 - River Ridge Golf Course

9 - Devon - River Valley
   Lions Campground

Start

The primary start for this reach is at Voyageurs Park in Devon just downstream of the Highway #60 Bridge on the west side of Devon, and on the east or right side of the river. Access to Voyageurs Park is via the north Devon access road, south of and just beyond the top of the hill from the river. This should put you on Athabasca Avenue, turn left/north onto Superior St, and then left/west onto Saskatchewan Avenue. This will take you back down the old highway hill to the park.

Finish

Finish for this run is at the Capilano Park – 50th Street Boat Launch in east central Edmonton, on the south side of the river. Virtually all main east/west roads in Edmonton between Nisku and the river lead to 50th St., and then it is just a matter of heading north to the river.

Intermediate Access and Distances

Location	Elevation meters	Km down	Km up	Km between	Access / Bank or Rapid / Class	MGRS datum NAD 1983 Zone 12 U	Gradient m/km
Voyageurs Park		49.6	0.0		right bank	UE 170 170	
Lion's River Valley Campground		45.8	3.8	3.8	right bank	UE 199 161	
	630	38.6	11.0				
Big Island - Upstream end		31.7	17.9		left bank	UE 241 239	
River Ridge Golf Club		31.2	18.4		right bank	UE 246 242	
Terwillegar Park		22.4	27.2		right bank	UE 270 291	
Fort Edmonton Hist. Site		18.6	31.0		right bank	UE 288 313	
	620	18.3	31.3				0.5
mouth of Whitemud Creek		17.2	32.4		right bank	UE 301 315	
Laurier Park Boat Launch		16.5	33.1	33.1	left bank	UE 307 318	
Emily Murphy Park / Groat Rd.		11.5	38.1	5.0	right bank	UE 317 349	
Rafters' Landing		6.4	43.2	5.1	right bank	UE 356 351	
Dawson Park		3.9	45.7		left bank	UE 364 363	
Capilano Park / 50 St Boat Launch		0.0	49.6	6.4	right bank	UE 398 375	0.3

Gradient

This is a gentle series of reaches and average gradients are less than .5 m/km over the whole length of this report.

River Volume and Flow Rate

Like the previous run, these reaches are best paddled with 150 to 300 cms or so. Flow rates at the Edmonton station vary from 2 km/hr at 100 cms to over 8 km/hr at 2000 cms.

Maps

1 - Probably the most useful maps for this run, are the *Alberta Road Map*, with the Edmonton street map on the backside, and the *Edmonton River Recreation Guide.* In addition the *North Saskatchewan River Guide* is not so much a river guide, as an interpretative manual to all you may see along the river, it is very informative on wildlife, history, and geology.

2 - NTS 1:250,000: 83H Edmonton
   NTS 1:50,000: 83H/5 Leduc, 83H/12 St. Albert,
      83H/11 Edmonton

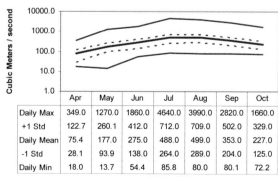

North Saskatchewan River at Edmonton

	Apr	May	Jun	Jul	Aug	Sep	Oct
Daily Max	349.0	1270.0	1860.0	4640.0	3990.0	2820.0	1660.0
+1 Std	122.7	260.1	412.0	712.0	709.0	502.0	329.0
Daily Mean	75.4	177.0	275.0	488.0	499.0	353.0	227.0
-1 Std	28.1	93.9	138.0	264.0	289.0	204.0	125.0
Daily Min	18.0	13.7	54.4	85.8	80.0	80.1	72.2

1911 to 2003

Camping

The only public campground on the river for this reach is the Devon Lion's River Valley Campground (780.987.477) on the east side of the town. Take the above mentioned Saskatchewan Avenue east through Devon and down the hill, through the golf course, and stay right for the campground. The river access is to the left just before the campground entrance. The other campground shown above is the Rainbow Valley Campground (780.434.5531) along Whitemud Creek in Edmonton. This campground is well off the river but it is central to Edmonton, and has some very fine tent and trailer sites along the creek

As I go to press (spring 2007) with this edition, Big Island is still provincial crown property with no leaseholder and thus is available for canoe camping. Most every spring the Ceyana canoe club offers a "first of the season" shakedown trip from Devon to Edmonton with camping on Big Island. We like to meet about 1:30 PM in Devon at the Lion's Campground river launch, return our vehicles to Laurier Park, catch a cab back and share the cost. This usually puts us on the river by about 3:30, and into Big Island by 6:30 or so for an evenings camp and hike around the island. We then are up early, and into Laurier park by noonish. This provides a pleasant paddle, camp and still gives two half days for those spring garden chores.

Wildlife

I am always surprised at how much wildlife one sees along these reaches of the river near and in the city. If you are out early or late in the day, beaver sightings are pretty much guaranteed. A wide variety of ducks, gulls, hawks, coyotes, fox and deer can be seen through much of the paddling season.

Trip Notes

These reaches are basic training and evening pleasure runs for Edmonton paddlers. Devon to Edmonton, the "local classic," often surprises novice paddlers with how long it can take. In the past during the K-Days Canoe Regatta the better teams often finished the run from the Lion's Campground in Devon to Whitemud Creek in well under two hours. On the other hand, in the late summer, at low flows or with an upstream breeze, novice paddlers have been known to take seven hours or longer to complete the same reach!

Possibly the most difficult short section is through the islands and bars above Big Island. There can be the occasional log jam here, and elsewhere. For most normal flows the bridge piers and odd boulder are the biggest hazards on this reach.

Now that the access portage at the mouth of Whitemud Creek has been extended, I can see Laurier Park becoming the primary SW Edmonton access. Laurier to Rafters' Landing should become the premier evening or ½ day paddle. Another reach that I use each fall with my Grant MacEwan paddling class is from Emily Murphy to Dawson Park, if a short run is desired, or through to 50th St. if a longer run is the choice of the crew.

For much of the season one does not need to arrange a shuttle. For an evening paddle at low to medium flows, pick any of the access points, throw your boat in and head upstream, either under paddle, or with a pole. Work the eddies along the bank on the inside of the corners, ferry across at the bends and spend an hour or two heading upstream; you'll be surprised at how far you can go. After the workout of the upstream paddling you have the pleasure of drifting back to your vehicle and the joy of NOT having to shuttle!

If you are looking for a practice run or site, one of my favorites is under Groat Road/Bridge. Access if from the south bank in Emily Murphy Park. Early and later in the season there are eddies on the south side, right under the bridge and a number along the north side. An especially large eddy forms just above the bridge at lower flows, and on river left at the outfall of the former Groat Creek. The bridge piers themselves provide a series of eddies for those working their way across the river. I have spent many hours here introducing novice paddlers to eddy turns, ferrying, and setting (back ferrying). If your schedule allows, the intro' session can be followed up with the run down to Rafters' Landing or Dawson Park.

Rentals & Shuttles

Rentals:
Mountain Equipment Co-op 780.488.6614
Totem Outdoor Outfitters 780.432.1223

Shuttles:
A number of taxi companies are available.
Edmonton Canoe 780.470.5352 *www.edmontoncanoe.com*

North Saskatchewan River

Edmonton to the Saskatchewan Boundary

Why Go
When the high flows of summer are past these are pleasant reaches for day to mult-day trips. These reaches offer scenic pastoral vistas, and both good wildlife and birding opportunities; and then there is the history!

Duration of Tour(s)
* 330 km
* 6-10 days with many day and weekend trip possibilities

Classification
1. Rapids: Class I to easy II
2. Skill of Paddlers: Novice River

Looking back at the Beverly Bridges in east Edmonton, August 1996

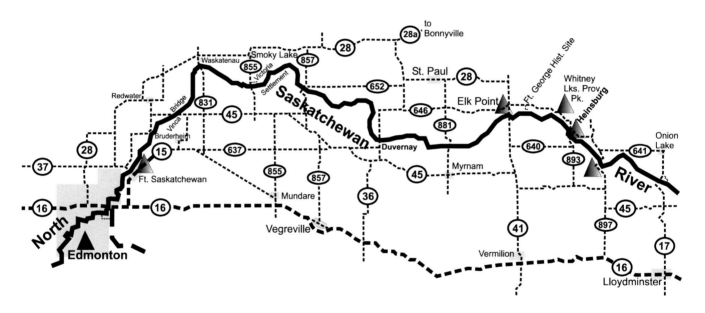

Start
The proposed start for this run is the Capilano Park / 50th Street boat launch in east central Edmonton. Once south of the river any main east-west road will take you to 50th Street, and then it is north to the river.

Finish
Finish for this run is at the former Highway #17 ferry north of Lloydminster, and south of Onion Lake. From the present highway bridge, go north approximately 800 m and take the first road on the east side, this is a sharp turn, and it quickly drops back into the river valley and down to the former ferry site.

Intermediate Access and Distances

Location	Elevation meters	Km down	Km up	Km between	Access / Bank or Rapid / Class	MGRS datum NAD 1983 zone 12U	Gradient m/km
Capilano Park / 50 St. in Edmonton		330	0		right bank	UE 398 375	
	610	315	15				
township road 540		313	17	17	right bank	UE 463 448	
Ft. Saskatchewan, Red Coat Landing, off Westpark Drive		303	27	10	right bank	UE 499 510	
	600	300	30				0.7
Highway #15 bridge		300	30		no access		
Turner Park / River Rd. & 104 St.		297	33	6	right bank, rather steep	UE 538 542	
Sturgeon River		290	40				
	594	284	46				0.4
Highway #38 / Vinca Bridge		271	59	26	left bank, under bridge	UE 702 728	
	587	259	71				0.3
	579	247	83				0.7
Highway # 831		245	85	26		UE 834 915	
	572	235	95				0.6
Highway # 855		223	107		poor access		
Victoria Settlement / Pakan		216	114	29	left bank	VE 083 848	
	564	214	116				0.4
Highway # 857		190	140	33	left bank, 500 m below bridge	VE 247 815	
	556	179	151				0.2
	549	168	162				0.6
	541	152	178				0.5
Highway #36 / Duvernay		141	189	49	right bank, above bridge	VE 546 603	
	533	122	208				0.3
former Beauvallon Ferry		119	211			VE 733 564	
Highway #881		107	223	34	either bank, old ferry crossing 500 m below bridge	VE 854 562	
Fort Island		104	226				
Highway #41 / Elkpoint		81	249	26	left bank	WE 067 680	
	526	78	252				0.2
Ft. George Historic Site		71	259		left bank	WE 155 679	
	518	68	262				0.8
Moosehills Creek		61	269			WE 239 677	
Highway #893 / Heinsburg		48	282	33	left bank, 500 m below bridge	WE 313 576	
Highway #897 / Vermillion River		29	301	19	right bank, under the bridge	WE 438 458	
Highway #17		1	329		dry weather access to either bank		
former ferry site		0	330	29	left bank, better all weather road access	WE 667 392	

Gradient

No average gradient on these reaches exceeds 1 m/km, though some stretches are a bit faster than others as the above table would suggest.

River Volume and Flow Rate

Again this is a good sized river and generally best paddled earlier or later in the season. Avoid the high water periods. Flows of 150 to 350 cms will provide more than adequate water and there will still be a decent beach at most locations for access and camping. These suggested flows may seem low relative to the flows reported in the graph and table to the right, but remember that this table reflects flows of nearly 100 years and flows have generally been diminishing over this whole period. At Edmonton flows vary from 2 km/hr at 125 cms to 8 km/hr at 2000 cms

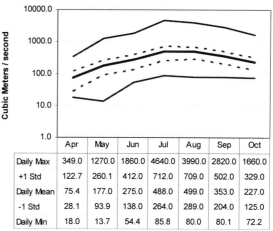

North Saskatchewan River at Edmonton

	Apr	May	Jun	Jul	Aug	Sep	Oct
Daily Max	349.0	1270.0	1860.0	4640.0	3990.0	2820.0	1660.0
+1 Std	122.7	260.1	412.0	712.0	709.0	502.0	329.0
Daily Mean	75.4	177.0	275.0	488.0	499.0	353.0	227.0
-1 Std	28.1	93.9	138.0	264.0	289.0	204.0	125.0
Daily Min	18.0	13.7	54.4	85.8	80.0	80.1	72.2

1911 to 2003

Maps & Guides

1 - *Alberta Road Map* - this may be all you need
2 - *North Saskatchewan River Guide* - this is not so much a guidebook, as an interpretative manual to all you may see along the river; it is very informative.
3 - NTS 1:250,00 - these are all getting rather old and the provincial series is not much better!

      83 H - Edmonton   83 I - Tawatinaw
      73 E - Vermillion
   NTS 1:50,000 - not necessary

Camping

On stream (or at least close) public campgrounds along this run are available: in Ft. Saskatchewan at Turner Park (780.998.4074), Highway #41 bridge (south of Elk Point), in the Hamlet of Heinsburg, and near the Highway #897 bridge at the Lea Park - Jubilee Regional Park (780.847.2273).

After the high waters of summer there are many idyllic stream side and island wilderness campsites for smaller groups. As always, one should ask permission of the local property owner or lease holder before camping above the highwater line, or near any occupied private property.

During the August '06 scouting trip, and when checking out the access on the south-side of the river at the former Beauvallon Ferry, I learned that the Alberta Snowmobile Association maintains a series of cabins along the Duvernay (Highway #36) to Highway #881 reach. Two cabins are available to the canoeing public at the former Beauvallon Ferry site, one on each side of the river. Individual paddlers are welcome to use these cabins, the south side cabin was open when we hiked down to it, a 25 minute walk each way from the first gate. The cabin is snowmobile and quad accessible, but it would be tough getting in a vehicle to drag out canoes. Road access is restricted (gates and locks) and groups should book in with the Alberta Snowmobile Association (780.427.2695) for the cabins and the Rannach Provincial Grazing Reserve Manager (780.645.6336) for access permission.

Wildlife

During consecutive trips in 1996, Lois and I saw more wildlife on the first few hours run out of Edmonton than we saw during a three day trip on Maligne Lake in Jasper National Park! Yes, these reaches are all through farm lands, but the wildlife is concentrated along the river and the viewing is grand. The pelicans alone make this run worthwhile. Over the years we have seen peregrine falcons, many other raptors, blue herons, cormorants, common and black terns, and a multitude of other bird life along these reaches. Mammals are well represented too: beaver and muskrat in the water, both deer species, moose and elk, coyotes, bears and maybe even a cougar may be spotted along these reaches.

Trip Notes

After or before the high water of summer these reaches offer great day, weekend or longer trips for the novice river paddler. The log jams and sweepers are few and far apart, the biggest problems may be the occasional gravel bar, or bridge pier that is off set to the current and creating some strong eddies. One paddler of these reaches has reported that some islands and bars may present more difficult riffles or rapids in one channel and not the other – it is always best to keep a sharp eye looking downstream -- and scout anything that is doubtful.

Lois and I have made a number of trips on these reaches, but have yet to paddle it all. In '96 we made the run down to Victoria Settlement from Edmonton. In '09 we had a pleasant overnight run from Shandro (Hwy #857) to Duvernay (Hwy # 36). In '06 we paddled the Heinsburg to Highway #897. On this last run I completed the shuttle by riding a bike back for the truck, 19 km of paddling and 23 km of riding! All of these runs were done with less than 200 cms for water flow. On both the Shandro and Heinsburg runs we were surprised by a number of gravel & boulder bar riffles. More than one of these riffles was loud enough I felt compelled to stand up in the canoe to scout the drop. On the Shandro run the riffles are on the higher gradient stretch, on the Heinsburg run the first drop was about 10 km below the start. Some of these riffles required maneuvering to stay in the deep water and to avoid the biggest of the boulders that broke the surface. An occasional wave even slopped into our canoe. Any one of these riffles, waves or boulders could catch an unwary paddler by surprise and provide a soaking, if not a swim or maybe even damage a canoe. It is always best to paddle with friends!

Other Reaches

Devon to Edmonton is in this guide. The North Saskatchewan river of course continues on and through Saskatchewan joining with the South Saskatchewan east of Prince Alberta. From the Saskatchewan border to The Battlefords there is approximately another 180 kms of similar paddling. There are numerous access points along the way.

Other Local Activities or Destinations

Whether you are on the river or not, all "old" voyageurs need to visit the historic sites of Victoria Settlement, and Ft. George & Buckingham House. Whitney Lakes Provincial Park has very nice individual and group campsites at Ross Lake that could be the base for a variety of activities and explorations in the eastern part of these reaches.

Rentals & Shuttles

Rentals:
Mountain Equipment Co-op 780.488.6614
Totem Outdoor Outfitters 780.432.1223

Shuttles: A number of taxi companies are available for reaches close to Edmonton and Fort Saskatchewan.

the "Shuttle Equipped" canoe on Bird Island, below Heinsburg, August, 2006

Sturgeon River

Bon Accord to the
North Saskatchewan River

First Surfing, mid-April, 2003 at 13.8 cms

Why Go
This is one of our local spring runs for Edmonton paddlers; it offers modest flows and modest whitewater through mid-April to early May most years. Much of this reach is through pleasant boreal & parkland forest scenery with active bird life in the spring paddling season.

Duration of Tour(s)
* 33 km

* These reaches of the Sturgeon make possible a number of short half- to full-day trips. Locals to the Sturgeon River have been known to do a short reach for an evening run.

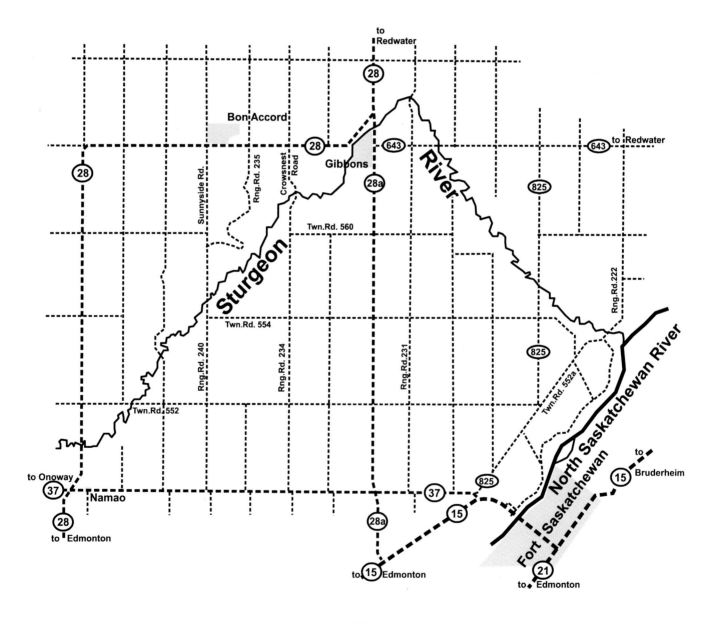

Classification
1. Rapids: Class I to II
2. Skill of Paddlers: Novice River Paddlers with good leadership, Intermediate River Paddlers at higher flows

Start
The upper run of the reaches reported here commences approximately 5.5 km south of Bon Accord on Range Road 240. On all the country roads here, be sure to pull your vehicle as far into the ditch as possible when loading, unloading and leaving your vehicle. For this run Edmonton paddlers often meet at North Town Mall, or in Bon Accord. The easiest approach is Highway #28 to Bon Accord and then south.

Finish
The finish of this run is most easily reached by taking Secondary Highway #825 north from Fort Saskatchewan (off Highways #15 & #37), then east onto Township Road 552a. Follow this road NE and then east again to meet Range Road 222, just where it crosses the Sturgeon. The river is quite deeply incised at this point and the access does require a good hike down to the water. The best parking is on the east side and off the main road, near the private railroad crossing.

Intermediate Access and Distances

Location	Elevation meters	Km down	Km up	Km between	Access / Bank or Rapid / Class	MGRS datum NAD 1927 Zone 12U	Gradient m/km
Sunnyside Rd./Rng.Rd. 240		33.1	0.0		right bank	UQ 405 617	
	640	27.9	5.2				
Crowsnest Rd./Rng.Rd.234		25.7	7.4	7.4	left bank	UQ 442 656	
	632	23.5	9.6				1.8
50 Ave. in Gibbons		22.0	11.1	3.7	either bank	UQ 464 669	
	625	20.7	12.4				2.5
Hwy. 28a / culvert		20.4	12.7		poor access		
Rng. Rd.231		18.1	15.0	3.9	left bank	UQ 488 689	
Hwy. # 643		15.7	17.4		left bank		
	617	11.1	22.0				0.8
Hwy. # 825		5.7	27.4	12.4	left bank		
	610	5.6	27.5				1.3
	602	1.1	32.0				1.8
Rng.Rd.222 /culvert		0.0	33.1	5.7	right bank	UQ 567 599	

Gradient
The gradients calculated above do not reflect where the most interesting paddling is. The run between Sunnyside and Crowsnest roads has historically been considered to be the most interesting paddle for whitewater, though a recent run would suggest the Highway #825 to Range Road 222 is well worth consideration.

River Volume and Flow Rate
Good paddling happens on this run with between 6 and 14 cms at the St. Albert Station on the Alberta Environment site. As with all streams, flows that are over the normal banks, or "running through the willows," should be avoided!

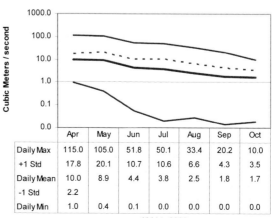

Sturgeon River near Ft. Saskatchewan

	Apr	May	Jun	Jul	Aug	Sep	Oct
Daily Max	115.0	105.0	51.8	50.1	33.4	20.2	10.0
+1 Std	17.8	20.1	10.7	10.6	6.6	4.3	3.5
Daily Mean	10.0	8.9	4.4	3.8	2.5	1.8	1.7
-1 Std	2.2						
Daily Min	1.0	0.4	0.1	0.0	0.0	0.0	0.0

1914 to 2003

Maps
1 - NTS 1:50,000: 83 H/14 Red Water

Camping
To date, in my runs along the upper two reaches of this report, and through my travels in the area, I have not discovered any commercial or public campgrounds along the river. All of the lands adjacent to this river are privately owned -- and many of the owners are very protective of their holdings. One should make camping arrangements before commencing on an overnight trip on this reach of the Sturgeon.

Trip Notes
Over the years Ceyana paddlers have always considered the upper reach included in this report as "the spring run!" Given recent experience with the lower runs, the Highway #825 to Range Road 222 is well worth a day paddle. Local paddlers from along the river have always used other reaches, and over the years I have learned of various school groups taking extended trips along all of the Sturgeon from Big Lake to the confluence.

Many sections of the river are very pretty with heavy growths of spruce along the banks, others sections wind through willow and oxbow flats where poplar, birch and rose bushes line the banks. Some sections of this river take you well away from the homes of the local acreages and for short periods the river can almost convince one that you are paddling a wilderness stream, and then the next bend will bring you right through a farm yard or an acreage development. Beware, one of the greater hazards along these reaches maybe the **barbed wire fences** that some farmers occasionally stretch across a corner of a bend, or even across the whole river at low water to keep their cattle in. Log jams have been known to come and go on these reaches, and some of the bridges and culverts that the river flows through can become plugged with debris. **I do not encourage paddling the culverts, at Highway 28a, or Range Road 222.**

The beaver dams are far more likely to provide the excitement of your trip. Some springs they provide enough of a drop that the "white water jocks" can even practice a little surfing below each dam, or "crank" some great turns on the "jets."

As I finish up this guide in Spring 2007, we were back on the Sturgeon and both of the hazards noted in these pictures, on this page, had washed out with the recent high water. But similar challenges will return from time to time. Paddlers must remain wary!

Tricky "S" bend due to recent bank slump, mid-April, 2003

Debris jam "portage", April, 2003, not too far above Crowsnest Road

Rentals & Shuttles
Rentals:
Mountain Equipment Co-op 780.488.6614
Totem Outdoor Outfitters 780.432.1223
Shuttles:
A number of taxi companies are available.

Blackstone River

Chungo Creek Road to
Gas Plant Bridge

Why Go
The Blackstone River offers good Class II to III whitewater through much of June and early July, all set in spectacular foothills scenery.

Duration of Tour(s)
* 42 km

* 2 days, with shorter day and ½ day runs possible.

Classification
1. Rapids: Class I to III
2. Skill of Paddlers: Intermediate River Paddlers at average to low normal flows.

Start
The primary start for these runs is up the Chungo Creek Road north of Nordegg. Go approximately 10.5 km north on the Forestry Trunk Road (FTR) (Highway #734) from Highway 11, just west of Nordegg. Turn left (west) onto the Chungo Creek road and follow it down Lookout Creek to the Blackstone River (stay right at the Wapiabi Creek road). One can start at a number of locations just downstream of the bridge

Finish
Approximately 1 km south of the FTR bridge over the Blackstone, head east towards the Blackstone Gas Plant. Stay left at the three main intersections, and just over 1 km beyond the Gas Plant you will find the last bridge over the Blackstone River.

Blackstone River below FTR, May, 1983

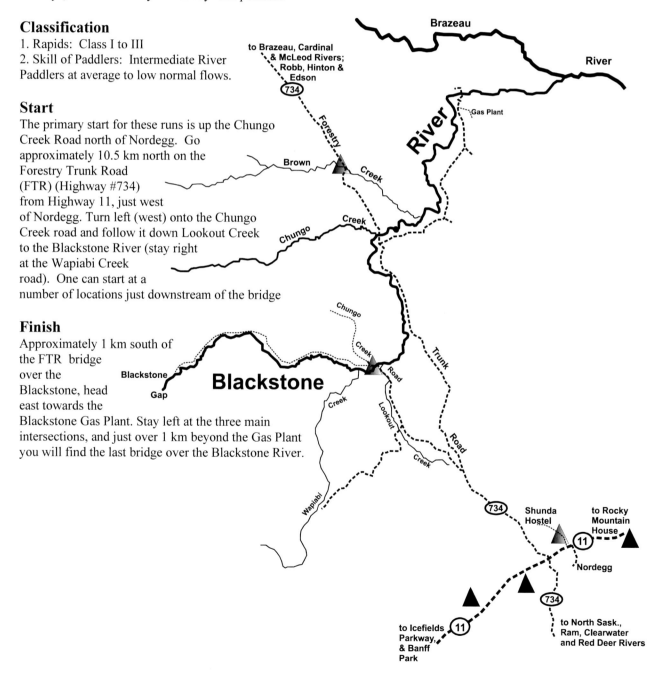

Intermediate Access and Distances

Location	Elevation meters	Km down	Km up	Km between	Access / Bank or Rapid / Class	MGRS datum NAD 1927 Zone 11U	Gradient m/km
	1360		-2.2				
Chungo Creek Road Bridge		42.3	0.0		right bank	NJ 456 295	
	1340	42.0	0.3				8.0
	1320	38.8	3.5				6.3
	1300	35.3	7.0				5.7
*access from FTR		33.8	8.5		right bank		
	1280	32.0	10.3				6.1
	1260	28.9	13.4				6.5
	1240	25.5	16.8				5.9
FTR Bridge		25.3	17.0		right bank		
beach below bridge		25.2	17.1	17.1		NJ 460 402	
	1220	22.5	19.8				6.7
	1200	19.4	22.9				6.5
Brown Creek		18.9	23.4		left bank		
	1180	16.1	26.2				6.1
	1158	12.7	29.6				6.5
	1128	7.7	34.6				6.0
	1113	3.1	39.2				3.3
	1097	0.9	41.4				7.3
Bridge north of Gas Plant		0.0	42.3	25.2	right bank	NJ 530 519	
	1082		45.2				3.9

* the river and road are very close together for about 2 km at this point and there are a number of trails down to the river. When coming from the south this is where the FTR road first drops into the Blackstone river valley and approaches the Blackstone.

Gradient
Given that this river is a mixture of ledges and long gravely chutes the gradient is pretty consistent, and may average out a little more than the numbers above suggest, particularly towards the lower end. The 7.3 m/km section seems a bit high for what is there.

River Volume and Flow Rate
This may be the only river in this guide for which there is not a gauging station. I would suggest that paddlers check the Brown Creek station for an indication of local high water. Brown Creek and the Blackstone share adjacent headwaters and a big rain storm on Brown Creek is likely to effect the Blackstone similarly. Given that the Brazeau to the north has considerable icefields in its headwaters, unlike the Blackstone or Brown Creek, mid to late summer high water on the Brazeau (due to hot weather) is not likely to indicate high water on the Blackstone.

I should also note that in mid-May 1983 I ran a very successful "Spring Camp" for the U of A, and a slalom race for the AWA on the Blackstone. In 1984 when I came back to repeat the experience we found the Blackstone absolutely dry at the Chungo Creek road bridge, and we had to move the class, race and canoe trip north to the Brazeau!

Maps
1 - NTS 1:50,000
        83 C/9 Wapiabi Creek   83 C/16 Blackstone River

Camping
The Blackstone Recreation Area on the Chungo Creek Road is considered by Ceyana Paddlers as the finest campground along the Blackstone. On many trips club members have "random" camped at the FTR bridge as it makes a convenient base for day tripping upstream and down of the FTR. In past years this site has been abused and some years it has been particularly unpleasant due to garbage. Like the Brazeau to the north, and the Saskatchewan to the south, this river does offer some fine wilderness campsites.

Wildlife
This is a whitewater stream, but we've always seen at least one small herd of elk on a weekend's paddle, and often much more.

Trip Notes
This is a fun, small volume stream, and a great stream for Novice River Paddlers with a little river experience – assuming the instructors/leaders know the river and can talk their "charges" down each drop. As noted above, this is a river of ledges, especially on the run above the FTR, and of long gravel chutes below the FTR. The paddling season can be short some years on the Blackstone. We Ceyana paddlers generally like to schedule our trips for mid-June to early July.

Other Reaches
The Blackstone has been paddled all the way from the Gap to the confluence with the Brazeau. Smith, S. (1996) provides write-ups for two runs above the Chungo Creek road. On my first visit to the Blackstone we walked our canoes down Cut-off Creek, roped them down the 1.5 m drop into the Blackstone and then paddled down to the Chungo Creek road bridge.

May, 1983

Brazeau River

Forestry Trunk Road (FTR) to the Brazeau Dam

Launch site below FTR, early September, 1995, at 45 cms

Why Go

The canyon below the Forestry Trunk Road (FTR) is one of the most challenging whitewater reaches in the province for open canoe tripping. It is "a notch or three" more difficult than the Nordegg to Rocky run on the North Saskatchewan.

Duration of Tour(s)

* 100 km
* 1-4 days, the whole run makes for a bit of a rushed long weekend and one day I am going to take four or five days so I have time to hike, bird, wildlife spot and really enjoy this paddle. There is a one day paddle through the canyon with access north of the Blackstone River Gas Plant.

Classification

1. Rapids: Class I to III+
2. Skill of Paddlers: Skilled River paddlers, especially if overnight tripping

Start

The start of this run is just below the FTR bridge in the Brazeau Recreation Area campsite.

Finish

The noted finish for this reach is at the Brazeau Dam campsite, boat launch. My last two runs on this river we drove out from Edmonton via Drayton Valley and Highway #620 and dropped of a shuttle vehicle. We then drove up the Elk River Road north of the Brazeau and out to the FTR, and then south to the Brazeau.

Intermediate Access and Distances

Location	Elevation meters	Km down	Km up	Km between	Access / Bank or Rapid / Class	MGRS datum NAD 1927 Zone 11U	Gradient m/km
	1260		-1.0				
Forestry Trunk Road		100	0.0		right bank	NJ 298 585	
	1240		3.3				4.7
	1220		8.1				4.2
	1204		11.6				4.6
	1189		13.5				7.9
	1173		15.1				10.0
	1158		19.7				3.3
	1143		21.5				8.3
	1128		25.5				3.8
* Cutline to Blackstone roads		70.7	29.3	29.3	right bank	NJ 480 561	
	1113		30				3.3
	1097		38.6				1.9
	1082		43.8				2.9
	1067		46.3				6.0
Blackstone River		52.4	47.6		right bank		
	1052		58.9				1.2
	1036		62.2				4.8
	1021		65.6				4.4
	1006		68.4				5.4
	991		72.5				3.7
	975		78.2				2.8
** access to Elk River roads		17	83		left bank	NJ 859 597	
Reservoir / start		13	87				
Brazeau Dam Campground Boat Launch		0	100	70.7		NJ 945 691	

* The Blackstone access, below the canyon and most of the whitewater, is reached by taking the Blackstone Gas Plant Road. This road leaves the FTR 1.1 km south of the Blackstone Bridge, and heads northeast. Stay left at all intersections. 1.2 km past the gas plant access road you again cross the Blackstone River. 800 m beyond the bridge stay left, then after another 1.8 km stay right. Follow this road for another 5.8 km. After you drop down a hill and cross a creek, you soon pass a well site/gas works on the right; continue on to, and through the old gravel pit and follow the trail and cutline north to the river. I strongly encourage you to buy the provincial 1:50,000 *83 C/16 Resource Access Map* and find the takeout before commencing and "flag it well!" Do not send some unwary novice down to pick you up! This takeout can require up to a 1 km portage depending on your vehicle and the condition of the trail and cutline.

** The Elk River access further downstream is reached from another gas plant road. 1.2 km west of the Wolf Lake Road head south, in 5.1 km you will pass the Gas Plant, continue 2.3 km (to NJ 750 649) and turn left. Go 4.4 km (to NJ 781 624) and turn left again. Continue 6.3 km (to NJ 828 624), turn right and go 4.1 km to a sour gas well site (at NJ 852 597). The river access is to the left/east and about 800 m across the small field and down a quad track to NJ 859 597. Again it is best to find this location before starting and flag it well! On Labor Day weekend 2007 we shortened the portage out a bit by paddling about 250 m up the creek to near the quad track and a "random" campsite.

** Note: due to gas field activity these roads are likely to change!

Gradient
The above gradients do reflect the character of the river.

River Volume and Flow Rate
Good paddling occurs on this run with 25 to about 100 cms, though the upper limit is very wet in an open canoe! I like about 40-50 cms for open canoe tripping on this run!

Maps
1 - NTS 1:50,000
    83 C/15 Cardinal River   83 C/16 Blackstone River
    83 B/13 Nordegg River
2 - Provincial 1:50,000 *83 C/16 Resource Access Map*

Camping
Public campgrounds are available at both ends of this trip. But this is really a river for wilderness camping, for canoe camping.

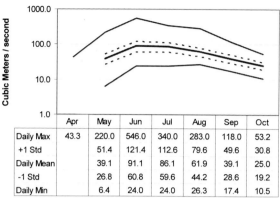

Brazeau River below Cardinal River

	Apr	May	Jun	Jul	Aug	Sep	Oct
Daily Max	43.3	220.0	546.0	340.0	283.0	118.0	53.2
+1 Std		51.4	121.4	112.6	79.6	49.6	30.8
Daily Mean		39.1	91.1	86.1	61.9	39.1	25.0
-1 Std		26.8	60.8	59.6	44.2	28.6	19.2
Daily Min		6.4	24.0	24.0	26.3	17.4	10.5

1961 to 2003

Wildlife
The Brazeau Canyon is home to both a herd of mountain goats and another of bighorn sheep, though I have to admit that when paddling in the canyon I've not had a lot of time to scan the cliffs to spot these critters. Further down I have had the opportunity to paddle by herds of elk. Moose, deer and both black and grizzly bears have all been spotted from the river. Dippers, kingfishers, great blue herons, bald eagles and spruce grouse have also been frequently sighted. The trick to seeing the wildlife is to take enough time, and to be out either early or late in the day.

Trip Notes
The run through the canyon from the FTR to the access off the lower Blackstone road involves much white water and rapids that are Class III to III+ at most water levels. The whitewater starts on the second corner below the bridge and just keeps getting better as one descends into the canyon. Approximately 6 km below the bridge there is a complex of two ledges that recently became easier than some years ago. In August '95, the next right bend presented the steepest ledge and chute combination I have ever remembered on the river. After a brief respite, the long, fun rapids begin through the high gradient sections down to the end of the canyon. From the canyon to the reservoir the river is pretty steady, with just a couple of short low gradient sections. There are even some fun, easy Class II rapids just upstream of the reservoir. The reservoir can be as much as 13 km of flatwater.

I have paddled this reach a number of times, and in '95 after two summers of long periods of highwater, I found most of the rapids to have been well scoured of gravel, to be much steeper than remembered, and the waves even bigger and stronger than most of my best lies. Rivers do change! After the pleasures of the canyon we were ready to relax on the flats down to the reservoir. But, all that high water had brought down many new trees, and there were many dangerous logjams that required precise maneuvering, and a very watchful eye downstream. I suspect that at some times, many of the braided channels could have been completely obstructed. I was back on this canyon run and down to the lower gas plant road in 2007 and my comments above still stand. You must remain vigilant on this river!

Other Reaches
Upstream of the FTR there are three reaches on the Brazeau. The highest reach requires a 14 km portage over Nigel pass from the Icefields Parkway, and then the river provides a very pleasant, but challenging week or more of paddling AND portaging, and some great side hikes. Edmonton area paddlers regularly travel to the Brazeau for day tripping on the whitewater between Small Boys Camp and the FTR. There is one intermediate access on this reach at an old ford. Smith, S. (1996) provides write-ups on each of these reaches and should be consulted. For open canoeists a better description of the run from Nigel Pass through to the Forestry Trunk Road can be found in: Parks Canada (1974) ***Wild Rivers: Alberta.***

Once with a University group we paddled the canal, portaged the powerhouse and followed the river all the way to Berrymore on the North Saskatchewan. In 2002 we paddled the 16 km from the powerhouse down to the North Saskatchewan, and then the additional 13 km down to the Boggy Hall access (see the Rocky to Drayton report). The run below the powerhouse is very scenic with the river deeply incised.

Pembina River

Reno Road to
Pembina River Provincial Park

Why Go
This is a fun spring paddle close to Edmonton, with easy Class II water in a deeply incised, and picturesque "near" canyon.

an easy riffle on the Pembina above Hwy #16
early June, 2003 with 15-16 cms

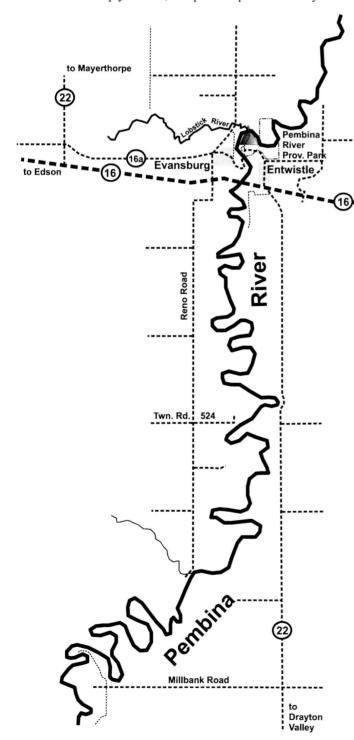

Duration of Tour(s)
* 37.6 km
* 1-2 days, with a short teaching run around the park .

Classification
1. Rapids: Class I to II+
2. Skill of Paddlers: Intermediate River Paddlers or Novice River Paddlers with good leadership – at most flows this is a great stream to teach on, especially around and just above Pembina River Provincial Park.

Start
The start for this run is approximately 14 km south of the town of Evansburg on Reno Road. Follow Reno Road south, down into the river valley. Once over a small stream bridge, look for the access to the river on the left. If you go too far you end up in a farm field high above the river. Access is just upstream of the small stream confluence.

Finish
Finishes are possible at both the day use area, on the upstream side of Pembina River Provincial Park, just below the Highway #16a Bridge; and near the downstream end of the park at the bottom of the hill and near the campground theater.

Intermediate Access and Distances

Location	Elevation	Km down	Km up	Km between	Access / Bank or Rapid / Class	MGRS datum	Gradient m/km
	meters					NAD 1983 Zone 11U	
Start / stream confluence		37.6	0		left bank	PV 306 253	
	762	34.0	3.6				0.8
	747	17.1	20.5				0.9
	732	7.2	30.4				1.5
Highway #16 bridge		2.7	34.9		no access		
Park - Day Use Beach		1.4	36.2	36.2	right bank	PV 319 409	
Lobstick River confluence		0.2	37.4		left bank		
lower Park access		0.0	37.6	1.6	right bank	PV 326 415	

Gradient

This run starts flat and lazy, less than 1 m/km, and then picks up the pace all the way to the park with some of the best water just above Highway #16.

River Volume and Flow Rate

During the summer months of June and July the river volume averages approximately 25 CMS, with a normal range (25 to 75 percentile) of approximately 10 CMS to 80 CMS. The extreme range of volumes reported between 1914 and 2003 is from less than 5 CMS to more than 1100 CMS for June and July at Pembina River Park. Good paddling occurs on this run with flows between 18 cms and 75 cms.

The rate of stream flow varies with volume, from less than 2 kmph with 20 CMS to 7 kmph with more than 500 cms. This data is for the hydrology station just below the Highway 16a Bridge, in Pembina River Park.

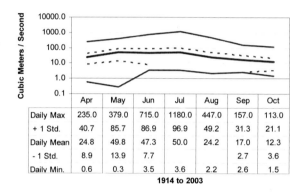

Pembina River near Entwhistle

	Apr	May	Jun	Jul	Aug	Sep	Oct
Daily Max	235.0	379.0	715.0	1180.0	447.0	157.0	113.0
+ 1 Std.	40.7	85.7	86.9	96.9	49.2	31.3	21.1
Daily Mean	24.8	49.8	47.3	50.0	24.2	17.0	12.3
- 1 Std.	8.9	13.9	7.7			2.7	3.6
Daily Min.	0.6	0.3	3.5	3.6	2.2	2.6	1.5

1914 to 2003

Maps

1 - NTS 1:50,000 sheets:

Easyford 83 G/6   Tomahawk 83 G/7
Isle Lake 83 G/10   Chip Lake 83 G/11

* four sheets are required as the river runs right down the edge! More of the river is on 83G 06 & 11 so one solution is to buy these two sheets and then sketch in the meander bends that run over and onto G 07 & 10. I would also suggest sketching Highway #22 as it is often the more logical road to hike out to if you get into trouble on any of the eastern bends of this stream.

Camping

Pembina River Provincial Park (780.727.3643) is the natural staging area for this run, or for making an extended stay in this area. The group campsite site at the Pembina River Provincial Park is wonderful! This group site is a great base for a canoe club, outdoor education class or scout troop. It also provides good access for the early spring white water on the nearby Lobstick River.

Random camping is generally available along the river but the private property owners must be respected. I have found that the beaches about ½ way down this reach make good campsites when the river is running at under 35 cms or so.

Wildlife
The Pembina has always provided a good range of wildlife viewing: from deer, elk and moose, to hawks, eagles and ospreys. Even the fishing for arctic grayling has been good on some trips!

Trip Notes
This a favorite run of the Ceyana Canoe Club. In past years we often have done this as a long day run of 6 - 7 hours, and once, in just over 3 hours at high water. More recently we have done this as an overnight trip, which has allowed for an easy Saturday start from Edmonton, and an early arrival home on Sunday.

The Pembina has a good reputation for hiding boat grabbing boulders. The muskeg colored, brown-tinged water camouflages the brown Pembina Formation sandstone that predominate in the river bed.

Other Reaches
Over the years we have paddled many other reaches of the Pembina. Upstream we once paddled on the Canada Day weekend the whole run from near Easyford through to Pembina River Park. We also once paddled, as an overnight trip, the reach from south of Wolf Lake down to the Wolf lake road – this was a more exciting run, but still certainly an open canoe run for Skilled River Paddlers. I have had other paddlers report on paddling the Pembina from the Forestry Trunk Road south of Robb right through to Pembina River Provincial Park - a week's paddle or longer.

Downstream we've paddled the run to Rangeton County Park as a Canada Day weekend trip – it proved to be a slow trip as over the weekend flows dropped from 19 cms to 11 cms and we had to walk our canoes through a number of riffles. In the early days of the club we also paddled the run at the very bottom of the Pembina, from near Flatbush through to the confluence with the Athabasca. At normal flows all of these lower runs should be well within the capability of Intermediate River Paddlers.

Rain clouds over the Pembina, early June, 2003

Lobstick River

Highway #22 west of Evansburg to Pembina River Provincial Park

Why Go
This is another of our local spring training runs for Edmonton paddlers. The Lobstick, like the Sturgeon River, offers modest flows and modest whitewater from late-April to after the June "monsoon" most years.

Duration of Tour(s)
* 13 km
* The Lobstick provides day and ½ day runs. The bottom run can be done in an hour or less.

Classification
1. Rapids: Class I to III-
2. Skill of Paddlers: Novice River Paddlers with skilled leadership at average to low normal flows, or Intermediate River Paddlers at above average, but normal flows.

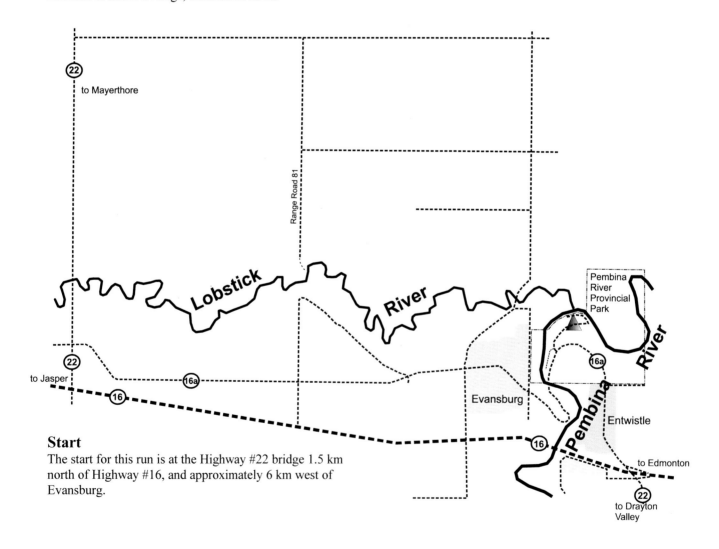

above Evansburg Bridge, July, 1996

Start
The start for this run is at the Highway #22 bridge 1.5 km north of Highway #16, and approximately 6 km west of Evansburg.

Finish

One can finish at either of the two intermediate points noted below, but the primary finish is at the bottom of the hill in the Pembina River Provincial Park campground. I usually try to park in the parking area for the interpretative theatre. Access to the park is gained from Highway #16a north of Entwistle, and east of Evansburg. The park gate is on the east side of the river, and part way down the hill. Once in the park, drive north past the campground booths and follow the main campground road down to the river terrace. Parking is right at the bottom of the hill.

Intermediate Access and Distances

Location	Elevation meters	Km down	Km up	Km between	Access / Bank or Rapid / Class	MGRS datum NAD 1927 Zone 11U	Gradient m/km
Highway # 22 bridge		12.8	0		left, downstream	PK 253 418	
	762	8.2	4.6				
Range Road 81, 400 m portage from end of road to river		7.1	5.7	6	left	PK 286 421	
	747	6.1	6.7				7.1
	732	2.0	10.8				3.7
access above bridge		1.9	10.9	5	right, almost continuous Class II to III- at most water levels to Pembina	PK 315 417	
Evansburg Bridge		1.5	11.3				
	716	0.5	12.3				10.7
Pembina confluence		0.4	12.4		right	PK 324 417	
Park take-out		0.0	12.8	1.9	right	PK 326 415	

Gradient

The above numbers are fairly representative of the river. The good paddling, or the good whitewater, starts about 3 to 4 kilometers below Highway #22, then the gradient eases off a bit below Range Road 81, and then picks up on the final downgrade to the confluence with the Pembina. This final downgrade starts just above the bridge north of Evansburg.

River Volume and Flow Rate

I have not been able to find the Lobstick flow data in Hydat and have estimated the table and graph to right from the Alberta Government, *Stream Flow Facts* (1996). Good paddling happens with about 5 to 12 cms, but flows are not published on the Alberta Government web site. The best bet is to ask other paddlers, or if you know someone in the area, have them take a look at the river for you. No discharge versus flow rate data has been published for this station.

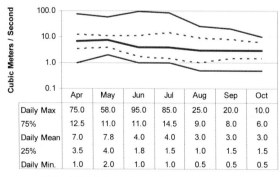

Lobstick River at Highway #22

	Apr	May	Jun	Jul	Aug	Sep	Oct
Daily Max	75.0	58.0	95.0	85.0	25.0	20.0	10.0
75%	12.5	11.0	11.0	14.5	9.0	8.0	6.0
Daily Mean	7.0	7.8	4.0	4.0	3.0	3.0	3.0
25%	3.5	4.0	1.8	1.5	1.0	1.5	1.5
Daily Min.	1.0	2.0	1.0	1.0	0.5	0.5	0.5

1957 to 1986 (all data estimated from "Stream Flow Facts," 1996)

Maps

1 - NTS 1:50,000   83 G 11 Chip Lake and 83G 10 Isle Lake (for just the last 500 m or so!).

Camping

One of the great features of this run is the campground at Pembina River Provincial Park, just across the Pembina from the confluence with the Lobstick. There are individual campsites that back onto, or face the river and two great group campsites part way up the hill from the river. Both the individual and group campsites can be booked by calling 780.727.3643 . Be warned, in the spring of 2007 I was out to paddle the Lobstick and after unloading and heading down to set the shuttle, we found the park, both the campground and the upstream day use area "locked up", and we ended up parking at the Highway #16a bridge and hiking, paddling and lining our canoes the 1.5 kms upstream after paddling down the Lobstick. We were paddling on Sunday April 29th, and the Park did not open until May 1!

Trip Notes (with assistance from Ted Bentley)

The Lobstick is a narrow river that puts the paddler in intimate contact with its surroundings. From the Highway #22 bridge the river gradually descends into scenic Paskapoo sandstone banks. The sandstone formations provide the variety of ledges and rock gardens which make the paddling interesting, and provide the modest whitewater challenges for new, or rusty paddlers. The challenges are significant enough that all groups should have some strong intermediate or skilled paddlers along for "fishing out" those who err at the practical lessons. The Lobstick is largely muskeg fed, and the brown sphagnum colored water nicley hides the brown Paskapoo sandstone boulders, all resulting in a visual challenge and a need for paddlers to stay alert. At all but the highest recommended flows a dump usually means a paddler can soon stand in most eddies and drag their boat out.

From Highway 22 to Range Road 81 the first few kilometers are placid, then some rock gardens and at least one interesting ledge that is usually rated Class II, but can go Class III with the right flow. From Range Road 81 to the Evansburg Bridge the river fluctuates between placid sections and a variety of whitewater features, none of which exceeds a Class II rating. This 6.7 km section is excellent for teaching new paddlers. Most first time paddlers can manage to practice in these features without being intimidated. From above the Evansburg bridge through to the Pembina River the stream is an almost continuous Class II rock garden, that can go to Class III with the right higher flow. At most early season flows the Lobstick provides excellent practice in reading water and boat maneuvering. At low water the Lobstick can be a very discouraging and tedious walk with some paddling above each beaver dam!

As noted above, the valley of the Lobstick has eroded into the Paskapoo Geological formation. Coal seams and the softly shaped sandstone beds provide some steep banks on the outside of the meander bends. These can be unstable after prolonged rain, or during the spring thaw and large blocks are know to tumble into the river. These can present new and challenging rapids for some years, and like log jams and sweepers, require paddlers to stay alert. The Paskapoo and related formations also include fossilized clams, petrified wood and iron concretions at various points along these reaches.

The Lobstick flows through a mixed spruce and aspen parkland ecosystem, and paddlers are likely to spot deer, moose, coyotes, beaver, and rarely black bears. A range of bird life may be seen, including great blue heron, mergansers, common goldeneye ducks, red tail hawks, osprey and bald eagles.

Historically the original trail to Jasper from Edmonton and Lac Saint Anne, the Foley Trail, crossed the Pembina in the area of the provincial park, and followed the north bank of the river to about the area of the Highway #22 crossing. Homesteaders moved into this area in about 1905 with the coming of the railway. Two transcontinental railways passed through this area in the early 20th century and both chose routes south of the Lobstick river, west of the Pembina. After the 1919 amalgamation that formed the CNR, and abandonment of one of the right-of-ways, the abandoned right-of-way became the first highway to Jasper.

Rentals

Mountain Equipment Co-op 780.488.6614
Totem Outdoor Outfitters 780.432.1223

McLeod River

Mercoal (Highway #40) to McLeod River Recreation Area

Why Go
At most summer flows this is a fun little river, with good whitewater, good fishing and some great wilderness camping.

Duration of Tour(s)
* 37 km
* 1-2 days, and if you like fishing and walking in picturesque meadows, three days!

Running the broken ledges above the confluence with the Gregg River, early July, 2005

Classification
1. Rapids: Class 1 to III-
2. Skill of Paddlers: Intermediate River, or at lower flows this can be a good introductory river for Novice River Paddlers under good leadership.

Logjams and sweepers can be a problem on this run.

Start
The start for this run is at the Highway #40 bridge just west of the former community of Mercoal. Access can also be had off of the Tri-Creeks Road near Mary Gregg Creek, and this allows for a very pleasant day run down to the Recreation Area.

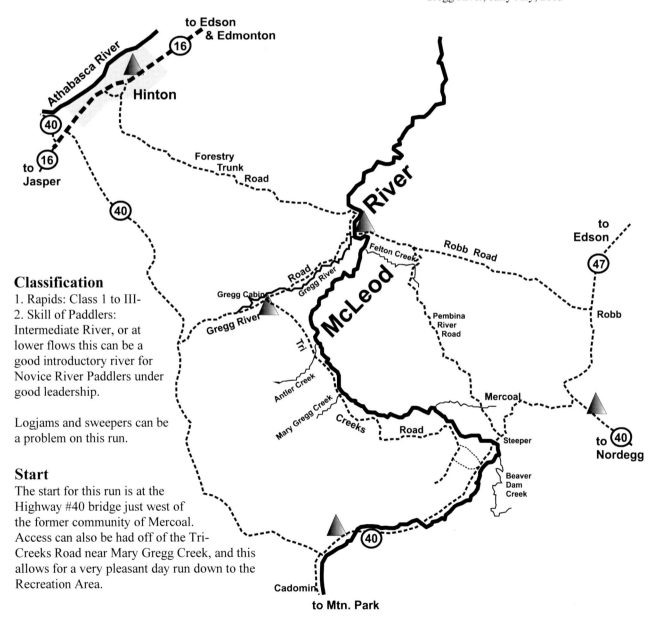

Finish

The end of this run is in the McLeod River Recreation Area, south of Hinton on the Forestry Trunk Road. There are a number of access points at and between the new (km 35) and old bridges (km 37) within the McLeod River Recreation Area.

Intermediate Access and Distances

Location	Elevation meters	Km down	Km up	Km between	Access / Bank or Rapid / Class	MGRS datum NAD 1927 Zone 11U	Gradient m/km
	1341		-4				
Steeper / Highway #40		37	0		left bank below bridge	MJ 929 876	
	1311	36	2				5.4
Mercoal Creek		30	7		right bank		
	1280	29	8				4.8
	1250	23	14				4.9
Mary Gregg Creek		20	17		left bank		
	1219	16	21				4.7
Antler Creek		15	22		left bank		
	1189	10	28				4.4
	1173	6	31				5.0
	1158	2	35				3.7
Gregg River confluence, & Forestry Trunk Road bridge		2	35		left bank, access on right bank above bridge	MK 813 044	
McLeod River Group Site		0	37	37	left bank below old bridge site	MK 818 059	
	1147		41				1.8

Gradient

Gradients on this run vary from over 5 m/km to under 3 m/km.

River Volume and Flow Rate

In 2005 we Ceyana paddlers had some very nice paddling with the Embarras River station reporting 80 - 100 cms. Good paddling occurs from about 30 cms up to 150 cms. Beware this river can change quickly. In June 2005 some colleagues of mine were on the river and had a fun day paddling down to near Antler Creek. They camped, did NOT tie their boats up and overnight the river rose over 1.3 m, washed their boats away, and then continued to rise for another day. It was three days before the river dropped enough to allow them to hike out to the Tri-Creeks Road.

At the Embarras River station flow rates range from under 2 km/hr at 30 cms to over 6 km/hr at 400 cms.

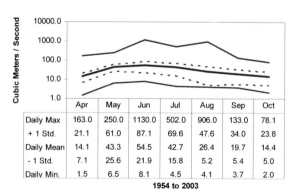

McLeod River above Embarras River

	Apr	May	Jun	Jul	Aug	Sep	Oct
Daily Max	163.0	250.0	1130.0	502.0	906.0	133.0	78.1
+ 1 Std.	21.1	61.0	87.1	69.6	47.6	34.0	23.8
Daily Mean	14.1	43.3	54.5	42.7	26.4	19.7	14.4
- 1 Std.	7.1	25.6	21.9	15.8	5.2	5.4	5.0
Daily Min.	1.5	6.5	8.1	4.5	4.1	3.7	2.0

1954 to 2003

Maps

1 - *Recreation and Activities: Hinton Forest Management Area* map produced by Hinton Wood Products. It is by far the best record of roads in the area and is usually available at the Tourist Information Office in Hinton in the upper town square.

2 - NTS 1:50,000: 83 F/3 Cadomin , and 83 F/6 Pedley

Camping

There are a number of campsites along Highways #40 on the approach to this run, and the large McLeod River Provincial Recreation Area (780.865.2154) at the finish. Once on the river, this is one of those fine foothill streams that offers a great campsite at nearly every bend — I cannot remember a poor campsite! The McLeod River Recreation Area includes a fine group campsite on river left at the old bridge site.

Wildlife

When I first started paddling this run in the mid-1970's we use to see a herd of wild horses on the McCardle Creek Flats. I've not seen these animals for some time, but this river is still a good place to spot moose, elk, mule deer, beaver, kingfishers and even the occasional eagle.

Trip Notes

This is a fun run. For a couple of years in the '70's we use to race this stretch, in about 3 hours — what a waste! Take more time. The run has lots of gravel chutes and pressure waves, and at various times there have been some complex rapids and ledges in the middle section. One 1.5 m ledge we called "Froggatt" falls, but in recent years the river has shifted channels and this ledge has been dry. This river does shift, and as a result there are often some pretty tricky, and downright dangerous logjams and sweepers.

Other Reaches

I have paddled this river from Cadomin down to the Steeper Bridge. The run is fast, but has even more logjams and sweepers than this reach! The run below the Recreation area to south of Marlboro and Highway #16 is also more prone to logjams and sweepers than this run. Then below Marlboro to Highway #47 the river is fairly flat and meanders some.

The Gregg River above the McLeod River Recreation Area also attracts some paddlers, but this too tends to be a shallow, tight stream prone to logjams and sweepers.

Other Local Activities or Destinations

If the McLeod is running high due to rains in the foothills, it is likely that other local streams are too. In June 2005, I cancelled weekend trips planned for the McLeod and other central foothills streams, three weekends in a row due to three consecutive multi-day storm "events". Caught in a big storm and looking for something else to do? Maybe the drive to Miette Hot Springs in Jasper National Park is just what your crew needs to lift their spirits, or maybe just a swim and shower at the pool in Hinton. If the rain has stopped and the rivers are still too high, consider a day hike up on the "High Divide" (or Cardinal River Divide) south of Cadomin and Mountain Park.

After June 2005 floods, the main channel just above Antler Creek blocked by
sweepers. As of 2009 this channel was completely dry at 40 cms.

McLeod River

Embarras River (Highway #47)
to north of Peers (Highway #32)

Why Go
This is a pleasant, or series of pleasant paddles in a near wilderness setting. With good leadership, and modest flows this can be a great first river for Novice River Paddlers.

Duration of Tour(s)
* 101 km
* 3-4 days with many shorter options

Classification
1. Rapids: mostly class I & easy II, Moose Creek rapids can be a III-
2. Skill of Paddlers: Intermediate River Paddlers, or Novice River Paddlers with good leadership

Looking back at the start of Moose Creek Rapids, June 2006 with approximately 30 cms of flow at the Embarras station

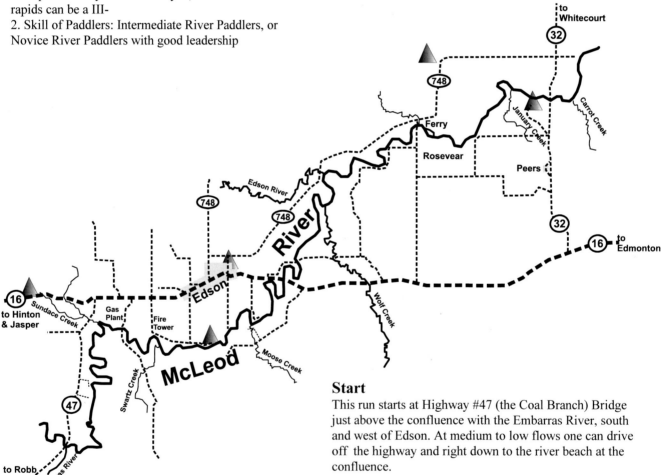

Start
This run starts at Highway #47 (the Coal Branch) Bridge just above the confluence with the Embarras River, south and west of Edson. At medium to low flows one can drive off the highway and right down to the river beach at the confluence.

Finish
One can of course finish at any of the intermediate access points. This report suggests the old gravel pit just downstream of the Highway #32 bridge, just north of Peers.

Intermediate Access and Distances

Location	Elevation meters	Km down	Km up	Km between	Access / Bank or Rapid / Class	MGRS datum NAD 1927 Zone 11 U	Gradient m/km
Highway #47, confluence with Embarras River		101	0		left bank, short drive in off of #47	NK 253 233	
	914	99	2				
	899	87	14				1.3
Sundance Creek / Big Eddy		78	23		left bank	NK 282 336	
Gas Plant Road		76	25	25	right bank, above bridge	NK 302 331	
	884	72	29				1.0
Swartz Creek		70	31		right bank		
Willmore Park Boat Launch		64	37	12	left bank	NK 381 318	
Moose Creek Rapids		59	43		Class II - III-, at most flows run right side of Island	NK 411 339	
Moose Creek		58	43		right bank	NK 413 333	
	860	57	44				1.6
Highway #16		49	52		poor access		
Highway #16a		43	58		no access		
Railway Bridge		39	63				
Wolf Creek		36	66		right bank	NK 475 430	
	840	35	66				0.9
road near Wolf Creek		34	67	37	right bank	NK 480 445	
Edson River		32	69		left bank		
Rosevear Ferry		18	83	16		NK 554 498	
	820	17	84				1.1
	800	5	96				1.6
January Creek		4	97		right bank		
		1	100				
Highway #32 north of Peers		0	101	18	left bank, below bridge off of old gravel pit	NK 669 517	

Gradient
The gradients for this run vary from 1.6 to 0.9 m/km.

River Volume and Flow Rate
At the hydrology station just upstream of the start of this run, the normal flows in May, June and early July vary from 20 cms to nearly 70 cms, with some peak flows exceeding 1000 cms. Good occurs with flows in the 25 to 70 cms range. Velocities at this station vary from just 2 km/hr at 25 cms to 4 km/hr at 100 cms and 6 km/hr at 300 cms.

McLeod River above Embarras River

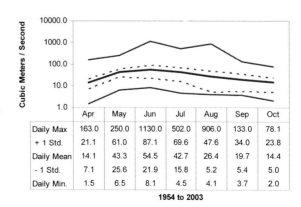

	Apr	May	Jun	Jul	Aug	Sep	Oct
Daily Max	163.0	250.0	1130.0	502.0	906.0	133.0	78.1
+ 1 Std.	21.1	61.0	87.1	69.6	47.6	34.0	23.8
Daily Mean	14.1	43.3	54.5	42.7	26.4	19.7	14.4
- 1 Std.	7.1	25.6	21.9	15.8	5.2	5.4	5.0
Daily Min.	1.5	6.5	8.1	4.5	4.1	3.7	2.0

1954 to 2003

Maps
1 - Alberta Road Map
2 - NTS - 1:50,000:
    83 F/7 Erith, 83 F/10 Bickerdike, 83 F/9 Edson. and 83 G/12 Carrot Creek

Camping
A public campgrounds is available on the river at Wilmore Recreation Area (780.723.7141) just south of Edson. Campgrounds within a few miles of the river occur at Bear Lake north of the Rosevear Ferry, and two near the Peers Bridges. Wilderness camping is available along much of the Mcleod. Once below Moose Creek rapids, islands may be the best locations for random camping.

Trip Notes
For the most part these are pleasant paddles that are occasionally interrupted with brief riffles. Nevertheless, at most water levels there may still be the occasional sweeper and logjam to be avoided. And in fact there are some longer stretches of low gradient ledges, one just below the start on the first long right hand bend. A number of such very low ledges will be found above Willmore Park, and between Willmore Park and Moose Creek Rapids.

The first modest hazard is the old bridge piers just below the put-in. They may even require scouting at highwer water levels. They are usually run-able without problem, and in June '06 they made some very nice eddies for our novice paddlers to practise on before heading downstream. Another sometime problem, at higher water levels, can be at "Big Eddy" at the confluence with Sundance Creek. This is usually just a very fine and popular fishing hole, but at high water it can demonstrate interesting hydrological dynamics – thus its name.

Possibly the most complex rapid and one that novices should certainly stop to scout would be the Moose Creek Rapids, at kilometre 43. These rapids start at the head of the island, and continue along the right bank all the way to Moose Creek at the left bend below the island. At most flows paddlers take the excitement on the right side of the Island, and at higher flows you may be able to sneak along the left channel. Some paddlers have even been known to portage through the farmyard on the left bank. One memorable group even borrowed the farmer's tractor, without permission. Paddlers were not popular with this farmer for some years — and likely even still so!

Other Reaches
The run above the Embarras River, from the Forestry Trunk Road down can be done in a couple of days. The first part offers much excitement with Class II - II+ rapids consisting of boulder gardens and broken ledges, the middle part is often thick with logjams and sweepers, and the lower third is a lazy meandering stream. Below the Highway #32 Bridge the river is mostly flat, with one exception, a small canyon about 2/3rds of the way to Whitecourt. It is just over 100 km from Highway #32 to Whitecourt by river.

A quiet pool, not far below the Embarras River, June, 2006.

Maligne Lake

Public Dock to Coronet Creek

Why Go
The mountains around Maligne Lake are spectacular; there is trout fishing, wildlife is abundant and the camping is grand.

Duration of Tour(s)
* 23 km
* 1 to 4 days - you go for the scenery and the hiking!

Classification
Intermediate Lake, with the risk of strong winds.

Spirit Island, August '96

Start & Finish
Maligne Lake is a forty minute drive east and south from the Jasper town site. Launch your own boat at the Maligne Lake public boat launch on the NW corner of the lake, or charter from the boat rental concession on the NE corner of the lake. You must drive pass Maligne Lake Lodge, and cross the Maligne river to reach the public boat launch.

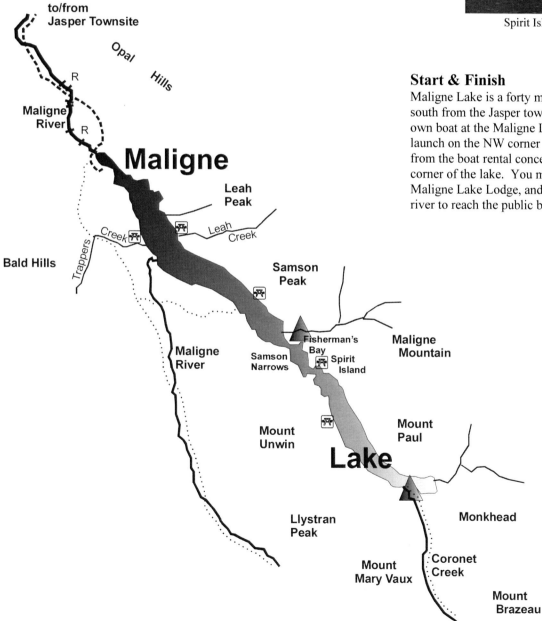

Intermediate Access and Distances

Location	Km down	Km up	Km between	Access / Bank or Rapid / Class	MGRS datum
					NAD 1983 Zone 11U
Public Boat Ramp	23	0			MU 565 419
Leah Creek / Picnic Site	18	6	6	east shore	
Samson Peak / Picnic Site				east shore	
Start Samson Narrows	11	13			
Fisherman's Bay / Campsite	10	14	8	east shore, southside of creek fan and deep in the bay	MU 565 419
Spirit Island / dock	8	16		east shore	MU 667 327
Coronet Creek Campsite	0	23	10	south shore / east side of creek fan	MU 713 273

*Distances were calculated using the east shore until opposite the Coronet Creek fan, and then crossing over to the campsite beach. Straight line distances down the middle of the lake, much riskier and far more boring to paddle, are about 2 km less for the whole trip.

Maps

1 - The Gem Trek Publishing *Jasper & Maligne Lake* at 1:100,000 is the only sheet you really need; it is very good!

2 - NTS 1: 250,000   83 C Brazeau Lake
   NTS 1: 50,000   83 C/12 Athabasca Falls   83 C/11 Southesk Lake

Camping

Car Camping: Wapiti (my favorite, down by the river) and Whistler campgrounds just south of Jasper make semi-convenient staging sites for this trip (National Park Campsite reservations 1.877.737.3783).

National Park Service Wilderness Camp sites:
    - Fisherman's Bay off the NE corner of Samson Narrows, eight tent pads.
    - Coronet Creek at the South end of the lake, eight tent pads.

Each of these sites includes picnic tables, fire rings (gather drift wood along the lake shore) and bear proof food storage cabinets. No unorganized camping is allowed. Many good park service campgrounds exist in the Jasper town site area for pre and post trip camping.

Beware, the parks service has restrictions on the campsites on the lake: campers are limited to only four nights on the lake, two each, at Fisherman's Bay in the narrows, and Coronet Creek at the south end. Group size is limited to six, and each campsite has only eight tent pads. Campsite permits are required, and reservations are accepted (for an additional fee!) and recommended. To book call the Jasper Trail Office at 780.852.6177. Other Park Information is at 780-852-6176.

Wildlife

Over my years on and around Maligne Lake, Lois and I have had the pleasure viewing birds ranging from osprey and loons to slate colored juncos, woodland caribou to thirteen-lined chipmunks, and on our last venture we just missed a morning black bear encounter. In 1996 our early rising campground neighbors told us with some "relish" of just how close the bear had been to our tent! Paddlers should be prepared for bear encounters. In 2008 I camped two nights at Coronet Creek and the campground had a significant population of resident deer. Fishermen will require a National Park License, those under 16 years fish on an accompanying adult's license.

Trip Notes

Maligne Lake is one of those spectacular spots one goes to paddle just for the scenery I have twice now taken advantage of the fine campsite that the National Parks service maintains in Samson Narrows, two-thirds of the way down the lake. The mountains around Maligne Lake are spectacular; there is trout fishing in the lake, wildlife is abundant and the camping is grand. On the negative side you must share this lake: fortunately only the wardens and the commercial tour operator are allowed power boats, and the commercial tours only go as far south as Spirit Island in the narrows. The best part of the lake for scenery and camping is in the southern third!

Maligne Lake is the longest lake, and third deepest lake in the Canadian Rockies. The parks service reports that the wind is often out of the south on the north two-thirds of lake, and out of the north on the southern third. Try to plan your paddling for the early morning.

Maligne Lake would appear to have been visited infrequently by the Native and Metis hunters in the late 19th century. The first reported European visitor would appear to have been the railroad surveyor Henry Mcleod, who in 1875 called it "Sorefoot Lake." In 1908, Mary Schäffer, with guides Bill Warren and Sidney Unwin, and using directions provided by the Stoney Indian, Samson Beaver, "rediscovered" Maligne Lake. Mary Schäffer revisited and mapped the lake for the Canadian Government in 1911, and later published a book, *Old Indian Trails of the Canadian Rockies* that provided early publicity of the beauties of the lake. This book has been reprinted as *A Hunter of the Peace*.

There is a hiking trail out of Coronet Creek up towards the glacier and another campsite about 6 km to the south. There are also many pleasant short walks and scrambles along the creeks, and avalanche paths flowing into the lake.

Rentals
On-Line Sport & Tackle 780.852.3630

Public Dock, northwest corner Maligne Lake, August 1996

Athabasca River

Athabasca Falls to Jasper

Why Go
The best open canoe whitewater in the park, and great mountain scenery!

Duration of Tour(s)
* 31.4 km
* ½ & 1 day runs; it can be done in one long day!

Author & daughter at bottom of Becker's Rapid, Sept. '04

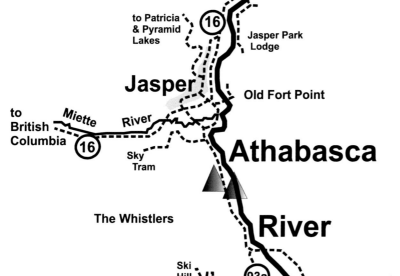

Classification
1. Rapids: Class I to III+
2. Skill of Paddlers: Intermediate River Paddlers in closed canoes and kayaks, Skilled River Paddlers in open canoes.

Start
Access to this run is just north of Athabasca Falls, off Highway #93A. Use the Geraldine Lakes Trailhead parking lot. Then portage across the old highway and down an old road/trail to the river and put in at the pool at the bottom of the gorge below the falls. I've been told that this old road down to the bottom of the gorge below the falls was cut for the shooting of some of the scenes in Marilyn Monroe's film *River of No Return*.

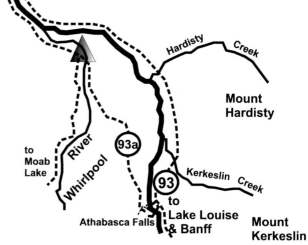

Finish
Old Fort Point is directly south of Jasper. Use the middle access road into Jasper from Highway #16. Instead of turning into Jasper, turn south, and then take the next left, and head east down to and across the river. There is a large parking lot next to the big pool just below the bridge on the east or right bank. Please park away from the river beach after dropping off your canoe. The commercial rafters arrive very frequently during the tourist season, with large crews, rafts and buses.

Intermediate Access and Distances

Location	Elevation meters	Km down	Km up	Km between	Access / Bank or Rapid / Class	MGRS datum NAD 1983 Zone 11U	Gradient m/km
	1160		0				
below Athabasca Falls		31	0		left bank - rapids to Class III+	MU 400 353	
Kerkeslin Creek		28	3		right bank - rapid to Class III+		
Hardisty Creek		26	6		right bank		
	1140	25	7				2.9
	1120	21	11				5.0
Whirlpool River / Picnic Site		20	12	12	left bank	MU 355 432	
	1100	18	14				6.7
Wabasso Campground		15	16		left bank	MU 333 468	
	1080	12	19				3.6
Dunk Corner		12	20		Class II+		
	1060	9	23				5.4
Icefields Parkway Bridge		8	23	11	left bank, below bridge	MU 298 518	
Beckers Rapid		6	26		Class III to III+	MU 287 536	
	1040	3	28				3.8
Alpine Bungalows - access		2	30		left bank	MU 275 570	
Miette River confluence		1	31		left bank		
Old Fort Point / Bridge		0	31	8	right bank, below bridge	MU 284 584	
	1020		37				2.2

Gradient

As with many whitewater rivers and reaches in shallow canyons, the gradients above can be questionable and I suspect that the higher gradient reaches maybe closer to the overall mean gradient on this reach of 3.7 m/km.

River Volume and Flow Rate

I really enjoy my paddling on these reaches with flows in the 100 to 250 cms range. Velocities vary from less than 2 km/hr at 30 cms to 7 km/hr at 350 cms. Flow rates will vary considerably on this run, and the hydrology station is located approximately 2 km above the finish. During the summer, temperature and glacier melt are the primary variables affecting flow rate. So when it is hot and dry in much of the rest of the province, the Athab' will likely be fun paddling!

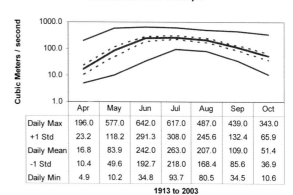

Athabasca River at Jasper

	Apr	May	Jun	Jul	Aug	Sep	Oct
Daily Max	196.0	577.0	642.0	617.0	487.0	439.0	343.0
+1 Std	23.2	118.2	291.3	308.0	245.6	132.4	65.9
Daily Mean	16.8	83.9	242.0	263.0	207.0	109.0	51.4
-1 Std	10.4	49.6	192.7	218.0	168.4	85.6	36.9
Daily Min	4.9	10.2	34.8	93.7	80.5	34.5	10.6

1913 to 2003

Maps

1 - My first choice for map on this reach would be the Gem Trek Publishing *Jasper & Maligne Lake* sheet at 1:100,000. Unfortunately this sheet only locates the rapids: Dunk corner, Beckers and Wapiti.

2 - NTS 1:50,000   83 C/12 Athabasca Falls   83 C/13 Medicine Lake
         83 D/16 Jasper
   *83 D/16 has most of the rapids marked, but the other two sheets show no rapids, and there are many!

Camping

Numerous public campsites are available in Jasper National Park, but one must often take what is available. For groups, such as canoe clubs or youth groups, the park does maintain a "limited services" group site on the Whirlpool river, just off of #93A, a kilometer or two above the confluence with the Athabasca. There is also a group site (Marmot Meadows) within Whistler Campground. Wapiti and Wabasso campgrounds are also situated along the river and both have some limited access to the river. All these campgrounds have an advance reservation system in place (1.877.737.3783 or www.pccamping.ca/parkscanada/). There are no "backcountry" campsites along this reach of the Athabasca.

Wildlife

On most trips on these reaches I have seen some wildlife, and over the years have seen all the common mammals and larger birds along these reaches. Ironically most of my sightings of big game have been of either black bears or elk in the campgrounds! Bear management has improved over the last decade and I've had few bear encounters these last few years. Elk and especially the big bulls can still be a problem in the fall. On our 2004 Labor Day weekend in Jasper, we had one bull maintaining his harem right within our campground loop in Wapiti Campground – and vigorously chasing out all the young guys who where sniffing around the edges.

Trip Notes

For us open boat paddlers, this is Alberta river paddling at its finest! Challenging, scenic, and few highway intrusions. What more could one ask for? Do note, the "Falls" run, and the "Beckers" run are NOT RECOMMENDED for open canoes, and DO require very good skills. I have made some awfully long rescues on both these sections, or, some paddlers have had some long cold swims! But if you are equipped with the skills, the boats and lots of flotation, go for it!

The first section below the falls has an impressive start. The pool at the bottom of the gorge below the falls swirls and boils and hisses with highly aerated water. This run can be intimidating; there is no time to warm-up, at most water levels you are immediately into a long class II to III rapid, all the way to the commencement of the next canyon, over 500 m. Once into the canyon the river is a mix of long quiet pools interspersed with a series of rapids. The best or biggest drops occur at Kerkeslin and Hardisty creeks. Various authors, including myself, would suggest at some water levels both of these drops can go "good" class III (good means big, from an open canoe perspective!). Kerkeslin in particular has earned a reputation because of the calm pool above, the horizon line, and the echoing of the rapid roar up the canyon walls. Kerkeslin can be scouted from the right shore unless the river is very high (not a good time to be there!).

There are two long stretches of boulder gardens with pushy, wet waves on this reach. One such rapid is just above and below the first appearance of Highway #93 (km 9), and the other just below the confluence with the Whirlpool (km 12).

Small rapids and gravel chutes occur regularly all along this reach. Between the Whirlpool and Mile 5 Bridge the most common "swimming" spot is "Dunk" corner (km 20). At this point the river makes a sweeping left turn, drops over a partial ledge and then makes a sharp right turn. The drop on the outside (right) by the ledge is considerable at most water levels, and the powerful boils "down the middle" usually require both some forward momentum and a good brace.

Below Mile 5 Bridge again is not recommended for open canoes by the Park Service. The first rapid of significance occurs at Becker's Bungalows and can go class III+. The whole stretch then down to km 29 is a series of rapids, often with large standing waves. The most complex rapid is opposite Wapiti Campground.

I have many, many fond memories of this reach and have used it for teaching and training many new paddlers. Possibly one of my best memories is my first time down. In '72 while with *Canoe Alberta* we hooked up with local paddlers, Bryn Thomas and Ron Steer. At that time they were providing commercial Klepper kayak tours of the Falls run and offered to take us along. Their hype had been such that I ended up paddling a slalom kayak, while two of my colleagues paddled with Bryn and Ron. Because my nylon spray cover tended to leak I thought, foolishly, that maybe a little Vaseline would help to water proof it. I was first into my boat and while waiting for the others I made the mistake of resting my paddle on my spray cover. And thus I paddled the run with a very slippery shaft, and with my arms stretched out to the side so that I could grip the blades to maintain proper blade orientation. The second good reason for never forgetting the run was that once we reached the canyon, Bryn and Ron stopped and searched each eddy. Only then did they mention that the wardens had asked them to look for the body of some unwary tourist who had backed into the falls while taking a picture. The body was found three months later near Whitecourt!

Historically this section of the river was not used by the voyagers as they usually traded their canoes for horses at Jasper House, east of Jasper Lake. Old Fort Point is probably a misnomer, as both Jasper and Henry House are usually reported as being to the east, and the name is usually ascribed to being a corruption of "old ford point."

Other Reaches
There is one other upstream run made regularly on the Athabasca, from the bend below Sunwapta Falls where the river meets the highway, down to Athabasca Falls. Parks Canada has developed a portage trail on the west/left bank around Athabasca falls, and conservative paddlers usually take out along the highway a kilometer or so above the falls along the highway if ending their run near the falls. There is a very good class III rapid just above the falls -- it is **not** a good place to "mess around." This run is approximately 15 km long, includes a number of good class II and III rapids and a few will go class III+ at some water levels. Many of these rapids can be "wet and pushy" for open canoe paddlers. The gradient averages 4.8 m/km, with a maximum gradient of 6.8 m/km.

Other Local Activities or Destinations
On an ugly paddling day in Jasper, we have been know to retreat to the Miette Hot Springs pool. And on a number of long weekends we have just paddled the Saturday and Sunday, and then on the holiday Monday, taken the Whistler Sky Tram to the top early for breakfast. After breakfast we have hiked up the ridge a kilometer or so, or considerably further once or twice. Then it is a late morning return to finish breaking camp, after the tents have dried. In the early fall the dew is usually heavy and a leisurely breaking of camp is a good plan.

Athabasca Falls, September 2004

Athabasca River

Jasper to Whitecourt

Why Go
These reaches provide scenic day tripping, and good wilderness tripping.

Duration of Tour(s)
* 292 km
* 1/2 day, full day and multi-day trips from 2 to 14 days, depending on how much time you want for fishing, hunting or hiking.

Classification
1. Rapids: Class I to II+
2. Skill of Paddlers: Intermediate River paddlers, or Novice River with good leadership

Start
Old Fort Point is directly south of Jasper. Use the middle access road into Jasper from Highway #16. Instead of turning into Jasper, turn south, and then take the next left and head east down to and across the river. There is a large parking lot next to the big pool just below the bridge on the east or right bank. Please park away from the river beach after dropping off your canoe. The commercial rafters arrive very frequently with large groups during the tourist season.

Old Fort Point, looking downstream, circa 1985

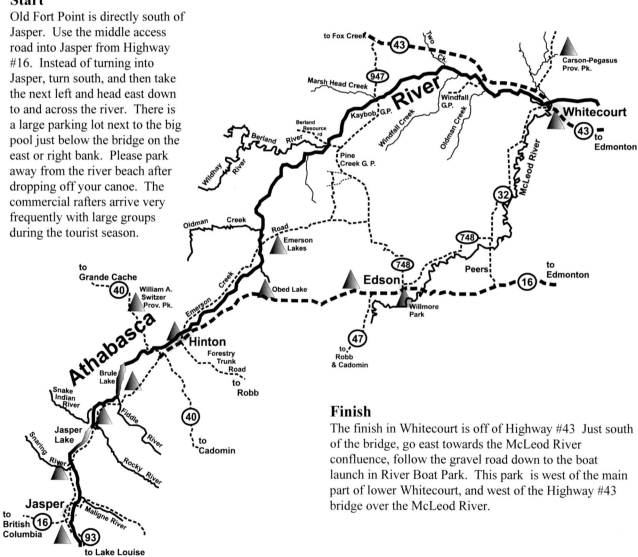

Finish
The finish in Whitecourt is off of Highway #43 Just south of the bridge, go east towards the McLeod River confluence, follow the gravel road down to the boat launch in River Boat Park. This park is west of the main part of lower Whitecourt, and west of the Highway #43 bridge over the McLeod River.

Intermediate Access and Distances

Location	Elevation meters	Km down	Km up	Km between	Access / Bank or Rapid / Class	MGRS datum NAD 1983 Zone 11 U	Gradient m/km
	1040		-4				
Old Fort Point		292	0		right bank	MU 284 584	
Maligne Road Bridge		287	5		poor access		
	1020	286	6				2.0
Maligne River		284	8		right bank	MU 305 653	
Snaring River		273	19		left bank		
	1006	272	20				1.0
Highway #16 Bridge		270	22	22	left bank, above bridge	MU 268 772	
Athabasca Island Campsite		268	24		on mid-stream island	MU 266 789	
Jasper Lake		264	28				
launch at bottom of Jasper Lake		254	38	16	right bank	MU 342 878	
Disaster Point		251	41		right bank	MU 349 911	
Snake Indian River		248	45		left bank		
Brule Tunnels Campsite		237	56		right bank	MU 420 982	
Fiddle River		236	56		right bank		
Brule Lake		235	57				
Ogre Creek / to canyon					left bank	MU 421 995	
Creek Fan / camping and access to abandoned RR station		227	65		right bank		
Solomon Creek / end of Brule Lake		224	68		left bank		
railway bridge		218	74				
Highway #40 bridge		212	80		no access		
Maskuta Creek		209	83		right bank	MV 565 148	
Pulp Mill / Haul Road Bridge		200	92	54	left bank	MV 626 198	
	960	198	94				0.6
	945	186	106				1.2
Obed Mine bridge		181	112				
	930	170	122				1.0
former Obed ferry site		165	127				
Obed Creek		161	131				
	914	158	135				1.3
Emerson Creek Road bridge		154	138	47	right bank, downstream of bridge	MV 892 504	
Oldman Creek		148	144				
	899	143	149				1.0
	884	138	154				3.1
	869	134	158				3.5
	853	118	174				1.0
	838	115	177				5.2

Location	Elevation meters	Km down	Km up	Km between	Access / Bank or Rapid / Class	MGRS datum NAD 1983 Zone 11 U	Gradient m/km
Berland River		102	190		left bank		
Berland Resource Rd. Bridge		101	191	52	left bank, downstream of bridge	NV 106 844	
	823	99	193				0.9
	808	91	201				1.9
	792	81	211				1.6
Marsh Head Creek		75	217		left bank		
Highway #947		75	217	26	left bank	NA 265 005	
RR bridge		75	217				
	777	64	228				0.9
	762	55	237				1.7
Two Creek		48	244		left bank		
	747	47	245				1.9
Windfall Creek		41	251		right bank		
Windfall Gas Plant Rd. Bridge		31	261		right bank	NA 612 069	
	732	30	262				0.9
	716	17	275				1.2
	701	8	284				1.7
Highway #43/32 bridge		1	291				
McLeod River / boat launch		0	292	75	right bank of Athab', left bank of McLeod	NA 848 010	
	686		298				1.1

Gradient

The overall average gradient on this run is 1.2 m/km. Once again I am suspect of some of the individual mean gradients noted above; there is no stretch that comes close to the difficulties that these numbers might suggest. On the other hand the run from Oldman Creek through to the Berland River does offer the most fun waves of the whole reach.

River Volume and Flow Rate

The Athabasca is a good size river, and it grows over the course of this run. You can see on the right that at Hinton the mean summer flow is about 500 cms; in Whitecourt this increases to about 650 cms. The range of flows at Whitecourt is even more striking, with floods of over 2100 cms having been reported. At Hinton flow velocities range from 2 km/hr at 100 cms to over 7 km/hr at 750 cms. Good paddling is had on this run with the Hinton Station reporting from about 125 cms through to about 450 cms.

Athabasca River at Hinton

	Apr	May	Jun	Jul	Aug	Sep	Oct
Daily Max	211	1080	1200	1000	997	660	487
+ 1 Std.	51.93	234.7	590.5	560.6	414.6	252.5	147.1
Daily Mean	43.9	175	491	472	351	207	117
- 1 Std.	35.87	115.3	391.5	383.4	287.4	161.5	86.9
Daily Min.	20.7	33.7	144	234	153	77.9	29.1

1961 to 2003

Maps

1 - ARCA in 2005 published the Alberta river guide *The Athabasca River: Rocky Mountain Region* which reports on this whole reach. With this sheet and the *Alberta Highways Map* most folks should be set.

For those just interested in only the first Jasper National Park reach, the Gem Trek Publishing sheet *Jasper and Maligne Lake* at 1:100,000 will see you through to the bottom of Jasper Lake.

2 - NTS 1:250,000   83 D Canoe River   83 E Mount Robson   83 F Edson

3 - For those wanting to explore the back roads and access options other than those noted here or in the ARCA map I would suggest getting the *Recreation and Activities Map* put out by the Hinton "mill" and usually available at the Hinton Tourist Information centre. For the reaches outside of Jasper National Park, the Alberta Lands & Forest *Whitecourt Forest* sheet at 1:250,000 is another good option.

Camping

This is a river for tripping. Yes, there is at least one day trip below Jasper, but this is really a river for loading the canoe up and going camping for a weekend, or for two weeks. There are only two primitive campsites where camping is permitted in Jasper Park, at km 24.6 on a island just above Jasper Lake (left bank, main channel), and just above the Fiddle River (km 53.3, right bank). Compounding this lack of allowed campsites within the park is the regulation that groups must be less than 12 in number. To confirm these park regulations and to book a primitive campsite call the Trail Office at 780.852.6177. Once out of the park there are many nice campsites. I have used one near the head of Brule Lake on Drystone Creek, and another 2/3 of the way along the east shore at km 65. Both these sites are near small creeks. Below Hinton there continues to be many good campsites. I have earlier reported that the first Oldman Creek site has been abused in the past but as of a Fall '97 Ceyana Canoe Club trip the site appeared to have been cleaned up. I think we owe a thank-you to some good Samaritans. In '07 a volunteer crew from MEC installed a Paddle Alberta "throne" at this site.

There are numerous public campgrounds near this river. In Jasper Park there is the Snaring River campground east of Jasper townsite. Between Jasper Park and Hinton there is Kinky/Wildhorse Lakes (780.866.2231) east of Brule Lake; two operated by the Town of Hinton (780.865.0876); at Emerson Lakes/Sundance Provincial Park (780.865.2154); and in Whitecourt, the Lion's Campground is along Highway #43 on the south edge of town (780.778.6782).

Wildlife

Take your time on this run. Try to do some of your floating in the early morning and late evening. Over the years I have seen moose, bear, wolves, elk, beaver, mink, bighorn sheep and mountain goats on these runs, all from my canoe. Bears can be a problem; just two years ago I suggested to a couple of developing paddlers who were working their way up the Alberta river progressions, that they were ready for the "Athabee". After a pleasant paddle down from Jasper, their first hour at the Athabasca Island campsite, involved visits from three bears and then a long, scary night. Between the bears and the head wind on Jasper Lake they opted to pull off the river and finish their trip on the east side of Jasper Lake.

Trip Notes

The runs in Jasper Park are fine scenic paddles. The river can be a little tricky and bouncy at average summer flows, especially between Brule Lake and the Windfall Gas Plant Bridge. In the various stretches where the river is braided, logjams and sweepers are often a significant hazard. In late August '97 on a Ceyana Canoe Club trip, we found that the river had cut the meander bend just below the first Oldman Creek, and above the former Gooseneck Rapid. This new channel was quite bouncy, with a strong current and many new sweepers. I especially like to return to the Athabasca in mid to late August, when the other rivers are starting to run low on water.

Beware and be alert! In the past couple of years we have had some big floods, the formation of new channels and log jams and sweepers will be a hazard. Above Whitecourt the river slows down, and this often means the dropping of logs, trees and other debris swept down from further upstream – all material for new logjams, and eventually river islands. This often leads me to ponder the age old question: Which came first, the logjam, or the island?

Jasper to Hinton can be a long two-day paddle. Often to shorten the run, and to get out of the park with large groups, I have started at the Jasper Lake outlet, and then camped at the head of Brule Lake. The run below Jasper to Mile 12 Bridge has been a popular day run for Ceyana families. Emerson Lakes Bridge to Whitecourt can make for a long three-day paddle, and for our '97 run mentioned above we pulled out at the Windfall Gas Plant bridge. Over the years many of us have avoided the first few miles immediately below the Hinton Pulp Mill due to the pollution and odour, though this situation has improved a lot since I first worked north of Hinton in the mid-'70s.

When paddling these runs there are three historical points worth visiting. Just upstream of Garonne Creek are the remains of the Moberly buildings. John Moberly constructed this farmstead starting about 1898, and farmed here until 1910 when the government bought him out for the establishment of the park. At approximately km 39 (left bank) is the last site of Jasper's House, the longest lived fur trade post in the area. The meadow in the area can make for a pleasant walk. Along the east shore of Brule lake, the abandoned railway line runs through a long series of sand dunes. At times the sand has buried the line to the depth of the telegraph posts, at others the wind has completely blown the railway bed away. Near the campsite at km 65 is an abandoned station that had been nearly covered by a sand dune when I first visited it in the '70s, now the wind has blown much of the sand, and the building away.

Other Local Activities or Destinations

Is the Athabasca too high due to glacial or high country snow melt? Give consideration to the Wildhay or McLeod Rivers for your trip. Is it too wet and cold? Check out the Miette Hot Springs. And if the paddling is failing there are plenty of hiking and mountain biking opportunities in the area. At the south end of Brule Lake is Ogre Canyon and the ridge walk – but be sure to supervise the kids (and older fools), more than one person has been rescued from, and more than one body has been pulled out of Ogre Canyon over the years. If you cannot paddle into the old train station on Brule Lake, you can hike in from the Kinky Lake side.

Moberly Cabins, 2001

Moberly Cabins, 1985

The difference between these two photos is a careless fire started by some persons seeking shelter in the cabins.

South end of Brule Lake from Ogre Ridge.

Rentals & Shuttles

Edmonton Canoe 780.470.5352 *www.edmontoncanoe.com*

Athabasca River

Whitecourt to Fort Assiniboine

Why Go
In the early or late season this is a most pleasant river for canoe camping, with some fine wilderness vistas and plenty of wildlife.

Duration of Tour(s)
* 90 km
* 1 to 3 days

Morning on the Athab', from under the fly, May '06

Classification
1. Rapids: Class 1
2. Skill of Paddlers: Intermediate River Paddlers, or at lower flows Novice River Paddler with good leadership.

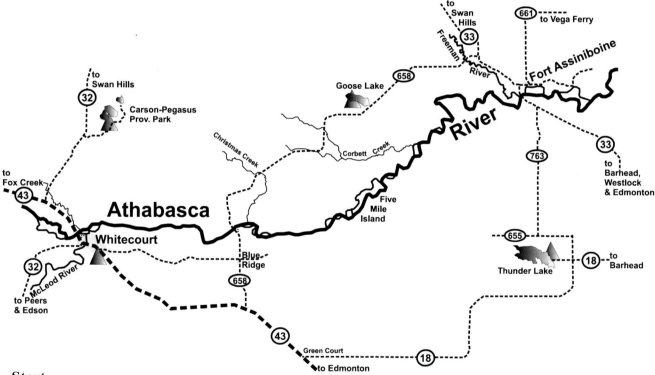

Start
This run starts at the River Boat Park boat launch in Whitecourt, which is at at the confluence of the McLeod and Athabasca Rivers. From Highway #43, on the south side of the Athabasca River bridge, take the east service road off Highway #43, and follow the park/boat launch signs, a bit north and then east and down stream to the confluence.

Finish
This run ends at the picnic site at the confluence of the Freeman and Athabasca Rivers. This is just over the bridge on the town (north) side of the Athabasca River. Take the west service road south to the picnic site by the bridge. If coming from the north, turn right before the town of Fort Assiniboine, and continue south on Highway #33. Just past the gas station turn onto the service road and follow it along the west side of the highway to the picnic site.

Intermediate Access and Distances

Location	Elevation meters	Km down	Km up	Km between	Access / Bank or Rapid / Class	MGRS datum NAD 1983 Zone 11 U	Gradient m/km
Riverboat Park in Whitecourt		90	0		right bank of Athab', left bank of McLeod	NA 848 010	
	686	84	6				
	671	71	19				1.1
Highway #658 north of Blue Ridge		66	24	24	right bank	PA 051 023	
	655	58	32				1.2
	640	52	38				2.5
start 5 Mile Island		46	44			PA 213 047	
Corbett Creek		29	61		left bank		
	625	29	61				0.6
	610	2	88				0.6
Freeman River, just above the Highway #33 bridge		0	90	66	left bank	PA 439 214	

Gradient

The average gradient over this whole run is 0.9 m/km, and I suspect that all of the above gradients are closer to this than the mean gradients between each contour line, especially that 2.5 mean gradient noted above.

River Volume and Flow Rate

This station is closer to Windfall than Whitecourt and does not reflect the McLeod River contribution to flow. In spring or early summer also check the McLeod River flows to ensure that neither river is in flood. Good paddling happens on these reaches with 125 to 500 cms of water being reported at this Windfall station. Velocities for this station vary from less than 2 km/hr at 200 cms to 10 km/hr at 4000 cms.

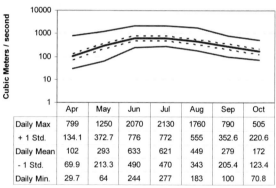

Athabasca River near Whitecourt

	Apr	May	Jun	Jul	Aug	Sep	Oct
Daily Max	799	1250	2070	2130	1760	790	505
+ 1 Std.	134.1	372.7	776	772	555	352.6	220.6
Daily Mean	102	293	633	621	449	279	172
- 1 Std.	69.9	213.3	490	470	343	205.4	123.4
Daily Min.	29.7	64	244	277	183	100	70.8

1960 to 2003

Maps

1 - I think that most folks will be adequately served by the NTS 1:250,000 sheet noted below and the *Alberta Road Map.* If you need a reference for additional access try the Alberta Lands and Forest *Whitecourt Forest* sheet at 1:250,000. It can be nice to have the 1:50,000 sheets, but on this run you need five of them!

2 - NTS 1:250,000: 83 J Whitecourt
    NTS 1:50,000: 83 J/ 4 Whitecourt, 83 J/ 3 Green Court, 83 J/ 2 Thunder Lake, 83 J/ 6 Christmas Creek, and
            83 J/ 7 Fort Assinboine

Camping

There are really no established public campgrounds right on the river to support this trip. In Whitecourt the campground is on the south edge of town, a long ways from the river. The picnic site at the Ft. Assiniboine bridge is not really a campground, and the Blue Ridge bridge is just a nice launch site. On the other hand, at medium to low water levels this is a fine run for wilderness camping. I suspect that most users are like myself: they come from within a few hours drive, drop a car off at the finish and drive the second vehicle to the start and paddle back, camping at least one night along the way. At medium to high flows you will have to read your map carefully and plan to check out all likely spots; the islands tend to be fairly overgrown and "thick!" Camping at higher water levels is limited.

Wildlife

On a May '06 run we spotted some deer but the biggest highlight were the eagles. We had at least two eagles, maybe more, one mature, and one immature that seemed to follow us down the river over our two day run from Blue Ridge to Fort Assiniboine. On the Sunday morning the mature eagle gave us an extended fishing demonstration right off of our breakfast beach. A prior canoe guide for this reach suggested that the walleye, and rocky mountain whitefish fishery were in good shape on this run. I would think that the eagles were a demonstration that this is still the case.

Trip Notes

Whitecourt to Blue Ridge is a little swifter, and very braided, relative to the run below Blue Ridge. Logjams and sweepers are a constant hazard on both reaches, unless you paddle as we did in May '06, at very low water levels and then most of the logjams and sweepers are "stranded" and well above the water line. There are a number of big islands on this run, with *5 Mile Island* being the largest. It is probably a good idea to keep your group together, and not split up to explore side channels. Not only are side channels more likely to harbor logjams and sweepers, but your separation can at times be rather extended.

Other Reaches

The reach above Whitecourt is available in this guide. From Ft. Assiniboine to well below the town of Athabasca, the "Athabee" is a pretty tame paddle. Vega Ferry is 41km, Smith 165 km, and Athabasca town 279 km below Fort Assiniboine.

Other Local Activities or Destinations

The senior's centre in Fort Assiniboine is a reconstruction of the original fur trade post, and is well worth the time of a tour.

Drifting and watching the eagles, May 2006

Athabasca River

Athabasca to Fort McMurray

Why Go
The history, the wilderness camping, the whitewater.

Duration of Tour(s)
* 394 km
* some one day paddles at each end are possible, but this is usually done as a historical run and the whole trip can take 7 to 10 days

Classification
1. Rapids: Class I to VI
2. Skill of Paddlers: Novice River on the first reaches out of Athabasca and down to the Calling River. The Grand Rapids to Fort McMurray reach requires strong, well equipped Skilled River Paddlers!

Start
Start for this run is along the river front in Athabasca. Rivers Edge Campground in Athabasca (4705-49 Ave) reports having a boat launch.

Finish
Finish for this whole run is on the west bank, just upstream of the Highway #63 bridge in Fort McMurray.

running right channel at Grand Rapids, circa 1900, PAA 3550

Intermediate Access and Distances

Location	Elevation meters	Km down	Km up	Km between	Access / Bank or Rapid / Class	MGRS datum NAD 1983 Zone 12U	Gradient m/km
Athabasca		394	0		right bank	UF 528 662	
Tawatinaw River		394	0		right bank		
Highway 813 Bridge		393	1				
	503	371	23				
Rnge Rd 202a Bridge		354	40			UF 744 910	
Pine Sands Natural Area		350	44		right bank	UF 779 928	
	495	340	54				0.3
La Biche River		333	61		right bank		
Calling River		318	77		left bank		
Township roads 705a & 704		317	77	77	left bank	UG 799 066	
	488	299	95				0.2
	472	268	126				0.5
	457	240	154				0.5
	450	230	164				0.7
Upper Wells Cabin		224	170		right bank	UG 991763	
Pelican Portage		213	181				
Pelican River		209	185		left bank		
	442	207	187				0.3
Pelican Rapids		206	188		Class I to II		
	434	203	191				2.0
Stony Rapids		201	193		Class I to II		
	427	197	197				1.2
	419	193	201				2.0
	411	182	212				0.7
						Zone 12V	
Rapides Du Joli Fou		169	225		Class 0 to I		
	404	163	231				0.4
House River		151	243		right bank		
	380	136	258				0.9
Grand Rapids		135	259		Class V - VI, portage on right bank, start above Grand Island	VH 009 434	
	370	134	260				5.0
Little Grand Rapids		134	260		Class II+ to III+		
	360	128	266				1.7
Pointe la Biche		119	275				
Buffalo Creek		105	289				
Brule Point		104	290				
	350	103	291				0.4
	340	94	300				1.1
Brule Rapids		93	301		Class III to IV		
	330	86	308				1.3
	320	75	319				0.9
	310	68	326				1.4
Algar River		65	329				
Boiler Rapids		59	335		Class II+ to III+		

Location	Elevation	Km down	Km up	Km between	Access / Bank or Rapid / Class	MGRS datum	Gradient m/km
	meters					NAD 1983	
	300	59	335				1.1
Middle Rapids		56	338		Class III to -IV		
	290	54	340				2.0
Long Rapids		50	344		Class III to -IV		
	280	48	346				1.7
Crooked Rapids		40	354		Class III to IV		
	270	37	357				0.9
Rock Rapids		36	358		Class III to IV		
Little Cascade Rapids		32	362		Class III+ to IV		
(Big) Cascade Rapids		29	365		Class III+ to IV+		
	260	24	370				0.8
	250	18	376				1.7
Mountain Rapids		13	381		Class III to IV		
Moberly Rapids		2	392				
Horse River		1	393				
Fort McMurray		0	394	317	left bank	VH 754 875	

Gradient

Gradients noted above correspond pretty well with the tough water
rapid section may more reflect the bedrock geology rather than gra

River Volume and Flow Rate

This is one of Alberta's largest rivers, and as such is probably best
summer. Good paddling and camping should be had in the range c
reports for this station range from under 2 km/hr at 300 cms to 10 l

Maps

1 - I'd suggest that unless you are planning on using one of the les:
run successfully with just the NTS 1:250,000 sheets and the *Albert*

2 - NTS 1:250,000: 83 I Tawatinaw, 83 P Pelican, 84 A Algar L;

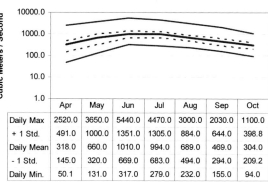

Athabasca River at Athabasca

	Apr	May	Jun	Jul	Aug	Sep	Oct
Daily Max	2520.0	3650.0	5440.0	4470.0	3000.0	2030.0	1100.0
+ 1 Std.	491.0	1000.0	1351.0	1305.0	884.0	644.0	398.8
Daily Mean	318.0	660.0	1010.0	994.0	689.0	469.0	304.0
- 1 Std.	145.0	320.0	669.0	683.0	494.0	294.0	209.2
Daily Min.	50.1	131.0	317.0	279.0	232.0	155.0	94.0

1913 to 2003

Camping

In Athabasca, Rivers Edge Campground (780.675.2063) is right downtown and on the river. There is a county
campground in or near the Pine Sands Provincial Natural Area, and a campground at the mouth of the Calling River.

Wildlife

Back in '72 when we paddled this reach for Canoe Alberta, we had our first experiences with swimming bears and
moose. Wildlife will be seen on this run, and any of the common mammals and birds of the boreal forest maybe spotted,
but it is a big river, in a big forest, such sightings will be by chance.

Trip Notes

There are two good reasons for making this run, the history, and the rapids. If you're into the history, you must start in Athabasca, and then take time at Grand Rapids to ferry over to Grand Island and check out the few remaining remnants of the wooden tram that use to run the length of the Island. Athabasca was the "trans shipment" point for all goods going north from about the 1880's through to the completion of the railroad to Fort McMurray - Waterways in 1916, and thus some of the most interesting material along the river relates to this river traffic.

If you are into the rapids, you might try to find and use an access closer to Grand Rapids and bypass much of the early flatwater. I know that some Fort McMurray paddlers have over the years both flown, or hired/caught a jet boat ride up the river for shorter trips through the rapids.

There is at least one good overnight's worth of paddling from Athabasca down to the Calling River access that just about any Novice River Paddler can handle at recommended flow levels. And there is at least one good access point that allows this to be turned into a most pleasant day run.

Paddling from the Calling River to Grand Rapids involves some whitewater. Pelican and Stony Rapids are the result of gradient increases and the river flowing through loose boulder bars. Generally these two rapids are not too challenging. Rapides du Joi Fou is reported to be voyageur's joke, and no problem at any water level.

Grand Rapids on the other hand is very serious. Over the years Grand Rapids has claimed the lives of numerous paddlers and other river folk who were unable to properly locate themselves, or so foolish as to try and run them. Virtually all paddlers portage the rapid on the right bank starting opposite the head of Grand Island. A few groups at the "right" water level have taken the old portage down Grand Island and then run the Little Grand Rapids from the bottom of the Island. Even finishing the longer portage on the right bank still requires that one runs a portion of the Little Grand Rapids. I still think that the cliffs at Grand Rapids are the best demonstration of boulder defoliation that I have ever seen. I have read recent reports that the boulders are concretions, and many have a core of fossilized wood in the centre. Some have described Grand Rapids as a boulder dam. My suspicion is that it is a combination of boulders and sandstone bedrock that the river is falling over and through. Some paddlers have lined and run the right channel around Grand Island, but this too is fraught with risks, and hard work! The portage is a rough haul but the better alternative for most of us.

The jaunt from Little Grande Rapids to Brule Rapids is fairly flat. Brule, Boiler, Middle and Long rapid are again largely the result of the interaction of the river with the Grand Rapids sandstone formation, and the most visible features are the sandstone boulders. Crooked Rapids marks the beginning of the interaction between the river and the next geological layer, a limestone formation. Thus Crooked, Little Cascade, Cascade and Mountain rapids involve the river falling over more defined ledges. At some higher water levels these are drowned out, but at most water levels there are significant ledges, some often nearly river wide, with very strong reversals. These too can be very dangerous and have claimed lives. Interestingly some paddlers have reported that the ledges are steepest on the inside of the corners. But rivers change, with water levels and over time and the only solid advice a canoe guide author can really provide is:
- know where the rapids should be, and where you are at all times.
- SCOUT – some of these are long rapids, measured in kilometers, and you must scout all the way to the bottom before committing.

In our Canoe Alberta trip of '72 we got tired of scouting ,so we often would just get out and start lining, thus in the end we only walked the rapid once, not down and back and down again. This though can get you into troubles at places like Crooked, Cascade and Mountain Rapids where the beaches turn into cliffs right at the water's edge at some water levels. I remember well our lifting of the canoes around the ledges of Cascade Rapid on river right, between the cliffs and the river "holes," an option that is not available at all water levels.

Other Reaches

Above the town of Athabasca the river makes a long loop to the north from Vega Ferry, through Smith and back to Athabasca. This whole reach of some 138 kilometers is pretty flat, and pretty much in one slow channel. It is not a trip I recommend to many. Below Fort McMurray the river grows in size, flattens and braids out, and until recently was maintained by the Canadian Government for commercial river traffic. Fort McMurray to Fort Chipewyan on Lake Athabasca is approximately 298 kilometers.

Jarvis Creek

Jarvis Lake Picnic site to
Gregg Lake campground

Why Go
Pleasant lake and creek paddling with scenic foothills vistas, great paddling for young and first time paddlers.

Jarvis Lake day use area, July 2002

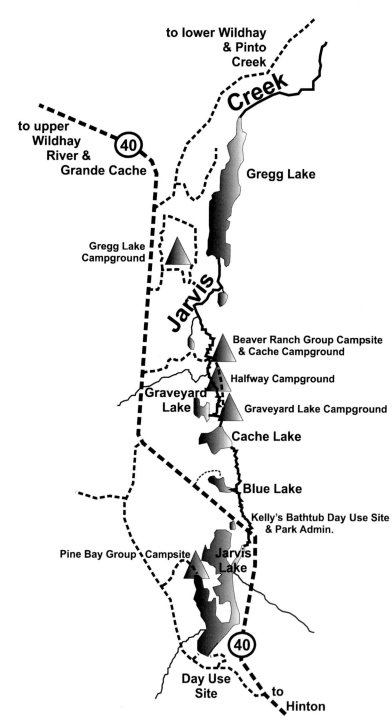

Duration of Tour(s)
* 13 km
* 1/2 day to one long day

Classification
1. Rapids: beaver dams
2. Skill of Paddlers: Novice Flatwater

Start
Start this trip at the Jarvis Lake Day Use Area at the south end of Jarvis Lake

Finish
The primary ending for this paddle is the Gregg Lake Campground & Day Use Area beach along the west shore of Gregg Lake. You may of course pull out at any of the intermediate road crossings or campgrounds.

-174-

Intermediate Access and Distances

Location	Km down	Km up	Km between	Access / Bank or Rapid / Class	MGRS datum
					NAD 1983 Zone 11U
Jarvis Lake Picnic Site	13.0	0.0			MV 468 222
entrance to creek	11.0	2.0		right/east shore	
Highway #40 culvert	9.8	3.2	3.2	use S culvert, portage across highway if water is too high	MV 477 250
Blue Lake	8.8	4.2			
Cache Lake	7.3	5.7			
entrance to creek	6.9	6.1			
Cache Lake campground	6.7	6.3	3.1		MV 470 275
channel to Graveyard Lake	6.6	6.4		left bank	
Winter Creek	5.5	7.5		left bank	
Campgrounds road bridge	4.8	8.2	1.9		MV 466 288
Gregg Lake	0.8	12.2			
Gregg Lake Campground	0.0	13.0	4.8	left/west shore	MV 466 316

Gradient
There must be some, but no contours lines are crossed on this run on my maps!

Stream Volume and Flow Rate
This is best done as an early to mid-summer run; it can get pretty dry later in some years. The reality is that for much of this run it is only possible if the beavers have been active and there are frequent, active dams. The Highway #40 Jarvis Creek crossing will give you a good sense of the creek level for the first half of this paddle.

Maps
1 - Use the Park Brochure and/or the two 1:50,000 NTS sheets below.
2 - NTS 1:50,000: 83 F/5 Entrance, 83 F/12 Gregg Lake

Camping
This trip is within William A. Switzer Provincial Park. There are a number of very nice campgrounds that one can use as a base to support this trip and all are on or very close to the water. NO random camping is allowed in the park. Gregg Lake Campground is the largest campground and has the most modern facilities. There are two group campsites (Beaver Ranch and Pine Bay) for group camping. All Park camping can be contacted at 780.865.5152.

Wildlife
Running the creek is a great way to introduce kids to fish, muskrats, beavers and kingfishers. Loons and grebes are likely to be spotted on the lakes and deer along the shore.

Trip Notes
The most commonly run section of this reach is from Jarvis Lake to Graveyard Lake Below Graveyard the creek can get shallow and some years can be pretty full of dead fall. Gregg Lake is the lake most likely to present wind problems in the park, but even it is pretty sheltered and really not very large.

on Jarvis Lake, July 2002

Wildhay River

Below Doctor Creek to above Jarvis Creek

Why Go
The Wildhay is a little river that offers one run of great whitewater for intermediate paddlers, runs for novice paddlers to learn on, and some fine scenic foothills tripping on other reaches.

Duration of Tour(s)
* 36 km
* ½ day to 2 days of tripping

Classification
1. Rapids: up to Class III-
2. Skill of Paddlers: Intermediate River Paddlers at most normal levels, great teaching river too!

Start
The Wildhay River is north of Hinton on Highway #40. After crossing the Wildhay River, continue on to the next intersection (4.1 km), and take the road west towards Rock Lake. Immediately after crossing Moberly Creek be sure to take the left turn at the "T." At the next intersection go straight through if going to the Wildhay Group Campsite, or turn right, to continue on to either Rock Lake or the upper former bridge site that is the start of this report. At the next intersection bear left and follow the dirt road to the river and the former bridge site.

Initial boulder garden on the start of the "Good Run" late June, 2003

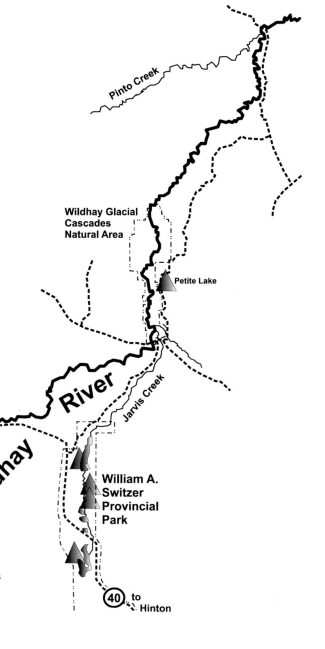

Finish

Access to the finish noted above is via the "Hay River Road." At the north end of W.A. Switzer Park take the "Hay River Road" east and north approximately 13 km to the intersection with Polecat Road, turn left and you will come to the bridge over "the Hay" within a few hundred metres.

Intermediate Access and Distances

Location	Elevation meters	Km down	Km up	Km between	Access / Bank or Rapid / Class	MGRS datum NAD 1927 Zone 11U	Gradient m/km
	1311		-2.4				
start of the "Good Run"		35.8	0.0		left bank	MK 315 284	
undercut cliff		34.4	1.4		right bank	MK 328 280	
	1280	32.8	3.0				5.7
Group Campsite		27.4	8.4	8	left bank	MK 371 305	
	1250	27.2	8.6				5.4
Moberly Creek		22.4	13.4		leftbank		
Highway #40		21.7	14.1				
access below bridge		21.6	14.2	6	left bank	MK 391 346	
	1219	20.4	15.4				4.6
old bridge piers above railway bridge		17.2	18.6		often bad log jams here	MK 425 356	
	1189	14.1	21.7				4.8
	1158	7.4	28.4				4.6
	1128	0.6	35.2				4.4
Polecat Rd. bridge		0.0	35.8	30	right bank	MK 527 418	

Gradient

Gradients are highest on the upper run reported on here, and easiest on the "day trip" below Highway #40.

River Volume and Flow Rate

Flows on the Wildhay taper off fairly quickly most years, with the best paddling in June and July. I really enjoy this run with flows of 15 to 20 cms. No Discharge-Velocity Relationship has been published. The gauging station is just below the group campsite.

Maps

1 - *Recreation and Activities: Hinton Forest Management Area* map produced by Hinton Wood Products. It is by far the best record of roads in the area and is usually available at the Tourist Information Office in Hinton in the upper town square.

2 - NTS 1:50,000: 83 E/9 Moberly Creek, 83 E/8 Rock Lake, 83 F/5 Entrance, and 83 F/12 Gregg lake (unfortunately the Wildhay flows back and forth across the corner of the first three sheets)

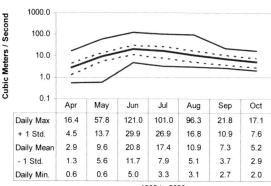

Wildhay River above Highway #40

	Apr	May	Jun	Jul	Aug	Sep	Oct
Daily Max	16.4	57.8	121.0	101.0	96.3	21.8	17.1
+ 1 Std.	4.5	13.7	29.9	26.9	16.8	10.9	7.6
Daily Mean	2.9	9.6	20.8	17.4	10.9	7.3	5.2
- 1 Std.	1.3	5.6	11.7	7.9	5.1	3.7	2.9
Daily Min.	0.6	0.6	5.0	3.3	3.1	2.7	2.0

1965 to 2003

Camping

There is a Provincial Forestry Group site on the river just above the first intermediate access point. This site can be booked at 780.865.2154. There are also public campgrounds on Rock Lake upstream and west of these reaches, and south of the river at Gregg Lake, off Highway #40. There is also much "random" camping in the area, particularly at the upper access point. There are also many good "wilderness" campsites along the river, on all three reaches reported on here.

Trip Notes

This is a fun little river. In my days as an instructor at the Blue Lake Centre I made over 70 runs on the "Good Run;" and I've added a good many more since then! Generally the 'Hay is not a powerful or fearsome river, but avoiding the rocks and headwalls does require good paddling skills.

The first reach is the most interesting. It starts with a little boulder garden, then a gentle kilometer or so, and then a number of tight fast turns. The first left turn leads into a severely undercut cliff, a right turn into a headwall, and then a right turn past the first ledge and surf site. The river eases off for a bit, then there is a boulder garden where the river bends left. At the following right bend is the largest ledge, stay right. Wherever this river braids out, or forms an island, be very watchful for logjams and sweepers. **Do not** enter any channel that you can not see a safe exit for.

The second run from the group site to Highway #40 is often the first run we take new river paddlers down, and the third run below Highway #40 (sometimes all the way from the group camp) makes for a very scenic day trip. We have often scared up a herd of elk in the meadows on this run, and we often enjoy an extended lunch in these same meadows. This run too has a couple of interesting chutes, but no really tricky rapids. Again the greatest danger lies in the logjams and sweepers that come and go with each major flood. As noted in the Access & Distance table there are often some complex and dangerous log jams upstream of, at and under the railway bridge.

Other Reaches

The Wildhay can be paddled from Rock Lake down. Exit Rock Lake on Rock Creek; it soon joins the river. In past years there were some good logjams on this first bit, necessitating a portage or two! It can make for a fine but very long day's paddle down to the group campsite. Below Jarvis Creek there is two to four days worth of tripping. The next available access is near Pinto Creek. The final egress in the past was at the Pine Creek Gas Plant Bridge on the Athabasca River, with the last dozen or so miles on the Berland River. It is a long dusty shuttle! In recent years both the "mill" and gas exploration in the area have added many new roads. A number of options may be available and the above mentioned *Recreation and Activities Map* from the mill operator is an essential requirement to find one's way through the new road network.

The undercut cliff, on the "Good Run"

Lakeland Provincial Park

Jackson, Kinnaird & Blackett Lakes Circuit

Why Go
This is a pleasant lake circuit, maybe Alberta's only lake circuit on relatively sheltered waters in our boreal forest.

Duration of Tour(s)
* 42 km
* 1 day trips are possible, 3 days minimum for the circuit and up to 5 days, or more if the fishing is good!

Classification
Novice Flatwater: this trip is on mostly sheltered lake water. The longest fetch is about 4 km east to west on Jackson Lake, and 4 north to south on Kinnaird Lake. Novice Flatwater Paddlers should be able to handle this lake, but do allow time in your schedule to be wind bound. I have reports that Jackson Lake is breezy most days, and suffers heavy winds on many. It is best to paddle the Jackson Lake reach either early or late in the day.

End of the portage - Fall 2001
photo by Mike Kuntz

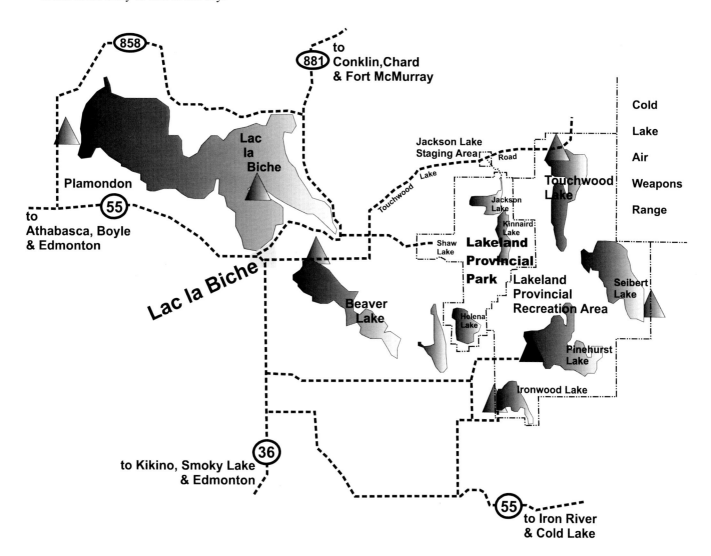

Jackson, Kinnaird & Blackett Lakes
Canoe Circuit

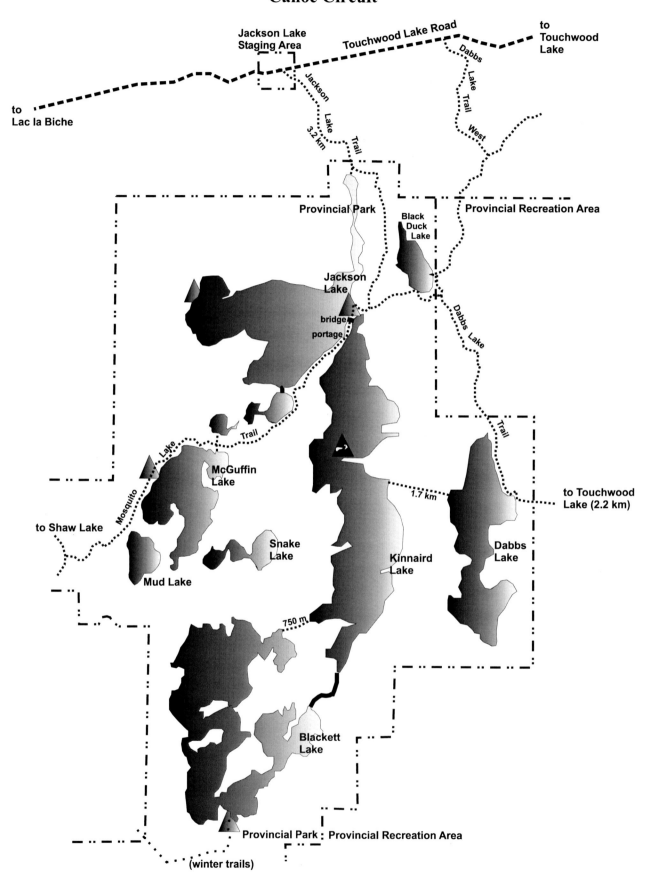

to
Lac la Biche

Jackson Lake
Staging Area

Touchwood Lake Road

to
Touchwood
Lake

Dabbs Lake Trail West

Jackson Lake Trail 3.2 km

Provincial Park

Provincial Recreation Area

Black Duck Lake

Jackson Lake

Dabbs Lake

bridge
portage

Trail

Mosquito Lake

to Shaw Lake

McGuffin Lake

Snake Lake

1.7 km

to Touchwood Lake (2.2 km)

Mud Lake

Kinnaird Lake

Dabbs Lake

750 m

Blackett Lake

Provincial Park : Provincial Recreation Area

(winter trails)

Start & Finish

This trip starts and finishes at the Jackson Lake Staging area approximately 35 km north-east of Lac la Biche on the Touchwood Lake road. It is 3.2 km portage to Jackson Lake. The park provides canoe carts (max. 270 kg load). I have reports that there are 13 or 14 carts available, but you can expect at least a few to have flat tires, and they may all be at the "other" end. Some parties have reported having to hike the whole 3.2 km to find a cart. And one couple who have made about a dozen trips on the circuit report it is best to take along a tire pump, and either rope or bungee cords to keep your canoe on the cart.

Intermediate Access and Distances

Location	Km down	Km up	Km between	MGRS datum
				NAD 1983 Zone 12 U
Jackson Lake Staging Area	42	0		VF 647791
Jackson Lake / N. arm	39	3		VF 664 770
Jackson Lake NE Bay	37	5		
Portage - very short	35	7		VF 661 732
Kinnaird Lake	35	7		
via west shore				
Kinnaird Island Campsite	33	10	10	VF 66 5709
Kinnaird Lake S arm	26	16		
Blackett Lake	25	17		
Blackett Lake Campsite	22	20	10	VF 637 625
return via Blackett/Kinnaird Portage				
Blackett Lk. Portage Start (750 m)	15	27		VF 648 667
Kinnaird Lake	15	28		VF 655 670
via east shore				
Portage	4	38		
Trailhead Jackson Lake	0	42	22	

Maps

1 - This trip is best supported by the *Lakeland Provincial Park & Provincial Recreation Area Back Country Map* which should be available from the Provincial Park office in Lac la Biche either by mail, or by dropping in during regular office hours (780.623.5235) Some Edmonton area map stores may have copies.
2 - NTS 1:250,000: 73 L Sand River (NAD 1983)
    NTS 1:50,000 (all NAD 1927)
        - 73 L/13 Lac la Bich, 73 L/12 Beaver Lake
            - all you need for Jackson to Blackett Lake
        - 73 L/14 Touchwood Lake, 73 L/11 Pinehurst Lake
            - are only necessary for the portage into, and paddling on Dabbs Lake

Camping

There are a number of public campsites in the area to support the staging of this trip. Probably my choice would be Sir Winston Churchill Provincial Park (780.623.4144) on the long point out into Lac la Biche. Others who have paddled this circuit regularly report that Touchwood is a nice camp to "stage" from.

Provincial Parks has established a number of campsites for canoeists on this circuit as noted below. I have a 2006 report that parks has established another 26 campsites in the park and is now discouraging random camping. In addition the use of stoves for cooking, and minimizing the use of open fires is encouraged. The original campsites on the circuit have bear poles, picnic tables and some form of a basic outhouse. The island campsite on Kinnaird Lake is very popular. My last report has it as very barren of firewood, and you must arrive early to claim one of the two campsites.

Wildlife

All of the common boreal wildlife species are present in Lakeland Provincial Park. Given the number of medium to large sized lakes in area, the fish eating winged predators (eagles, osprey, cormorants, loons and pelicans) are very likely to be spotted. The park has a wide variety of micro climates and in the spring all of the birds that commonly nest in the boreal forest may be seen. In addition I have reports that bear, moose and deer are commonly seen. My birding colleagues also suggest the park is very good for owl spotting. They also provided a report on a mouse-in-tent incident, which should be a reminder to all about not having food in one's tent. It could as easily have been a bear!

Trip Notes

My sources tell me that the carts generally require two paddlers to successfully push and pull them over the initial. In 2006 the trail in was reported to be in very good repair. One source suggests that trying to bypass the trail and paddle in on the creek is a very bad idea. It took at least ½ a bottle of wine to hear their full 6 hour horror story of trying to paddle the creek and drag their gear over dry beaver dams bigger than their house. Use the trail and the carts!

I would suggest that the biggest danger on this lake may be a westerly wind when trying to paddle down the east shore of Jackson Lake. If the water is up, you can paddle from Jackson into Kinnaird under the bridge that is north of the portage.

Given the drought of the past few years one can expect the N arm of Jackson Lake and the stream up to Blackett Lake to be shallow. The Park guide does note that there is at least one beaver dam near the outlet of Blackett that you must drag your canoe over or around.

Bridge and channel between Jackson Lake and Kinnaird Lake, Spring, 2004
photo by Mike Kuntz

A 2006 crew from Fort McMurray found that the beaver dam on the Blackett Lake channel was gone, but there was still enough water to paddle and float one's canoe from Blackett to Kinnaird Lake. This crew has also reported that the NE bay portage from Blackett back to Kinnaird Lake was spongy, and the board walk has sunk in places. And NO carts! This portage is about 750 m long.

As of August 2009 I have a report that the Dabbs Lake portage trail is overgrown and hard to find in places. This couple also reported small motor boats in the park and this they felt certainly reduced their wilderness experience.

Kinnaird Lake Island Campsite, mid-June, 2004
photo by Werner Groschel

Sand River

Highway #55 to confluence with the Beaver River

Why Go

This 22 kilometer paddle is a pleasant day trip with a modest amount of excitement for Novice and Intermediate River Paddlers This trip usually provides many opportunities for wildlife viewing.

Duration of Tour(s)

* 22 km
* 1 - 2 days

On the Sand River, August, 2001, at 30 cms.

Classification

1. Rapids: Class I to II+
2. Skill of Paddlers: Intermediate River Paddler or Novice River Paddlers with good leadership

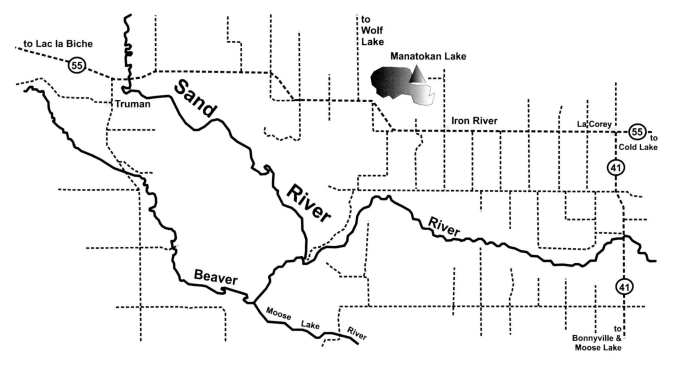

Start

The start for this run is at the Highway #55 Bridge just north and east of Truman, or west of Iron River.

Finish

The finish for this run is 3.2 km south of Iron River, 4.8 km west, and then another 5 km south and west on an unimproved (beware in wet weather) road down to the confluence of the Sand and Beaver Rivers.

Intermediate Access and Distances

Location	Elevation *meters*	Km down	Km up	Km between	Access / Bank or Rapid / Class	MGRS datum NAD 1927 Zone 12 U	Gradient m/km
	549		-9.4				
Highway #55		21.2	0.0		left bank	VR 880 352	
	541	18.2	3.0				0.6
	533	9.2	12.0				0.9
Beaver River		0.6	20.6		right bank		
End/Access		0.0	21.2	21	left bank	VR 980 253	

Gradient

This is a relatively flat paddle, with most of the rapids and riffles in the middle stretch.

River Volume and Flow Rate

The Sand River hydrology station is near the confluence, and reports data for the years 1967 to 2003. Best paddling seems to be from flows of 15 cms up to about 40 cms.

Maps

1 - NTS 1:50,000: 73 L/6 Goodridge (for the River) and 73 L/7 Bonnyville (for the shuttle)

Camping

There are a number of public campgrounds in the area, four on Moose Lake, and one north of Iron River. My favorite is Moose Lake Provincial Park (780.826.5358). I just love the jack pine, reindeer moss and sand dunes that dominate this park.

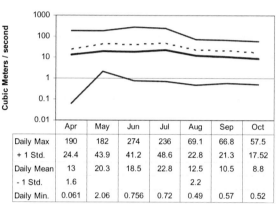

Sand River near the mouth

	Apr	May	Jun	Jul	Aug	Sep	Oct
Daily Max	190	182	274	236	69.1	66.8	57.5
+ 1 Std.	24.4	43.9	41.2	48.6	22.8	21.3	17.52
Daily Mean	13	20.3	18.5	22.8	12.5	10.5	8.8
- 1 Std.	1.6				2.2		
Daily Min.	0.061	2.06	0.756	0.72	0.49	0.57	0.52

1967 to 2003

For wilderness camping the west bank of the Sand River is still relatively wild, and the long series of sand dunes along the west bank makes for very poor farmland, but provides nice campsites. The banks do tend to be a bit overgrown so start your campsite search early.

Wildlife

Our memories are not only of a pleasant paddle on this reach, but of warm summer days with the bees buzzing through the multitudes of flowers, of us following a series of great blue herons down the river, of the occasional osprey stealing a fish from just in front of us and on our last run – of spotting a pair of otters playing along the bank.

Trip Notes

As I peruse old reports and the *Bedrock Topography* map that I have collected, I see that previous authors and map makers have reported as many as 13 rapids on this reach. None of these rapids are really significant, just easy boulder gardens and minor chutes. At some water levels these can be tricky to find the way through, and at high flows the water can be rough. But remember, it only takes one boulder to "wrap" a canoe. Yes, there are times that one must be awake on the Sand River. One spot to note is the old bridge piers that occur at about km 1.5. They can be tricky at some water levels.

Other Reaches

Past guides have encouraged paddlers to start as high as Wolf Lake on the Sand River system. I have received mixed reports of the paddle down the Wolf River, but logs and wading seem to be a common thread through most of them. Various reaches on the Beaver are also possible, though it is much like the Battle River, a "misfit" stream flowing, or rather lazily meandering, through an old glacial spillway. It can be a nice paddle at the right water levels, and if your goal is not great distance!

Cold Lake

Why Go
Cold Lake offers some of the longest sandy beaches in the province, deepest waters, finest lake trout fishing and many opportunities for great provincial park (Alberta & Saskatchewan) and wilderness camping.

Duration of Tour(s)
* 102 km
* 3-5 days

Classification
1. Lake water - BIG lake water
2. Skill of Paddlers: Skilled Flatwater Paddlers, experienced in rough lakewater!

Beach just north of the Medley River mouth

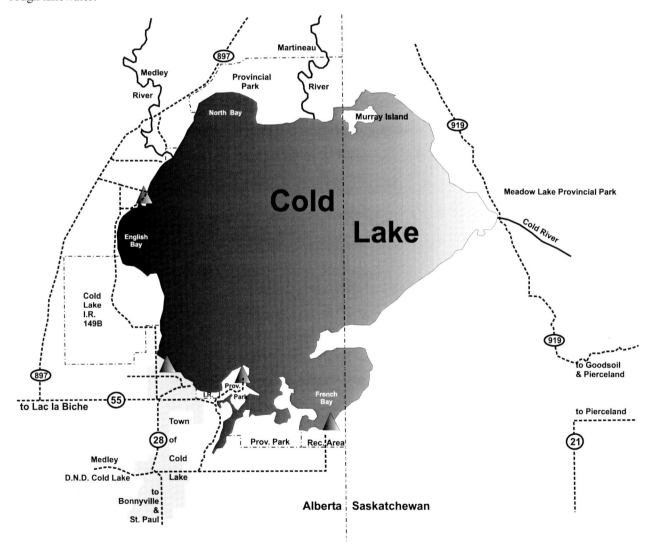

Start & Finish
For the start and finish of this report I have used the municipal campground on the north edge of the town of Cold Lake.

Intermediate Access and Distances

Location	Km down	Km up	Km between	Access Comments	MGRS datum
					NAD 1927 Zone 12U
Start - Municipal Campground	102	0			WR 520 365
South Point - English Bay	95	7			
English Bay Campground	87	15	15	boat launch	WR 506 478
Medley River - mouth	83	19	4		WR 526 509
North Bay	77	25			
Martineau River - mouth	70	32	13		WR 623 532
NW point - Murray Island	67	35			WR 641 538
Alberta/Saskatchewan Boundary	67	35			
Cold River - outlet	51	51	19		WR 748 468
Saskatchewan/Alberta Boundary	38	64			
French Bay - east point	33	69			
French Bay	23	79	28		WR 630 323
Cold Lake Prov. Pk. Boat launch	8	94	15	boat launch	WR 578 360
Prov. Park Picnic Site	4	98			
Marina - downtown Cold Lake	2	100		boat launch	
Municpal Campground	0	102	8		

Maps

1 - NTS 1:50,000   73 L/08 - Cold Lake   73 L /09 - Marie Lake

73 K/05 - Pierceland   73 K/12 - Cold River

Camping

For those who prefer to "car camp" there are many choices around Cold Lake: the municipal campground (780.639.4121) on the north fringe of the town of Cold Lake, English Bay to the north of town, the Provincial Park and French Bay Recreation Area to the south of the town (are all available at 780.594.7856), and over on the Saskatchewan side camping is allowed on the east shore of the lake in Meadow Lake Provincial Park (306.236.7680).

Much of the lake shore along the north and east sides is available for random/wilderness camping. Beware - the Alberta side of Murray Island is designate a provincial natural area, with a day use area, but no designated camping area. My Cold Lake friends also tell me that the 6-7 km of shore north and west of the Cold River outlet is very swampy, and offers no dry camping options.

Wildlife

Cold Lake is still renowned for its fishing and for the feathered predators: bald and golden eagles, osprey, kingfishers, western grebes and great blue herons. One should not be surprised to see moose and bear. Fish stocks in the lake as of the 2006 were still strong enough to support a limited catch (rather than catch and release) on lake trout, walleye, pike, perch, burbot and lake whitefish.

Trip Notes

I've paddled a number of times on and around Cold Lake. Some five years ago our good friends were kind enough to include young Hans on a circumnavigation of the lake. But – they did resort to small motors on their boats and Hans only recollects one night out on the lake. I say; I've paddled "around" Cold Lake, because more than once we've been in the area with intentions to paddle on the lake and have chosen not to do so due to conditions. Cold Lake is over 25 km across on both the axes south to north, and west to east – IT DOES "blow up!" If you plan to paddle and trip on the lake, you must be experienced with rough water, landing in surf, and prepared to be "wind bound!"

Other Reaches

On at least two of the breezy occasions we have taken the day and paddled on the "T" shaped lagoon on the south side of the Provincial Park campground, near town.

Cold River

Cold Lake to Pierce Lake

Why Go
This is a great little whitewater run and well worth the effort if in the area. If one is in Meadow Lake Provincial Park for a paddling holiday, this is the "icing-on-the-cake".

Duration of Tour(s)
* 14.7 km
* ½ to 1 day

An easier riffle, early August, 1981

Classification
1. Rapids: Class I to III
2. Skill of Paddlers: Intermediate Whitewater Paddlers

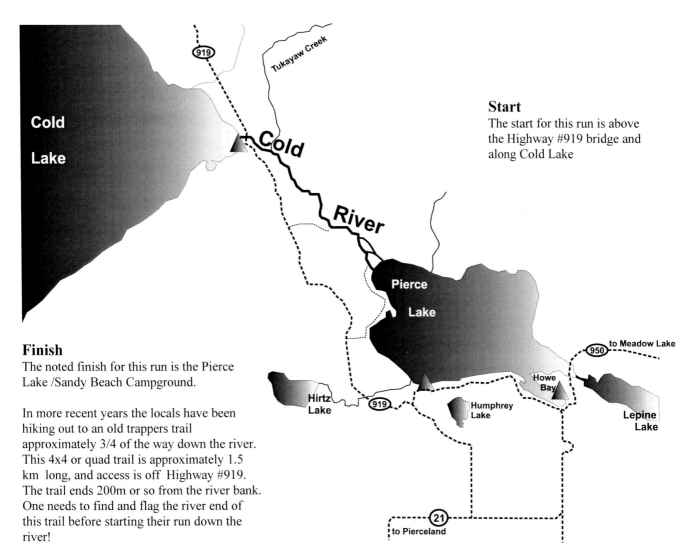

Start
The start for this run is above the Highway #919 bridge and along Cold Lake

Finish
The noted finish for this run is the Pierce Lake /Sandy Beach Campground.

In more recent years the locals have been hiking out to an old trappers trail approximately 3/4 of the way down the river. This 4x4 or quad trail is approximately 1.5 km long, and access is off Highway #919. The trail ends 200m or so from the river bank. One needs to find and flag the river end of this trail before starting their run down the river!

Intermediate Access and Distances

Location	Elevation	Km down	Km up	Km between	Access / Bank or Rapid / Class	MGRS datum	Gradient m/km
	meters					NAD 1927 Zone 12U	
Cold Lake/river outlet	534	14.7	0.0		Left bank	WR 748 468	
	533	13.3	1.4				0.7
	518	10.3	4.4				5.0
Pierce Lake/river inlet	508	6.6	8.1	8.1		WR 798 420	2.7
Sandy Beach Campground		0.0	14.7	6.6		WR 816 379	

Gradient

As the gradient numbers above report, the best part (highest gradient, best whitewater) of this run is the middle section!

River Volume and Flow Rate

This river is best paddled at flows between about 15 and 45 cms. High flows on this river are well known for swamping open canoes, and the submerged boulders for "wrapped" canoes!

Maps

1 - NTS 1:50,000: 73 K/12 Cold River, 73 K/5 Pierceland

Camping

This trip is all within Meadow Lake Provincial Park (306. 236.7680), and there are park campgrounds at both ends of this run, at Cold Lake near the outlet and on the south shore of Pierce Lake.

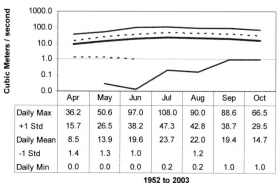

Cold River at outlet of Cold Lake

	Apr	May	Jun	Jul	Aug	Sep	Oct
Daily Max	36.2	50.6	97.0	108.0	90.0	88.6	66.5
+1 Std	15.7	26.5	38.2	47.3	42.8	38.7	29.5
Daily Mean	8.5	13.9	19.6	23.7	22.0	19.4	14.7
-1 Std	1.4	1.3	1.0		1.2		
Daily Min	0.0	0.0	0.0	0.2	0.2	1.0	1.0

1952 to 2003

Wildlife

Meadow Lake Provincial Park is on the boundary between the parkland and farmlands to the south and the great Canadian Shield and boreal forest to the north. Thus it is home to wide variety of wildlife. One of my more memorable experiences is paddling out onto Pierce Lake after a most exhilarating whitewater paddle, and then drifting in the sun and watching a pair of immature (teenage) bald eagles practice their fishing skills along the lake in front of us.

Trip Notes

As noted above this is primarily a run for Intermediate or better whitewater paddlers. The rapids are continuous for long stretches. The risks of swamping and boulder bashing are cumulative. Paddlers must be able to make quick decisions and be able to slow the canoe for the waves, while side-slipping through the boulders.

Other Reaches

This is the primary whitewater run in Meadow Lake Provincial Park The other runs further down on the Waterhen River (really the continuation of the Cold River) tend to be flat, pleasant runs with some great birding opportunities.

Other Local Activities or Destinations

My past trips to Meadow Lake park have been "all toy" excursions. This has meant sail boards, fishing tackle, hiking boots and all car camping supplies have been taken for multi-day stays. The lakes are well know for both their fishing, and great sandy beaches. In the Ceyana Canoe Club we have often thought of Meadow Lake Provincial Park as the Jasper Park east alternative vacation destination. Jasper and Meadow Lake are both four hours driving from Edmonton.

Christina River

Chard to Fort McMurray

Duration of Tour(s)
* 209 km
* 4-7 days

Classification
1. Rapids: Class I to III
2. Skill of Paddlers: Skilled River Paddlers

Camp above Christina Crossing, June 1990

Start
The start of this run is at the Chard access road bridge off Highway #881.

Finish
The finish of this run is in downtown Fort McMurray, on "the Snye", off main street, at the Jean Family Boat Launch

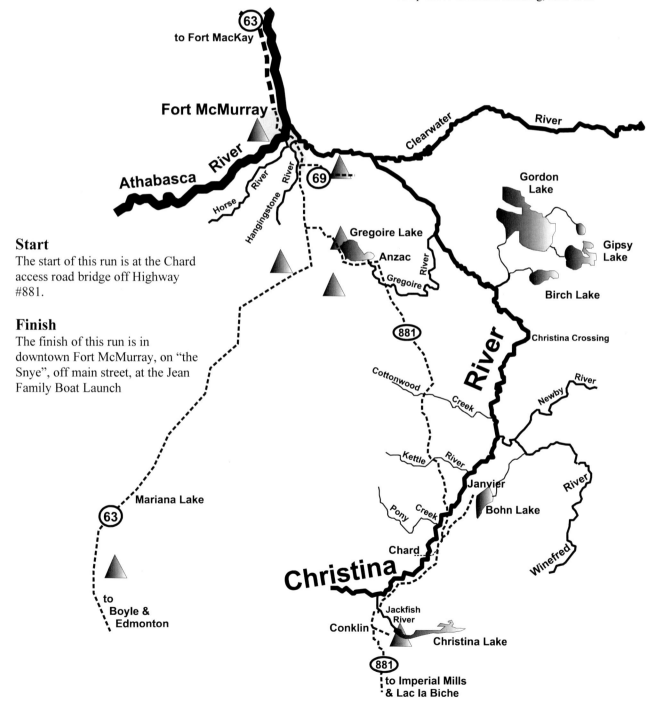

Intermediate Access and Distances

Location	Elevation meters	Km down	Km up	Km between	Access / Bank or Rapid / Class	MGRS datum NAD 1983 Zone 12 U	Gradient m/km
	457		0				
TwnshpRd 792a / Chard Bridge		209	0		right bank	WG 082 879	
Pony Creek		205	4		left bank		
Highway 881 Bridge		196	13	13		WG 117 924	
	450	187	22				0.3
Kettle River		175	35		left bank		
	442	171	38				0.5
						Zone 12 V	
Winefred River		149	60		right bank		
Cottonwood Creek		144	65		left bank		
	440	134	75				0.1
Christina Crossing		112	97				
	430	108	101				0.4
	420	99	110				1.1
	410	95	114				2.5
Gordon River		90	119		right bank		
	400	88	121				1.4
	390	79	130				1.1
	380	75	134				2.5
	370	68	141				1.4
	360	65	144				3.3
	350	63	146				5.0
Gregoire River		61	148		left bank		
	340	61	148				5.0
	330	59	150				5.0
	320	58	151				10.0
	310	55	154				3.3
	300	51	158				2.5
	290	47	162				2.5
	280	43	166				2.5
	270	39	170				2.5
	260	35	174				2.5
	250	30	179				2.0
Clearwater River		29	180		right bank		
Saprae Creek		16	193		left bank		
The Snye		1	208		left bank		
Fort McMurray / Main St.		0	209	196	left bank	VH 770 876	

Gradient

This trip is flat, damn exciting, and then flat again. I'm not sure if the gradient really reaches the noted 10m/km above, but the increases in gradient above certainly do correlate with my recollections, and the rapids as noted on the 1:50,000 and 1:250,000 sheets. These sheets do NOT note ALL the rapids.

River Volume and Flow Rate

In June 1990 we paddled the Christina with the river falling from 65 cms on our first day out. Three days earlier the river had been another 10 cms higher, which I believe would have translated into fearsome water in the canyon above and below the Gregoire river. At the level we had, most of the finer features of the rapids were washed out. We did have some multi-kilometer, fun stretches of continuous Class II+ to III water. I would suggest that good paddling occurs with the water flow between 20 and 60 cms as reported at the Chard station.

The graph and table to the right demonstrate one problem of using standard deviation to define mid range flows. The skew is such on the distribution of flows for some days and months on the Christina that minus one standard deviation is less than the minimal flows ever reported! Thus I have removed these calculations to develop this graph.

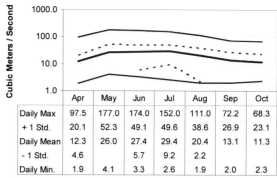

Christina River near Chard

	Apr	May	Jun	Jul	Aug	Sep	Oct
Daily Max	97.5	177.0	174.0	152.0	111.0	72.2	68.3
+ 1 Std.	20.1	52.3	49.1	49.6	38.6	26.9	23.1
Daily Mean	12.3	26.0	27.4	29.4	20.4	13.1	11.3
- 1 Std.	4.6		5.7	9.2	2.2		
Daily Min.	1.9	4.1	3.3	2.6	1.9	2.0	2.3

1982 to 2003

Maps

1 - I see from my trip log that I carried both 1:50,000, 1:250,000 sheets for this run, and air photos for the expected difficult sections! Given my notes I would suggest that most folks will find it adequate to carry just the 1:250,000 sheets on the river, and the *Alberta Road Map* for getting to the start. At least one of the 1:50,000 sheets is still a monochrome sheet!

2 - NTS 1:250,000   73 M Winefred Lake   74 D Waterways
    NTS 1:50,000   73 M/15 Bohn Lake   74 D/2 Quigley   74 D/1 Watchusk Lake
    74 D/8 Gipsy Lake   74 D/7 Cheecham   74 D/10 Hollies Creek (mono.)
    74 D/11 Fort McMurray

*note that the 1:250,000 sheets are all based on NAD 1983, and the 1:50,000 sheets (except 74D/11) on NAD 1927.

Camping

This trip is all "random" camping. On our 1990 trip we camped on the pipeline that parrallels the road into Chard by the bridge, and then camped on the river as we found sites. Given the high water you will note in the picture above (pg. 189) that at least once we were confined to a pretty narrow bank side camp. As the trip progressed and the water dropped, we were able to find some good river side camping on the "point bars." On the Clearwater River we found a very nice limestone outcropping, about 2 hrs out of Waterways for our last camp.

Wildlife

As I read through my trip notes I see that we had many wildlife encounters, bears in the river, many moose, deer and eagles. I have three vivid memories of this trip. First we were asked to keep an eye out for peregrine falcons nesting on the canyon reach near the Gregoire River. The whitewater kept us so busy, we reached the bottom the canyon, and then remembered what we were supposed to be looking for. Second, on the first two days the river banks were all just a blanket of wild roses and other sweetly-scented flowers. My third memory is of the bird life; mid June is still mating season and the woods were just alive with bird song.

Trip Notes

One can avoid some of the flat water paddling by putting in at the Highway #881 bridge, or even more by requesting access permission through the Janvier Reserve (Chipewayn Prairie Band).

The river flows gently, and meanders for the whole run from the Chard bridge through to Christina Crossing. After the crossing it begins to pick-up and the first riffles are reached around the Gordon River. Towards the Gregoire River every bend has some sort of rapid. At 50+ cms they are mostly standing waves, but other paddlers have reported some complex ledges and large boulder bar rapids (up to Class III+). Given that the Christina is falling through the same geological formations that give us the Grand and Cascade Rapids on the Athabasca River to the west, and Whitemud Falls and the rapids of the Clearwater river to the N.E., ledges and sandstone boulder bar rapids should be expected. At most water levels you can expect to line, and maybe even carry your boat for some short stretches.

We camped on a point bar a bend or two above the Gregoire River and I remember that last couple of good hours into camp involved much scouting, eddy to eddy, and whitewater. Similarly the first hour or so out of the camp also involved some long stretches of whitewater.

Other Reaches
The run from the Jackfish River to the Chard bridge has been done and there are reports of Class II (to III?) rapids in the middle section, their existence is supported by the 1:50,000 top sheets, and recent reports from the Tar Sands Canoe Club.

Bottom of one of the rapids below the Gregoire River, June, 1990

Clearwater River

Warner Rapids (Highway #955 Bridge), Saskatchewan
to Fort McMurray, Alberta

Whitemud Falls from the Air
courtesy of the Alberta Government

Why Go
History, extended wilderness tripping, whitewater, portages, waterfalls, scenery and wildlife!

Duration of Tour(s)
* 216 km
* 7 to 10 days

Classification
1. Rapids: Class I to VI & Falls
2. Skill of Paddlers: Skilled River Paddlers, with good wilderness camping and navigation skills. This run includes at least four major waterfalls, a minimum of 7 portages and up to 13 for those with less than adequate whitewater skills.

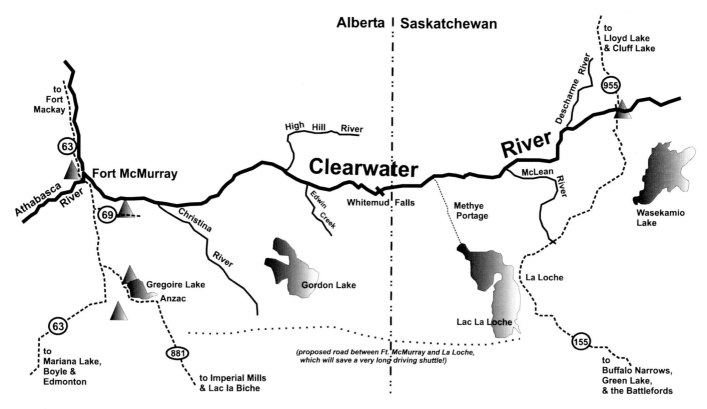

Start
The proposed start for this run is at the Warner Rapids Bridge on Highway #955 north and east of La Loche, Saskatchewan.

Finish
The suggested finish for this run is on "the Snye" in Fort McMurray, just north of downtown on Main street, at the Jean Family Boat Launch.

Intermediate Access and Distances

Location	Elevation meters	Km down	Km up	Access / Bank or Rapid / Class	MGRS datum NAD 1927 Zone 12 U	Gradient m/km
Highway #955		216	0	right bank	XU 230 076	
Warner Rapids		216	0	Class III - III+ / may start right under #955 bridge	XU 209 070	
	390	200	16			
Descharme River		198	18	right bank	XU 088 029	
Gould Rapids / Portage		189	28	Class III - IV	066 953	
Smooth Rock Falls / Portage					057 930	
	380	186	30			0.7
	370	186	30			33.3
	360	181	35			2.3
Skull Canyon / Waterfall / Portage					985 931	
	350	178	38			2.6
	340	173	43			2.3
Simonson Rapids		172	44	Class II - III, very long up to 5 km	WT 941 913	
McLean River / Contact Rapids		167	49	Class III - V	WT 925 893 922 887	
	330	165	51			1.3
	320	165	51			7.0
Methye Portage NO camping allowed at portage terminus		132	84	left bank	696 865	
	310	132	84			0.3
Ab/Sask Border		117	99		609 846	
Flower Pot Island					575 836	
Whitemud Falls / Portage		111	105		WT 574 834	
	300	111	105			0.5
	290	107	109			2.5
Pas rapid		107	109			
Pine rapids / portage		106	110	Class III - III+	WT 537 851	
Gros Roche Rapid		101	115	Class II - II+	487 859	
	280	100	116			1.4
Le Bon Rapid / Portage		98	118	Class II - III	474 848	
Cascade Rapid / Portage		95	121	Class III - III+	446 843	
	270	95	121			2.0
Edwin Creek		89	127	left bank		
High Hill River		78	138	right bank		
	260	61	155			0.3
Hollies Creek		39	177	right bank		
	250	30	186			0.3
Christina River		29	187	left bank	VT 960 804	
The Snye		0	216	left bank		
Main St., Ft. McMurray		0	216	left bank	VT 770 874	

Gradient

As you can see from the above table, gradients vary – and I believe on this stream high gradients do reflect the waterfalls and rapids. BUT, the correlation is not perfect and as always paddlers must be alert and always looking downstream for the next episode of excitement.

River Volume and Flow Rate

As I prepare this report and look at these hydrographs, both to the right and on the Alberta Environment web site I am amazed at how stable the late summer flows are relative to the eastern slope streams I am far more familiar with. This river promises good paddling well into fall most years. Good paddling should be had in the range of 70 to 150 cms as reported by this station. Archer (2003) reports that float plane charters are reluctant to pick-up on the river below Cascade Rapids with less than 60 cms of flow.

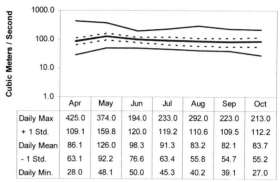

Clearwater River above Christina River

	Apr	May	Jun	Jul	Aug	Sep	Oct
Daily Max	425.0	374.0	194.0	233.0	292.0	223.0	213.0
+ 1 Std.	109.1	159.8	120.0	119.2	110.6	109.5	112.2
Daily Mean	86.1	126.0	98.3	91.3	83.2	82.1	83.7
- 1 Std.	63.1	92.2	76.6	63.4	55.8	54.7	55.2
Daily Min.	28.0	48.1	50.0	45.3	40.2	39.1	27.0

1966 to 2003

Maps and Guidebooks

1 - I believe given the number of waterfalls, portages and hazards on this river one would should carry a full set of NTS 1:50,000 sheets for this run, as listed below. I would also VERY STRONGLY recommend that groups take along either:

Saskatchewan Canoe Trips #40: Warner Rapids to Fort McMurray guidebook, available from the Saskatchewan Department of Tourism & Renewable Resources, available on line at: www.se.gov.sk.ca/saskparks/canoe/ or,

Archer, L. (2003) *Northern Saskatchewan Canoe Trips: a guide to fifteen wilderness rivers.* Erin, Ontario. Boston Mills Press (I find this book easier to read and follow than the government report above!)

2 - NTS 1:50,000
    74 C/11 McLean River   74 C/12 Wallis Bay
    74 C/14 Tocker Lake   74 C/15 Mackie Rapids
    74 D/9 Bunting Bay   74 D/10 Hollies Creek
    74 D/11 Fort McMurray   74 D/15 (no tittle)
        * all of these sheets EXCEPT 74 D/11 use NAD 1927

Camping

This run is noted for it's great wilderness camping on the Saskatchewan side. Once below the rapids in Alberta campsites can be a bit hard to find, especially at high water. In the 1980's the Alberta Forest Service established campsites at: Whitemud Falls, Cascade Portage, Engstrom, Miseieutin, Greentree, and at the Christina River. My understanding is that this sites have not been well maintained.

Wildlife

This run has a great reputation as a trip for viewing wildlife. Over the course of this trip you have a very good chance of seeing all of the common mammals and birds of the boreal forest. This river is supports a highly reputed sport fishery for arctic grayling, mountain whitefish, walleye, pike, burbot and goldeye. Remember you will need both Saskatchewan and Alberta fishing licenses!

Trip Notes

I have NOT made this run – it is on my list of "to dos." This report is based on previous guides and reviews by paddlers who have been down the river recently.

As noted above this is a river for skilled paddlers and outdoors folks. You must be 100% confident in your map reading and navigational skills, and especially your river reading skills; I would not depend upon a GPS!

I have limited my trip notes to these few comments and would again very strongly recommend that any one contemplating this run acquire the one of the above recommended Saskatchewan river guides. It would also be useful to go over a set of maps with someone who has been down the river. Within the major canoe clubs in Edmonton and Calgary there are such folks who will share their knowledge, though it may cost you a good bottle of wine!

Other Reaches

For those with more time the Clearwater is often run from Lloyd Lake down to Warner Rapids. This is a trip of up to 147 kilometers depending on how and where you choose to access the river. This reach is also in the Canadian sheild and offers a mix of rapids, waterfalls and required portages.

Rentals & Shuttles

All of the Saskatchewan materials strongly recommend that folks who access the river by vehicle, make arrangements with the taxi service in La Loche for secure vehicle storage and shuttle return to the river. Once your trip is completed you can then fly back to La Loche and make the long drive just once, or as I have often contemplated, drop your crew off at the Warner Rapids Campground, drive to McMurray and fly back to La Loche, and catch a cab up to the river.

For the reach below Whitemud Falls there are jet boat outfitters who will either shuttle paddlers up the river, or pick-up paddlers for a quick trip home.

Flying in to Saskatchewan and landing on much of this reach is NOT an option as the river is closed to non-emergency landings. I have some reports that float plane pick-ups are allowed for a short stretch of river, a short distance below the Methye Portage terminus.

Voyage Air 780.743.0255

McMurray Aviation 780.791.2182

Smoky River

Bezanson (Highway #43) to
the Town of Peace River

Why Go
This is a wilderness canoe trip that is relatively close to
Alberta's population centres.

Duration of Tour(s)
* 194 km
* 2 - 6 days

lower Smoky River, late July 2000

Classification
1. Rapids: Class I to II+
2. Skill of Paddlers: Intermediate River, or Novice River at low water with
good leadership.

Start
The start for this run is just below the Highway #43 bridge east of
Bezanson.

Finish
The finish for this run is at the
downtown dock in Peace
River, east side of the river,
and near the
memorial to
12 Foot Davis
and the
Rowing &
Sailing Club.
An alternative finish is
available across the river,
nearer the Lion's
Campground.

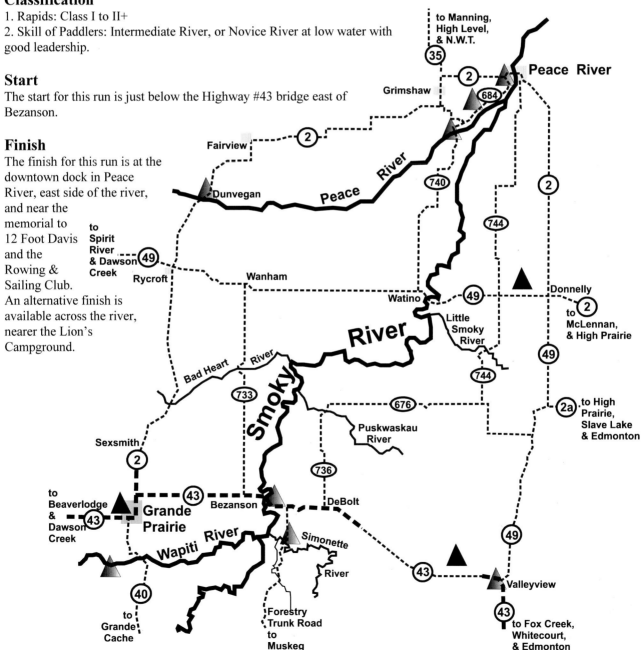

Intermediate Access and Distances

Location	Elevation	Km down	Km up	Km between	Access / Bank or Rapid / Class	MGRS datum	Gradient m/km
	meters					NAD 1983 Zone 11U	
	472		-3				
below #43 bridge		194	0		right bank	MB 200 218	
	457	176	18				0.7
	442	157	37				0.8
Pukwaskau River		153	41		right bank		
Bad Heart River		144	51		left bank		
	427	137	57				0.8
	419	125	69				0.7
	411	120	74				1.6
	404	111	83				0.8
	396	99	95				0.7
	389	90	104				0.8
Confluence with Little Smoky		87	107		right bank		
	381	81	113				0.9
Watino / Highway #49 Bridge		75	119	119	right bank for access	MB 607 745	
abandoned RR bridge		73	121				
	373	71	123				0.8
	366	60	134				0.6
	351	48	146				1.3
	335	33	161				1.1
	320	12	182				0.7
						Zone 11V	
Peace River - town dock			194	75	right bank	MC 816 321	

Gradient

Calculated "average gradients" for this run vary from as little as .6 m/km, to 1.6 m/km.

River Volume and Flow Rate

The Smoky is a big river and as I look at the table to the right it is very apparent how the spring and summer snow and icefield melt in the mountains and foothills of the upper Smoky watershed contribute to the overall flow of this river. As I write this report I have just checked back on the flows we experienced in late July 2000, and I see that at Watino, for the three days we were on the Smoky, the flows dropped from 658 to 515 cms. These were low flows and yet we had lots of water. Earlier reports on this run of the Smoky report that it is a powerful dangerous river at high normal, and above normal flows. This again is a run best left for mid to late summer, or even fall. I would suggest that the best paddling on this river would be with flows in the 300 to 1000 cms range.

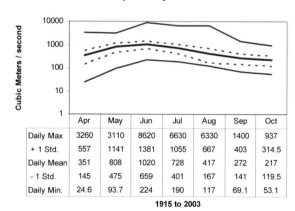

Smoky River ay Watino

	Apr	May	Jun	Jul	Aug	Sep	Oct
Daily Max	3260	3110	8620	6630	6330	1400	937
+ 1 Std.	557	1141	1381	1055	667	403	314.5
Daily Mean	351	808	1020	728	417	272	217
- 1 Std.	145	475	659	401	167	141	119.5
Daily Min.	24.6	93.7	224	190	117	69.1	53.1

1915 to 2003

Maps

1 - This is a big river and unless you are using an access not listed in this guide, you should be able to safely navigate this river with the following three NTS 1:250,000 sheets, and the *Alberta Road Map*.

NTS 1:250,000: 83 M Grande Prairie, 83 N Winagami, 84 C Peace River

Camping

Again the camping is best after the high flows of early summer, once the mud has had some time to dry. Wilderness or random camping is available all along this trip. There are some farms on the river benches, especially on the first half of this run and in the Watino area, and it is appropriate to hike up and ask permission to camp if you've chosen a site near a farmyard.

Wildlife

You should expect bears, moose and deer at any point on the run, and the high valley walls provide great soaring for the large hawks and eagles common to this area. It is a big river and your chances for spotting wildlife will be enhanced if you spend time drifting closer to one shore, instead of "hammering" down the middle!

Trip Notes

As I look back at other reports for this reach, and my own experience on this river below the Little Smoky confluence, the rapids of note appear to be below Watino. Around the first bend below the #49 Highway Bridge is an abandoned railway bridge, and not far below on the first right bend there is, at medium to low waters, a modest Class II rapid. Then 4 km or so further along on the left bend is another Class II rapid, and again approximately four more kilometers on the next left bend there is a more significant rapid. At our July 2000 flows some very large boulders, or bedrock remnants were exposed providing for us the most exciting water of our trip. My notes of July 2000 suggest there were at least two or three more easy Class II rapids that involved infrequent boulders and some pressure waves.

One highlight for us on this trip was a grand evening spent a few short kilometers above the confluence with the Peace. We camped on the sand bars and in the early evening crossed the river and hiked up on the ridge that separates the Peace from the Smoky. As the sun began to set we had a glorious view of the two river valleys, upstream and down, including in the distance the town of Peace River.

Other Reaches

The Smoky is a great paddlers' river and has been paddled (with some notable portages) all the way from Adolphus Lake in the shadows of Mount Robson to its confluence with the Peace. Grande Cache to Bezanson (approx. 210 km) is a notable wilderness paddle and includes some major rapids. These rapids rate up to Class IV+, and are primarily on the stretch from upstream of the Kakwa confluence through to and below the confluence with the Cutbank River.

Shuttles

As noted on all of these Peace River basin reports, I have had good service from Peace River Taxi (780.624.3020) If paddling this whole reach I would be tempted to check the scheduled bus (www.greyhound.ca/) options.

Note the mid-stream boulders, this is about 13 km below the abandoned RR bridge.

Bottom of the biggest rapid below Watino, late July, 2000.

Little Smoky River

Guy (Highway #49) to Watino (Highway #49)

Why Go
Like the big Smoky to the west this is another wilderness canoe trip that is easily accessible to Alberta's population centres. The Little Smoky is a smaller stream and at most flows less intimidating than the big Smoky.

Duration of Tour(s)
* 72 km
* 1 to 3 days (can easily be combined with the big Smoky and make for a four or five day paddle down to Peace River)

Classification
1. Rapids: Class I to II
2. Skill of Paddlers: Intermediate River

Camp along the River, July 2000

Start
The start for this run is about 500 m below the Highway #49 bridge, accessed through the old campsite on the north side of the bridge.

Finish
The finish for this run is at the former Watino Provincial Recreation Area, off Highway #49 on the south bank of the Smoky River, across the river from the hamlet of Watino.

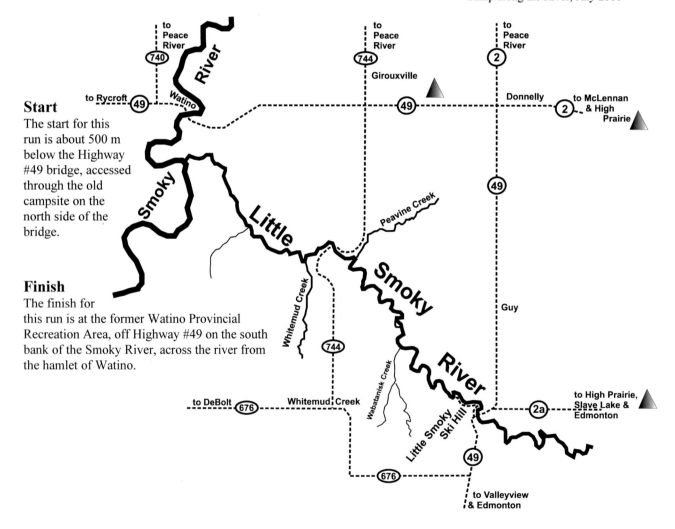

Intermediate Access and Distances

Location	Elevation meters	Km down	Km up	Km between	Access / Bank or Rapid / Class	MGRS datum NAD 1927 Zone 11U	Gradient m/km
	488		-7				
below Highway #49		72	0		right bank	MM 899 455	
	472	55	12				1.1
	466	52	15				1.9
Wabatanisk Creek		50	17				
	457	48	19				2.6
	450	46	21				2.5
	442	43	24				3.2
gradient suspect	434	42	25				7.3
	427	37	30				1.5
Peavine Creek		34	33		right bank		
Highway #744 Bridge		31	36	31	right bank	MM 755 615	
	419	31	36				1.2
Whitemud Creek		27	40		left bank		
	411	25	42				
	404	18	49				1.0
	396	14	53				2.0
	389	9	58				1.5
confluence with Smoky River		7	60		left bank	MM 606 697	
	381	1	66				1.0
#49 Bridge at Watino		0	72	36	right bank	MM 608 743	
overall mean gradient							1.4

Gradient
I am suspect of some of the gradient calculations above, both from the *Topo Canada* and my study of the actual NTS sheets. Yes, the section above Peavine Creek is a little faster, and could be the most exciting stretch with medium to high water, but there is NO stretch that runs at 7.3 m/km!

River Volume and Flow Rate
We paddled this run in late July with approximately 45 to 60 cms of water and found this provided a good paddle, with modest current and no "scary bits." This is on the low end of normal for this run and it could be considerably more difficult (logjams, sweepers, and standing waves) with lots of water. I would suggest that good paddling occurs with between 50 and 150 cms

Maps
1 - There are not many map option for this run and I'd not leave home without the *Alberta Road Map* and the following three topo's.

NTS 1:50,000:   83 N/6 Whitemud Creek,   83 N/11 Donnelly,   83 N/12 Watino

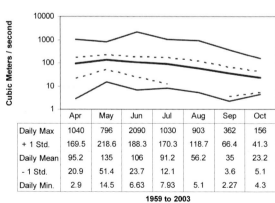

Little Smoky River near Guy

	Apr	May	Jun	Jul	Aug	Sep	Oct
Daily Max	1040	796	2090	1030	903	362	156
+ 1 Std.	169.5	218.6	188.3	170.3	118.7	66.4	41.3
Daily Mean	95.2	135	106	91.2	56.2	35	23.2
- 1 Std.	20.9	51.4	23.7	12.1		3.6	5.1
Daily Min.	2.9	14.5	6.63	7.93	5.1	2.27	4.3

1959 to 2003

Camping

This is a fine run for wilderness camping. There is some farm land, at least one grazing reserve, and even one short stretch with cottages, but for the most part this is wilderness and random campsites are reasonably frequent. As always high water limits the camping options.

Wildlife

In July 2000 we thought we had hit the wildlife bonanza – in the first hour we spotted a number of deer, a herd of elk, a couple of eagles, kingfishers, Canada geese and other bird life. After the first hour our spotting rate dropped back to more normal for this kind of country. Bears should be expected!

Trip Notes

In late July 2000 we paddled this run plus continued through to Peace River on the big Smoky River. We were two nights on the Little Smoky and two nights on the big Smoky. The Little Smoky proved to be a fun paddle, and at the low water it tested our channel reading capabilities. At higher waters I suspect our maneuvering skills for avoiding logjams and sweepers may have been in higher demand. There are some fun riffles on this run and some longer boulder garden rapids, which at higher water may result in larger pressure waves.

Other Reaches

There is an additional 160 kilometers, or more of the Little Smoky available for paddlers upstream of this reach. From the hamlet of Little Smoky to and including this reach was reported on in the 1978 version of Canoe Alberta, and in Macdonald (1985) *Canoeing Alberta*. In addition Hurlbut & Cameron (1996) wrote *A Guide to the Little Smoky River* covering a number of short (1 to 3 day) reaches above the hamlet of Little Smoky.

Shuttles

As mention in each of these Peace River country reports I have had positive experiences with Peace River Taxi (780.624.3020) for shuttles from the town of Peace River.

Along the Little Smoky, July 2000

Peace River

Clayhurst Bridge to Peace River

Why Go
Wilderness canoe tripping, and big valley scenery!

Duration of Tour(s)
* 237 km
* ½ to 7 days

Classification
1. Rapids: easy Class II
2. Skill of Paddlers: Intermediate River, or Novice River with good leadership

Dunvegan Bridge, July 2002

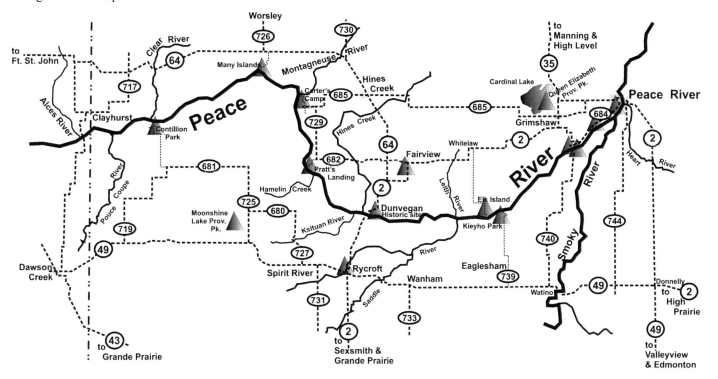

Start
Clayhurst Bridge is almost due north of Dawson Creek, and is the last crossing of the Peace River in British Columbia. If access at the bridge is difficult (too wet?), there is a picnic area approximately 4 kms downstream of the bridge on the north or left bank.

Finish
The finish noted here is at the town dock in Peace River, near the small park for 12 Foot Davis and the Rowing/Sailing Club. This access is approximately 400 m below the mouth of the Heart River. There is also a boat launch across the river from downtown Peace River which is closer to the town (Lion's) campground.

Intermediate Access and Distances

Location	Elevation	Km down	Km up	Km between	Access / Bank or Rapid / Class	MGRS datum	Gradient m/km
	meters					NAD 1983	
						Zone 10V	
Clayhurst Bridge		237	0			FH 830 240	
Clayhurst Picnic Site		233	4		left bank	FH 858 261	
	381	229	8				
						Zone 11V	
Pouce Coupe River		227	10		right bank	LC 190 245	
Clear River		212	25		left bank	LC 319 287	
Contillion Park / range road 120		211	26		right bank	LC 329 278	
	366	177	60				0.3
Many Islands Park / range road 80		171	67	67	left bank	LC 671 433	
Carters Camp / range road 65		153	84		left bank	LC 791 348	
	351	134	103				0.3
Pratt's Landing / township road 820		129	108		left bank	LC 810 127	
Ksituan River		105	132		right bank		
						Zone 11U	
Dunvegan Bridge		101	136	70	either	LB 996 984	
	335	73	164				0.3
Saddle (Burnt) River		70	167		right bank		
Elk Island Park, south of Whitelaw		60	177		left bank	MB 382 970	
Kieyho Park, north of Eaglesham		54	183		right bank	MB 435 989	
						Zone 11V	
Shaftbury Ferry		25	212	76	either	MC 646 167	
	320	14	223				0.3
Strong Creek Park		13	224		left bank	MC 739 239	
Smoky River		7	230		right bank		
Peace River - downtown dock		0	237	25	right bank	MC 816 321	

Gradient

Gradients on this reach are pretty consistent at 0.3 m/km! But surprisingly, on the run south down to Dunvegan Bridge there can be some pressure waves, kinda bouncy and kinda fun.

River Volume and Flow Rate

This is a BIG river. For the Dunvegan station in the middle of this reach, flows in the 700 to 2600 cms range should provide good paddling, though the larger flows may reduce the banks for camping. This really is a run best left for August or later when other streams start getting too low for good paddling.

During a mid-July run in 2002, with approximately 2500 cms, our GPS unit reported velocities of 6-9 km/hr when drifting and we had no problem averaging 8-10 kms per hour on the river during our trip. At Dunvegan the reported velocity ranges from 3 km/hr at 500 cms to 7 km/hr at 6000 cms.

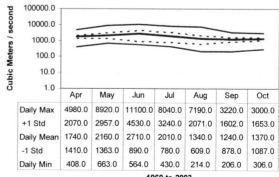

Peace River at Dunvegan

	Apr	May	Jun	Jul	Aug	Sep	Oct
Daily Max	4980.0	8920.0	11100.0	8040.0	7190.0	3220.0	3000.0
+1 Std	2070.0	2957.0	4530.0	3240.0	2071.0	1602.0	1653.0
Daily Mean	1740.0	2160.0	2710.0	2010.0	1340.0	1240.0	1370.0
-1 Std	1410.0	1363.0	890.0	780.0	609.0	878.0	1087.0
Daily Min	408.0	663.0	564.0	430.0	214.0	206.0	306.0

1960 to 2003

Maps

1 - The *Alberta Road Map*, and a set of 1:250,000 sheets may be all you need. If you are planning on using some of the lesser traveled to access points I would suggest purchasing the relevant county/municipality maps, or at least referring to them and annotating your NTS sheet with the up-dated road info.

2 - NTS 1:250,000

94 A Charlie Lake	84 D Clear Hills
83 M Grande Prairie	83 N Winagami (very little - I'd borrow this sheet and draw it in!)
84 C Peace River	

Camping

There are a number of very nice public campgrounds along these reaches to support either day tripping or the start or end of a longer trip. In the 1990s it appears the local municipalities got together to develop the Upper Peace Valley Recreation Area. Contillion Park, Many Islands, Carters Camp, Pratt's Landing, Elk Island Park and Kieyho Park are the result. Each of these parks has unserviced (no power) camping, cook shelters and boat launches. Many Islands Park also has a group camp area (780.685.2560 to reserve). Other campsite contacts include: The Lion's Club Campground (780.624.2120) in Peace River, Strong Creek Park (780.338.3845), and the Dunvegan Historic site (780.538.5350)

This is a river for tripping and the best camping comes in the late summer and fall when the high waters are past and the banks have had some time to dry out. On our July 1983 paddle with the family, I have some vivid memories of one camp where everyone lost their rubber boots in the deep, sucking mud. Many of the side stream fans provide a gravel beach and can provide acceptable campsites. Below the Shaftsbury Ferry be aware that Highway #684 does parallel the river so pick a campsite on the opposite side of an island. There is also considerable private land on both sides of the river below the Shaftsbury Ferry so the islands are the best campsite choices.

Wildlife

In 2002 when we paddled the Dunvegan stretch, we were just about always in visual contact with at least one small family group of mule or whitetail deer. Moose and bear are also common to the Peace Valley, and bears should be considered a risk in all camps along these reaches.

The Peace River valley is so deep, nearly 300 m in places that it has generated its own micro climate. Dunvegan has long been a centre for market gardening. The valley is also the most northerly limit of garter snakes and prickly pear cactus (on the south facing slopes) in Alberta.

Trip Notes

As noted, save this river for mid to late season paddling. Go for the scenery and a leisurely paddle, or for the sense of history. This river was part of the trans-continental fur trade route, and was used by McKenzie in his historic crossing of North America.

Other Reaches

In the above mention 1983 trip we paddled from just above Hudson's Hope right through to Dunvegan with our young family of the time. Except for some easy Class II water just above Hudson's Hope it is a pretty flat paddle, but very scenic right through to this reach reported on here. There is approximately 120 km of paddling available from Hudson's Hope to the Clayhurst Bridge.

Other Local Activities or Destinations

The historic site at Dunvegan is well worth the time to visit. In the town of Peace River, be sure to check out one of the memorials to 12 Foot Davis. Alexander Mackenzie wintered just above "the forks" in 1793 on his way to the Pacific Ocean, and a memorial to this fort is located along Highway #684 south of Peace River towards the Shaftsbury Settlement and Ferry.

Shuttles

On both my canoe trips into the town of Peace River I have used Peace River Taxi (780.624.3020) for both the shuttle and vehicle storage during the trip.

Peace River

Peace River to Fort Vermillion

Why Go
More big river, historic, wilderness canoe tripping.

Duration of Tour(s)
* 430 km
* 1 to 12 days - mostly multiple day reaches.

Classification
1. Rapids: Class I
2. Skill of Paddlers: Intermediate River

Start
The downtown dock in the town of Peace River, next to the Rowing & Sailing Club, and the memorial to 12 Foot Davis.

Finish
The suggested finish is on the river front in the village of Fort Vermillion.

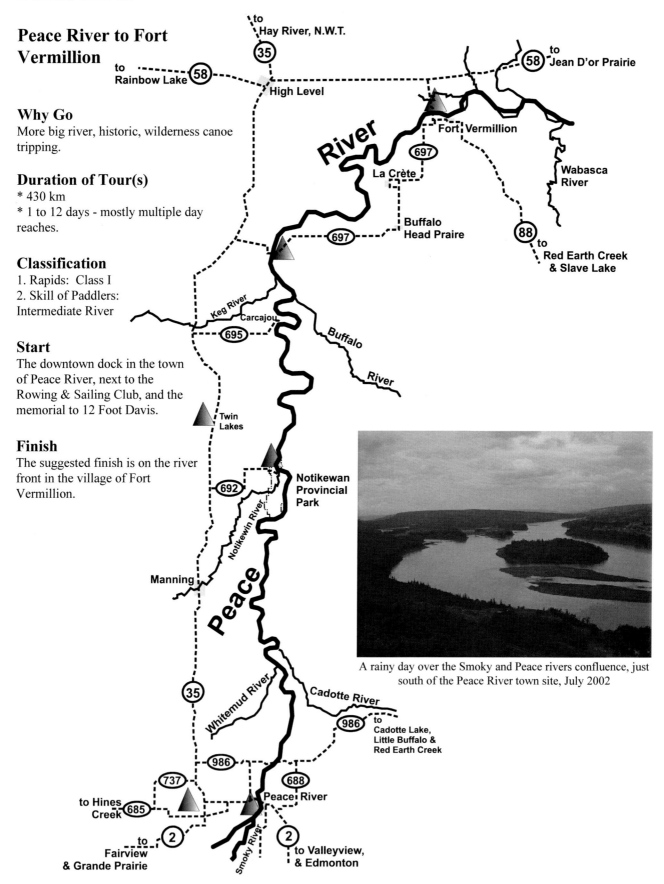

A rainy day over the Smoky and Peace rivers confluence, just south of the Peace River town site, July 2002

Intermediate Access and Distances

Location	Elevation meters	Km down	Km up	Km between	Access / Bank or Rapid / Class	MGRS datum NAD 1983 Zone 11V	Gradient m/km
Peace River - downtown dock		430	0		right bank	MC 816 321	
Highway #986 Bridge		412	18	18	right bank	MC 887460	
	305	400	30				
Whitemud River		372	58		left bank		
Cadotte River & Remote Prov. Rec. Area		360	71		right bank	MC 892 866	
	290	348	82				0.3
	274	279	151				0.2
Notikewin River		263	167		left bank		
Notikewin River Prov. Park Campground		262	168	150	left bank	MD 908 495	
	267	250	180				0.2
Carcajou		179	251		left bank	MD 980 999	
Buffalo River		154	276		right bank		
Keg River		146	284		left bank		
Highway #697 Ferry Crossing		136	294	126	right bank	ME 916 257	
	259	122	308				0.1
	251	68	362				0.1
Highway # 88 Bridge		8	422			NE 509 741	
Fort Vermillion		0	430	136	right bank	NE 583 734	

Gradient
The Peace River gradually slows down (.3 m/km to .1/ m/km), but maintains a good flow rate until late fall or very low water.

River Volume and Flow Rate
This is a big river and good paddling can be had from between about 1000 to 4000 cms. At the Peace River station, in Peace River velocity ranges from approximately 2 km/hr at 1000 cms up to 7 km/hr at 6750 cms.

Maps
1 - A recent *Alberta Road Map* plus the three 1:250,000 NTS sheets listed below would be my first choice.

2 - NTS 1:250,000
        84 C Peace River
        84 F Bison Lake
        84 K Mount Watt

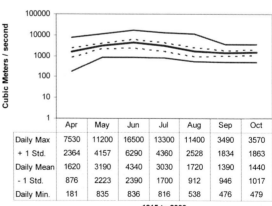

Peace River at Peace River

	Apr	May	Jun	Jul	Aug	Sep	Oct
Daily Max	7530	11200	16500	13300	11400	3490	3570
+ 1 Std.	2364	4157	6290	4360	2528	1834	1863
Daily Mean	1620	3190	4340	3030	1720	1390	1440
- 1 Std.	876	2223	2390	1700	912	946	1017
Daily Min.	181	835	836	816	538	476	479

1915 to 2003

Camping

On river, or near-to-the-river campgrounds for supporting the start or finish of these runs are available at: the Lion's Club Campground (780.624.2120) on the west side of the town of Peace River, at Notikewin Provincial Park (780.836.2048), and at the Highway #88 Bridge just upstream of Fort Vermillion.

Again, this run has grood wilderness camping, but it is best during the late summer and fall seasons after the high water has come and gone.

Wildlife

As with most of the Peace River, this reach is deeply incised. Even though the west bank to Highway #697, and then the south bank after Highway #697 are in the Alberta agricultural "white" zone, sightings of the common mammals and birds of this area should be expected. In particular, paddlers must consider that they are in "bear country" and must take the normal precautions. These reaches of the Peace River above and below the town of Peace River do support a number of commercial hunting and fishing guides. In the fall you can expect to see (& hear) hunting parties along the river. After the summer high waters, this river is notable for producing good numbers of a wide variety of fish including: arctic grayling, mountain whitefish, walleye, burbot and goldeye. For further sport fishing information be sure to check the annual *Alberta Guide to Sportfishing Regulations*.

Trip Notes

This is a river for canoe tripping. Plan your adventure for the late summer and take your time. Plan to fish and explore the many side streams. In this day and age you should carry and filter any water source.

Other Reaches

Fort Vermillion to Peace Point in Wood Buffalo National Park is another 307 kilometers and includes the difficulties of portaging and navigating the Vermillion Chutes AND Falls some 23 km below the Wabasca River. And then there is yet another 224 km of the Peace and Slave River from Peace Point to make Fort Fitzgerald and the start of the portage around the Slave River Rapids.

Shuttles

To shuttle for this whole run I would consider some combination of Taxi service out of Fort Vermillion or High Level, and then the bus (Greyhound) or scheduled air service south to Peace River. For a shorter trip at the south end of these reaches, I would again contact Peace River Taxi (780.624.3020) for shuttle and vehicle storage.

Appendix A
Safety Code of the American Whitewater Affiliation

Five decades of service to the paddlers of America.

"Our mission is to conserve and restore America's whitewater resources and to enhance opportunities to enjoy them safely."

first adopted 1959   this revision 2005

Eric Nise - Safety Chairman
Charlie Walbridge - Safety Vice-chairman
Mark Singleton - Executive Director

Introduction
This code has been prepared using the best available information and has been reviewed by a broad cross-section of whitewater experts. The code, however, is only a collection of guidelines; attempts to minimize risks should be flexible, not constrained by a rigid set of rules. Varying conditions and group goals may combine with unpredictable circumstances to require alternate procedures. This code is not intended to serve as a standard of care for commercial outfitters or guides.

I. Personal Preparedness and Responsibility

1. *Be a competent swimmer*, with the ability to handle yourself underwater.
2. *Wear a life jacket -- a snugly-fitting vest-type life preserver* that offers back and shoulder protection as well as the flotation needed to swim safely in whitewater.
3. *Wear a solid, correctly-fitted helmet when upsets are likely.* This is essential in kayaks or covered canoes, and recommended for open canoeists using thigh straps and rafters running steep drops.
4. *Do not boat out of control.* Your skills should be sufficient to stop or reach shore before reaching danger. Do not enter a rapid unless you are reasonably sure that you can run it safely or swim it without injury.
5. *Whitewater rivers contain many hazards which are not always easily recognized.* The following are the most frequent killers.
    1. *High Water.* The river's speed and power increase tremendously as the flow increases, raising the difficulty of most rapids. Rescue becomes progressively harder as the water rises, adding to the danger. Floating debris and strainers make even an easy rapid quite hazardous. It is often misleading to judge the river level at the put in, since a small rise in a wide, shallow place will be multiplied many times where the river narrows. Use reliable gauge information whenever possible, and be aware that sun on snowpack, hard rain, and upstream dam releases may greatly increase the flow.
    2. *Cold.* Cold drains your strength and robs you of the ability to make sound decisions on matters affecting your survival. Cold-water immersion, because of the initial shock and the rapid heat loss which follows, is especially dangerous. Dress appropriately for bad weather or sudden immersion in the water. When the water temperature is less than 50 degrees F., a wetsuit or drysuit is essential for protection if you swim. Next best is wool or pile clothing under a waterproof shell. In this case, you should also carry waterproof matches and a change of clothing in a waterproof bag. If, after prolonged exposure, a person experiences uncontrollable shaking, loss of coordination, or difficulty speaking, he or she is hypothermic, and needs your assistance.
    3. *Strainers.* Brush, fallen trees, bridge pilings, undercut rocks or anything else which allows river current to sweep through can pin boats and boaters against the obstacle. Water pressure on anything trapped this way can be overwhelming. Rescue is often extremely difficult. Pinning may occur in fast current, with little or no whitewater to warn of the danger.

4. *Dams, weirs, ledges, reversals, holes, and hydraulics.* When water drops over a obstacle, it curls back on itself, forming a strong upstream current which may be capable of holding a boat or swimmer. Some holes make for excellent sport. Others are proven killers. Paddlers who cannot recognize the difference should avoid all but the smallest holes. Hydraulics around man-made dams must be treated with utmost respect regardless of their height or the level of the river. Despite their seemingly benign appearance, they can create an almost escape-proof trap. The swimmer's only exit from the "drowning machine" is to dive below the surface when the downstream current is flowing beneath the reversal.

6. *Broaching.* When a boat is pushed sideways against a rock by strong current, it may collapse and wrap. This is especially dangerous to kayak and decked canoe paddlers; these boats will collapse and the combination of indestructible hulls and tight outfitting may create a deadly trap. Even without entrapment, releasing pinned boats can be extremely time-consuming and dangerous. To avoid pinning, throw your weight downstream towards the rock, this allows the current to slide harmlessly underneath the hull.

7. *Boating alone is discouraged.* The minimum party is three people or two craft.

8. *Have a frank knowledge of your boating ability*, and don't attempt rivers or rapids which lie beyond that ability.

9. *Be in good physical and mental condition, consistent with the difficulties which may be expected.* Make adjustments for loss of skills due to age, health, fitness. Any health limitations must be explained to your fellow paddlers prior to starting the trip.

10. *Be practiced in self-rescue, including escape from an overturned craft.* The Eskimo roll is strongly recommended for decked boaters who run rapids Class IV or greater, or who paddle in cold environmental conditions.

11. *Be trained in rescue skills, CPR, and first aid* with special emphasis on the recognizing and treating hypothermia. It may save your friend's life.

12. *Carry equipment needed for unexpected emergencies*, including foot wear which will protect your feet when walking out, a throw rope, knife, whistle, and waterproof matches. If you wear eyeglasses, tie them on and carry a spare pair on long trips. Bring cloth repair tape on short runs, and a full repair kit on isolated rivers. Do not wear bulky jackets, ponchos, heavy boots, or anything else which could reduce your ability to survive a swim.

13. Despite the mutually supportive group structure described in this code, *individual paddlers are ultimately responsible for their own safety, and must assume sole responsibility for the following decisions:*
    1. The decision to participate on any trip. This includes an evaluation of the expected difficulty of the rapids under the conditions existing at the time of the put-in.
    2. The selection of appropriate equipment, including a boat design suited to their skills and the appropriate rescue and survival gear.
    3. The decision to scout any rapid, and to run or portage according to their best judgment. Other members of the group may offer advice, but paddlers should resist pressure from anyone to paddle beyond their skills. It is also their responsibility to decide whether to pass up any walk-out or take-out opportunity.
    4. All trip participants should consistently evaluate their own and their group's safety, voicing their concerns when appropriate and following what they believe to be the best course of action. Paddlers are encouraged to speak with anyone whose actions on the water are dangerous, whether they are a part of your group or not.

II. Boat and Equipment Preparedness

1. *Test new and different equipment* under familiar conditions before relying on it for difficult runs. This is especially true when adopting a new boat design or outfitting system. Low-volume craft may present additional hazards to inexperienced or poorly conditioned paddlers.

2. *Be sure your boat and gear are in good repair before starting a trip.* The more isolated and difficult the run, the more rigorous this inspection should be.

3. *Install flotation bags* in non-inflatable craft, securely fixed in each end, designed to displace as much water as possible. Inflatable boats should have multiple air chambers and be test-inflated before launching.

4. *Have strong, properly sized paddles or oars* for controlling your craft. Carry sufficient spares for the length and difficulty of the trip.

5. *Outfit your boat safely.* The *ability to exit your boat quickly* is an essential component of safety in rapids. It is your responsibility to see that there is absolutely nothing to cause entrapment when coming free of an upset craft. This includes:
    1. Spray covers which won't release reliably or which release prematurely.
    2. Boat outfitting too tight to allow a fast exit, especially in low volume kayaks or decked canoes. This includes low-hung thwarts in canoes lacking adequate clearance for your feet and kayak foot braces which fail or allow your feet to become wedged under them.
    3. Inadequately supported decks which collapse on a paddler's legs when a decked boat is pinned by water

pressure. Inadequate clearance with the deck because of your size or build.

4. Loose ropes which cause entanglement. Beware of any length of loose line attached to a whitewater boat. All items must be tied tightly and excess line eliminated; painters, throw lines, and safety rope systems must be completely and effectively stored. Do not knot the end of a rope, as it can get caught in cracks between rocks.

6. *Provide ropes which permit you to hold on to your craft* so that it may be rescued. The following methods are recommended:

1. Kayaks and covered canoes should have grab loops of 1/4" + rope or equivalent webbing sized to admit a normal-sized hand. Stern painters are permissible if properly secured.

2. Open canoes should have securely anchored bow and stern painters consisting of 8 - 10 feet of 1/4" + line. These must be secured in such a way that they are readily accessible, but cannot come loose accidentally. Grab loops are acceptable, but are more difficult to reach after an upset.

3. Rafts and dories may have taut perimeter lines threaded through the loops provided. Footholds should be designed so that a paddler's feet cannot be forced through them, causing entrapment. Flip lines should be carefully and reliably stowed.

7. *Know your craft's carrying capacity*, and how added loads affect boat handling in whitewater. Most rafts have a minimum crew size which can be added to on day trips or in easy rapids. Carrying more than two paddlers in an open canoe when running rapids is not recommended.

8. *Car-top racks must be strong and attach positively to the vehicle.* Lash your boat to each crossbar, then tie the ends of the boats directly to the bumpers for added security. This arrangement should survive all but the most violent vehicle accident.

III. Group Preparedness and Responsibility

1. *Organization.* A river trip should be regarded as a common adventure by all participants, except on instructional or commercially guided trips as defined below. Participants share the responsibility for the conduct of the trip, and each participant is individually responsible for judging his or her own capabilities and for his or her own safety as the trip progresses. Participants are encouraged (but are not obligated) to offer advice and guidance for the independent consideration and judgment of others.

2. *River Conditions.* The group should have a reasonable knowledge of the difficulty of the run. Participants should evaluate this information and adjust their plans accordingly. If the run is exploratory or no one is familiar with the river, maps and guidebooks, if available, should be examined. The group should secure accurate flow information; the more difficult the run, the more important this will be. Be aware of possible changes in river level and how this will affect the difficulty of the run. If the trip involves tidal stretches, secure appropriate information on tides.

3. *Group equipment* should be suited to the difficulty of the river. The group should always have a throw-line available, and one line per boat is recommended on difficult runs. The list may include: carabiners, prussic loops, first aid kit, flashlight, folding saw, fire starter, guidebooks, maps, food, extra clothing, and any other rescue or survival items suggested by conditions. Each item is not required on every run, and this list is not meant to be a substitute for good judgment.

4. *Keep the group compact,* but maintain sufficient spacing to avoid collisions. If the group is large, consider dividing into smaller groups or using the "buddy system" as an additional safeguard. Space yourselves closely enough to permit good communication, but not so close as to interfere with one another in rapids.

1. *A point paddler sets the pace.* When in front, do not get in over your head. Never run drops when you cannot see a clear route to the bottom or, for advanced paddlers, a sure route to the next eddy. *When in doubt, stop and scout.*

2. *Keep track of all group members.* Each boat keeps the one behind it in sight, stopping if necessary. Know how many people are in your group and take head-counts regularly. No one should paddle ahead or walk out without first informing the group. Paddlers requiring additional support should stay at the center of a group, and not allow themselves to lag behind in the more difficult rapids. If the group is large and contains a wide range of abilities, a "sweep boat" may be designated to bring up the rear.

3. *Courtesy.* On heavily used rivers, do not cut in front of a boater running a drop. Always look upstream before leaving eddies to run or play. Never enter a crowded drop or eddy when no room for you exists. Passing other groups in a rapid may be hazardous; it's often safer to wait upstream until the group ahead has passed.

5. *Float Plan.* If the trip is into a wilderness area or for an extended period, plans should be filed with a responsible person who will contact the authorities if you are overdue. It may be wise to establish checkpoints along the way where civilization could be contacted if necessary. Knowing the location of possible help and planning escape routes can speed rescue.

6. *Drugs.* The use of alcohol or mind-altering drugs before or during river trips is not recommended. It dulls

reflexes, reduces decision-making ability, and may interfere with important survival reflexes.

7. *Instructional or commercially guided trips.* In contrast to the common adventure trip format, in these trip formats, a boating instructor or commercial guide assumes some of the responsibilities normally exercised by the group as a whole, as appropriate under the circumstances. These formats recognize that instructional or commercially guided trips may involve participants who lack significant experience in whitewater. However, as a participant acquires experience in whitewater, he or she takes on increasing responsibility for his or her own safety, in accordance with what he or she knows or should know as a result of that increased experience. Also, as *in all trip formats, every participant must realize and assume the risks associated with the serious hazards of whitewater rivers.*

8. It is advisable for instructors and commercial guides or their employers to acquire trip or personal liability insurance:
   1. An "instructional trip" is characterized by a clear teacher/pupil relationship, where the primary purpose of the trip is to teach boating skills, and which is conducted for a fee.
   2. A "commercially guided trip" is characterized by a licensed, professional guide conducting trips for a fee.

IV. Guidelines for River Rescue

1. *Recover from an upset with an Eskimo roll* whenever possible. Evacuate your boat immediately if there is imminent danger of being trapped against rocks, brush, or any other kind of strainer.

2. *If you swim, hold on to your boat.* It has much flotation and is easy for rescuers to spot. Get to the upstream end so that you cannot be crushed between a rock and your boat by the force of the current. Persons with good balance may be able to climb on top of a swamped kayak or flipped raft and paddle to shore.

3. *Release your craft if this will improve your chances*, especially if the water is cold or dangerous rapids lie ahead. Actively attempt self-rescue whenever possible by swimming for safety. Be prepared to assist others who may come to your aid.
   1. When swimming in shallow or obstructed rapids, lie on your back with feet held high and pointed downstream. Do not attempt to stand in fast moving water; if your foot wedges on the bottom, fast water will push you under and keep you there. Get to slow or very shallow water before attempting to stand or walk. Look ahead! Avoid possible pinning situations including undercut rocks, strainers, downed trees, holes, and other dangers by swimming away from them.
   2. If the rapids are deep and powerful, roll over onto your stomach and swim aggressively for shore. Watch for eddies and slackwater and use them to get out of the current. Strong swimmers can effect a powerful upstream ferry and get to shore fast. If the shores are obstructed with strainers or under cut rocks, however, it is safer to "ride the rapid out" until a safer escape can be found.

4. *If others spill and swim, go after the boaters first.* Rescue boats and equipment only if this can be done safely. While participants are encouraged (but not obligated) to assist one another to the best of their ability, they should do so only if they can, in their judgment, do so safely. The first duty of a rescuer is not to compound the problem by becoming another victim.

5. The use of rescue lines requires training; uninformed use may cause injury. Never tie yourself into either end of a line without a reliable quick-release system. Have a knife handy to deal with unexpected entanglement. Learn to place set lines effectively, to throw accurately, to belay effectively, and to properly handle a rope thrown to you.

6. When reviving a drowning victim, be aware that cold water may greatly extend survival time underwater. Victims of hypothermia may have depressed vital signs so they look and feel dead. Don't give up; continue CPR for as long as possible without compromising safety.

V. Universal River Signals

Stop: Potential Hazard Ahead. Wait for "all clear" signal before proceeding, or scout ahead. form a horizontal bar with your outstretched arms. Those seeing the signal should pass it back to others in the party. -

Help/Emergency: Assist the signaler as quickly as possible. Give three long blasts on a police whistle while waving a paddle, helmet or life vest over your head. If a whistle is not available, use the visual signal alone. A whistle is best carried on a lanyard attached to your life vest.

All Clear: Come ahead (in the absence of other directions proceed down the center). Form a vertical bar with your paddle or one arm held high above your head. Paddle blade should be turned flat for maximum visibility. To signal direction or a preferred course through a rapid around obstruction, lower the previously vertical "all clear" by 45 degrees toward the side of the river with the preferred route. **Never** point toward the obstacle you wish to avoid.

I'm okay: I'm okay and not hurt. While holding the elbow outward toward the side, repeatedly pat the top of your head.

Other signals I've collected, and use. [ML]

Medical Attention Required. Stand vertical and hold your arms or paddles overhead in an "X", straight and crossed over.

Group-UP. Use repeated short blasts, or "chirps" on the whistle to indicate that the lead canoe or kayak should stop and all should wait for the sweep boat. This signal often is initiated at the "back of the pack" and moves forward through the group. This signal is repeated by all until the lead boats have clearly received the message, and can be seen heading for a group sized eddy or beach. If whistles are unavailable then thump the sides or deck of ones boat to join the chorus.

VI. International Scale of River Difficulty

This is the American version of a rating system used to compare river difficulty throughout the world. This system is not exact; rivers do not always fit easily into one category, and regional or individual interpretations may cause misunderstandings. It is no substitute for a guidebook or accurate first-hand descriptions of a run.

Paddlers attempting difficult runs in an unfamiliar area should act cautiously until they get a feel for the way the scale is interpreted locally. River difficulty may change each year due to fluctuations in water level, downed trees, recent floods, geological disturbances, or bad weather. Stay alert for unexpected problems!

As river difficulty increases, the danger to swimming paddlers becomes more severe. As rapids become longer and more continuous, the challenge increases. There is a difference between running an occasional class-IV rapid and dealing with an entire river of this category. Allow an extra margin of safety between skills and river ratings when the water is cold or if the river itself is remote and inaccessible.

The six difficulty classes:

Class I Rapids
Fast moving water with riffles and small waves. Few obstructions, all obvious and easily missed with little training. Risk to swimmers is slight; self-rescue is easy.

Class II Rapids: Novice
Straightforward rapids with wide, clear channels which are evident without scouting. Occasional maneuvering may be required, but rocks and medium-sized waves are easily missed by trained paddlers. Swimmers are seldom injured and group assistance, while helpful, is seldom needed. Rapids that are at the upper end of this difficulty range are designated "Class II+".

Class III Rapids: Intermediate
Rapids with moderate, irregular waves which may be difficult to avoid and which can swamp an open canoe. Complex maneuvers in fast current and good boat control in tight passages or around ledges are often required; large waves or strainers may be present but are easily avoided. Strong eddies and powerful current effects can be found, particularly on large-volume rivers. Scouting is advisable for inexperienced parties. Injuries while swimming are rare; self-rescue is usually easy but group assistance may be required to avoid long swims. Rapids that are at the lower or upper end of this difficulty range are designated "Class III-" or "Class III+" respectively.

Class IV Rapids: Advanced
Intense, powerful but predictable rapids requiring precise boat handling in turbulent water. Depending on the character of the river, it may feature large, unavoidable waves and holes or constricted passages demanding fast maneuvers under pressure. A fast, reliable eddy turn may be needed to initiate maneuvers, scout rapids, or rest. Rapids may require "must" moves above dangerous hazards. Scouting may be necessary the first time down. Risk of injury to swimmers is moderate to high, and water conditions may make self-rescue difficult. Group assistance for rescue is often essential but requires practiced skills. A strong Eskimo roll is highly recommended. Rapids that are at the lower or upper end of this difficulty range are designated "Class IV-" or "Class IV+" respectively.

Class V(5): Expert
Extremely long, obstructed, or very violent rapids which expose a paddler to added risk. Drops may contain large, unavoidable waves and holes or steep, congested chutes with complex, demanding routes. Rapids may continue for long distances between pools, demanding a high level of fitness. What eddies exist may be small, turbulent, or difficult to reach. At the high end of the scale, several of these factors may be combined. Scouting is recommended but may be difficult. Swims are dangerous, and rescue is often difficult even for experts. A very reliable Eskimo roll, proper equipment, extensive experience, and practiced rescue skills are essential. Because of the large range of difficulty that exists beyond Class IV, Class 5 is an open-ended, multiple-level scale designated by class 5.0, 5.1, 5.2, etc... each of these levels is an order of magnitude more difficult than the last. Example: increasing difficulty from Class 5.0 to Class 5.1 is a similar order of magnitude as increasing from Class IV to Class 5.0.

Class VI: Extreme and Exploratory Rapids
These runs have almost never been attempted and often exemplify the extremes of difficulty, unpredictability and danger. The consequences of errors are very severe and rescue may be impossible. For teams of experts only, at favorable water levels, after close personal inspection and taking all precautions. After a Class VI rapids has been run many times, its rating may be changed to an appropriate Class 5.x rating.

American Whitewater Affiliation
Share the River: Protect Our Ability to Enjoy Them

Positive, cooperative relationships between river users are important to the future of paddlesports and to the future of rivers themselves. Please follow the guidelines below in an effort to establish or maintain positive relationships with other river users. Unnecessary conflicts may result in unwanted regulations and enforcement actions that may limit opportunities and enjoyment of the river.

Rules of the Road:

* At put-ins and take-outs behave in a friendly, positive manner toward others and be helpful to those who might need assistance. Be mindful of the time that you are spending occupying the launch or take-out area so that you do not unfairly restrict opportunities for others.

* Allow for spacing up and downstream of others, particularly in a rapid, and seek to avoid collisions. Colliding boaters should not leave the scene without checking with the other paddlers and making sure that they are unhurt. Do not take any action that escalates conflict.

* When entering a rapid, and especially when entering from an eddy, the upstream craft has the right of way. Those entering the current should yield to those already in it. Never cut in front of an oncoming boat.

* When exiting the current, avoid eddies that are full, if possible, and take care when entering occupied eddies. Exit an eddy when you see approaching boats, to facilitate your safe exit and entry, respectively.

* When playing, avoid blocking navigation by yielding to oncoming, upstream craft. Exit a play spot after a reasonable time to allow someone else to use it.

* Always provide assistance to others who are in trouble or who are injured. Provide whatever assistance you are qualified to give or help them in obtaining assistance.

* When traveling on rivers and camping overnight, consult with other groups on the water about their stopping and camping intentions, and strive to cooperate by spreading out among desirable locations. Do not invade another party's campsite. If darkness, emergency or other factors require you to set a camp close to others, always explain the situation and attempt to gain their understanding while respecting their privacy.

Appendix B - Glossary

Access, Access point - a point beside a river, stream or lake to which boats and gear can easily be brought to by vehicle, usually a bridge, boat launch, old ferry site, campground, picnic site, or along side of, or end of a road allowance.

Attain, Attainment - paddling upstream, generally by the intelligent use of eddies and ferrying from the inside of one corner to the inside of the next.

Back Ferry, Setting - using the current to push the canoe or kayak sideways while one paddles backwards to negate the downstream push of the river. The opposite of a *front ferry*.

Boils - an up-welling of water, usually associated with, and down stream of strong eddies, or where two strong currents collide or join.

Bow - the front of a boat.

Brace, Bracing stroke - a paddle stroke that stabilizes a boat, used to counteract the anticipated rolling force of the current, or to react to the start of a tip, or prevent the further tipping of a boat.

Braided stream - a river that spreads out over gravel flats in many diverging and converging shallow channels. Such channels are often separated by alluvial (gravel) material. Dangerous logjams and sweepers are often associated with braided streams. Braided streams are often "depositional" and mark the point where a river gradient is reduced and the river slows down. Such channels are often found in Alberta where streams break out of the mountains or foothills and onto the great plains.

Broach, Broaching - to turn broadside to the current, usually due to the unequal forces on the canoe in waves (either wind or rapids). To turn broadside to a rock, boulder, or bridge pier and become pinned on the upstream side of such.

C-1/2/4/15/x - Canoe paddled by the designated number of paddlers. May be a flatwater, touring, or whitewater version - decked or not decked.

Canoe - small (4 - 12m long) double ended boat usually propelled by a single bladed paddle, and derived from the bark or dugout craft of aboriginal peoples. May be paddled by one or more paddlers. Canoes come in a near infinite variety of flatwater, touring, tripping, recreational, competitive, playboat and whitewater models.

Carve - to use a lean to the outside of a turn to assist the turning of a canoe; most commonly used in marathon racing canoes; can be used by all paddlers and is most useful when cruising on flat water.

Channel - 1 - the deepest part of a river bed, the location of the main current, 2 - a paddle-able route through a section of the river or rapid.

Chute - the steep, fast channel through a rapid or ledge. Usually delivers the main current of the stream into the tail or standing waves at the bottom of a rapid. May be recognized by the "down stream" aligned "V" patterns in the water.

Confluence - where two streams join.

Correction Strokes - the strokes that include a later portion that reverses a push to one side or the other caused by the first part of the stroke. The "J" stroke, in all its variations is the granddaddy of correction strokes. Bow paddlers will often use a Reverse "J" stroke when back ferrying, also a correction stroke.

Crown land - land owned by the government of Alberta, and usually available to citizens to access. Crown land may be occupied by those holding grazing or other surface right leases.

Deck - 1 - the small solid triangle of wood, plastic or fiberglass at the ends of a canoe where the gunwales join. 2 - a fabric, or solid structure that covers all or most of the upper portion of a canoe or kayak. Decks may or may not be permanently attached.

Depositional - where the gradient of a stream is reduced, the slower flowing water is not able to carry as great a load of gravel, silts, or even logs and other debris. Thus where a river flattens out, as in where it leaves the foothills and flows onto the prairies, one tends to find braided streams with the river bed made up of gravels, and often the logs and other debris that the slower stream can no longer carry.

Distributary - a channel flowing out of a river rather into it, most commonly found, and the term used, in deltas, such as the Embarrass Channel on the Athabasca River.

Downgrade, Entrench - when flowing water carves and erodes the stream bed down to the lowest possible point. Streams tend to downgrade above confluences. This action often results in canyons, gorges, rapids and waterfalls.

Downstream 1- the direction in which a stream or rivers flow. 2 - The side of one's craft that is facing the same direction as the stream flows. Opposite of *upstream.*

Draw stroke(s) - the family of canoe strokes that involve the pulling water towards the side of the boat, strokes that move the whole boat, or one end of the boat to the side. May be used (and with a partners pry stroke in tandem canoes) for sideslipping (moving the whole boat sideways), or turning one's craft (both paddlers drawing in a tandem canoe).

Dry suit - a modern convenience, a suit of vinyl coated nylon, with neoprene gaskets that keeps a paddler dry, even when immersed.

Eddy - the usually quieter water, or gentle reverse flow, downstream of an obstruction or on the inside of a corner. As current speed increases eddies too become stronger. With the right geology, gradient and flow, eddies can become violent whirlpools.

Eddy line - the often sharp boundary between the downstream flow of the main current and the upstream flow of a eddy.

Entrench - see *downgrade*

Falls - 1 - a drop over which water falls freely. 2 - any steep or vertical section of river. Bow Falls at Banff does not include much free falling water, where as Athabasca Falls near Jasper does.

Ferry, front ferry - a manoeuver carried out with the bow pointed upstream. The paddlers negate the downstream force of the current and use the current force to push the boat to one side or the other of the stream. The opposite of a *back ferry, or set.*

Gradient - the steepness of a slope, the average rate of descent of a river, usually expressed in metres per kilometer by Canadian and European paddlers, feet per mile by Americans, and in % slope by highway and railway engineers (i.e. 10 m/km = 50 ft/mi. = 1% slope with some rounding off).

Haystacks, Standing waves, Tail waves - the large waves usually found at the foot of a rapid caused by the deceleration of the current due to a reduction in stream gradient.

Hole - a vertical reversal that is downstream of a large boulder or partial ledge. A small *keeper.* A river feature some do their best to avoid, and some seek to play with.

Horizon Line - the visual line formed upstream of significant drops such as ledges, falls and weirs. From upstream the river seems to disappear, and the further away the river appears beyond the horizon line, the more significant the drop!

Kayak - a usually-decked craft, derived from the skin boats of the Inuit, and paddled with a double bladed paddle. Like canoes, kayaks come in near infinite variety of designs for touring, tripping, recreational, flatwater, ocean, river, creek, whitewater and play-boat paddling. And like canoes come in K-1/2/4/x variations for different numbers of paddlers.

Keel 1 - the lowest longitudinal centre line of the canoe along the bottom. 2 - the lower longitudinal structural member of the craft. 3 - a protective strip of wood or metal along the bottom of a boat. Structural keels provide rigidity to the hull, keels that extend below the bottom of a boat may provide some directional stability.

Keeper - a wave with a strong vertical reversal that traps paddlers and boats. Keepers that form behind river wide ledges, or worse, weirs can be very dangerous. Because weirs are manmade, and very symmetrical, they form the strongest of all keepers and have been referred to as "drowning machines."

Ledge - a solid rock strata over which the river flows. Ledges cause a temporary vertical reversal in flow and often create a *hole* or *keeper*. Ledges may be a impediment to travel, or worse, a major hazard to paddlers on the stream. Or a ledge just may be a fun spot to play and develop surfing skills. The difference is judgement, skill and equipment.

Lining - the use of ropes to work one's canoe downstream through a rapid, usually to avoid a portage, a sure swim, or worse. The opposite of *tracking*.

Logjam - one, a number of, or even thousands of logs caught on some obstruction. Logjams are often in the main current and allow the water through, but not boats, paddlers or swimmers. Logjams can be extremely dangerous and are a prime cause of on-river drownings in Alberta.

Meander, Meander bend - the sinuous winding course of a stream or river.

Ox-bow lake, abandoned meander - a lake created by the cutting off of an extreme meander bend. Meanders and ox-bows are usually found where a river has much reduced gradient, even if just for short stretches. Ox-bow lakes can be found all across Alberta including on the Bow River above Banff, and on the lower Athabasca towards the delta.

Painter - a rope attached to the ends of a boat. Here in Alberta it is consider wise to have a painter of 1.5 m to 2 m attached to one's canoe to assist with rescue and the tying up of one's boat when tripping. Such painters should be secured so that they do not float free in a unplanned swim and become a source of entanglement for swimming paddlers.

Pillow - a smooth, thin mound of water usually hiding a rock or boulder.

Pool - a quiet section of river, possibly a large eddy, or a slow, deep section of river between rapids or shallower faster flowing sections of the stream.

Portage 1 - to carry one's boat and gear overland and around an obstacle such as a rapid, falls or a dam. 2 - the path along which one carries one's boat and gear to avoid a rapid, falls or a dam.

Random camping - in Alberta, camping where allowed on *Crown land*. Random camping may or may not be road accessible. Camping on *Crown land* requires the camper to clean the site on departure, and to be considerate of other campers and *Crown land* users.

Rapid - a section of river characterized by waves, obstructions, whitewater, and other forms of turbulence. Usually but not always associated with an increase in gradient AND/OR a change in river bed geology.

Reach 1 - a stretch of river, between two access points. 2 - a stretch of river between two bends or locks. 3 - to sail with the wind abeam, or a distance sailed with the wind abeam, or abaft of the beam.

Riffle - a small rapid, or a long stretch of easy, shallow rapid caused by the stream flowing over gravel bars or small boulders. Riffles often require a sharp eye to avoid the shallows and boulders and to find the best route through. Usually if you run aground you can step out of your canoe and push off.

River right, River left - the left and right side of a stream are determined from the downstream view. Assume a mid-stream position, look downstream, to the right, is river right, to left, river left.

Rock Garden 1 - a rapid with many exposed boulders that require constant maneuvering to avoid. 2 - a rapid that is so shallow one can not avoid scrapping bottom very frequently, also sometimes referred to as "boney."

Rollers - mid-rapid waves caused by the acceleration and deceleration of the current in the rapid. Rollers are often caused by the river flowing over a series of rocky shelves or ledges. Many of the rapids on the North Saskatchewan above Rocky Mountain House have mid-rapid rollers, as does the Maycroft Rapid on the Oldman River.

EXTREME DANGER
SUBMERGED WEIR

THE DROWNING MACHINE

•Venturing over the weir is RISKING CERTAIN DEATH.
•Escape is IMPOSSIBLE once caught in the whirling water.
•Portage as directed.

Sieves - usually a rocky feature that breaks up the flow of a channel, and does not allow the passage of boats, or swimmers. The rock version of a *strainer*.

Spillway - the channel, usually concrete, which carries water over or around a dam at times of high flow. In the past some spillways were unprotected and were a danger to water craft and stream users.

Splash cover - a fabric cover used to keep water out of a open canoe. Splash covers may be partial, or full.

Spray skirt - Usually a nylon or neoprene fabric cover used to close the cockpit in a closed canoe or kayak. A paddler wears the spray skirt, and the skirt attaches by means of a heavy elastic to the rim of the cockpit.

Strainer, Logjam - the wooden version of a *sieve* and far more common in Alberta. Usually a collection of trees, sometimes one is enough, through which the water goes, BUT a boat or swimmer will be caught, and pinned, usually below the surface. Logjams often occur in the main flow of a channel, or adjacent to the main flow.

Stern - the back of a boat

Swamp - 1 - the filling of one's canoe with water by crashing through large waves in a rapid. May be followed by a tip and a swim for the paddlers. 2 - another term for "muskeg," a wet area of black spruce trees, willows, and moss.

Sweepers - in Alberta, usually spruce trees, hanging horizontally, about "kidney height" above the river, over the main flow, on the outside of bends. Sweepers tend to sweep the unwary into the river. Best avoided by staying well to the inside of a corner. Logjams may have sweepers protruding over the navigable channel.

Sweep Boat - the last boat in a tour group. Usually a more skilled, and fully equipped paddler who can help those who fall behind.

Tracking - working a canoe upstream with the aid of ropes. The canoe is attached to ropes which are held as one walks along the bank.

Tufa - the porous rock largely comprised of calcium carbonate that forms at some mineral springs.

Undercurrent, Under-tow - 1 - a current that tends to pull a paddler or floating objects below the surface. 2 - the downstream flow at the bottom of a keeper.

Upstream 1- the direction from which a river flows, opposite of *downstream*. 2 - The side of one's craft that is facing towards the source of the stream.

Weir - a small man-made dam which the river **normally** flows over. Usually created in Alberta to provide the head, and head-works for irrigation facilities. All the weirs I have visited in Alberta have a serious reversal or keeper downstream, and are "drowning machines."

White water - the result of rapids, waves and river turbulence. The water appears white because of the introduced air from the turbulence. This usually results in a mixture that is too thick to breath, and too thin for buoyancy!

Wilderness Campsite - a campsite, usually on Crown land that has no road access. A form of *random camping*. Campers are fully responsible for cleaning and maintaining any site they use, and packing out all garbage and debris that they create. Responsible campers clean up after those less so.

Appendix C - Selected Paddling Manuals

American Canoe Association (2008) *Canoeing: outdoor adventures*. Human Kinetics, Champaign, IL.
ISBN #978-0-7360-6715-7

American Red Cross (1977) *Canoeing*, **Doubleday & Co., Garden City, New York**
This is the classic text for canoeing and covers many aspects that other manuals completely forget, such as canoe sailing and poling. Some of the material is becoming dated, but still a text I occasionally refer to. If you can find it — buy it!

British Canoe Union (2002) *Canoe and Kayak Handbook 3ʳᵈ Edition*, **Pesda Press, Bangor Gwynedd, Great Britian**
ISBN # 0-9531956-5-1
This is a great manual, but it does have a British/European orientation. I do find it at least at the MEC paddling rack and would recommend it to any serious paddling instructor or coach.

Conover, G. (1991) *Beyond the Paddle:a canoeists guide to expedition skills: poling, lining, portaging and maneuvering through ice.* **Willowdale, Ont., Firefly Books** ISBN # 0-921820-29-1

Harting T. (2000) *Shooting Paddlers,* **Toronto, Ont., Natural Heritage**
ISBN # 1-896219-62-4
A manual for the paddling photographer

Jacobson, C. (2000) *Canoeing & Camping: beyond the basics,* **Globe, Pequot, US**
ISBN # 0-7627-0668-6
Cliff Jacobson is the "Dean" of American canoe tripping.

Johnson, S. (2002) *The complete sea kayaker's handbook*, **Ragged Mountain Press, Camden Me.,**
ISBN 3 0-07-136210-X
This manual is a very good introduction to the skills and requirements of kayak touring, and is not just for "sea" paddlers.

Lessels, B. (1994) AMC Whitewater Handbook 3rd ed., Boston, Appalachian Mountain Club Books
This is getting a little dated too – but is still the best canoe - kayak combo book I've found and up to 2006 still used it as my text for my fall paddling course at Grant MacEwan College.

Mason, B. (1980) *Path of the Paddle - an illustrated guide to the art of canoeing*, **Van Nostrand Reinhold Ltd., Toronto, Ontario** ISBN # 1 55013 654 2
This is the Canadian classic. Bill passed away some years ago, and his son Paul, an even better paddler, has recently brought out a revised edition. A must have, for every paddler!

Mason, B. (1988) *Song of the Paddle - an illustrated guide to wilderness camping*, **Key Porter Books, Toronto, Ontario** ISBN # 1 55263 579 1
This is Bill's guide to canoe camping. The information is good, and the pictures and illustrations are wonderful.

Mason, P. & Scriver, M. (1999) *Thrill of the Paddle: the art of whitewater canoeing*, **Key Porter Books, Toronto, Ontario** ISBN # 1-55263-039-0
Paul, "son of Bill," continues the family tradition and with Mark Scriver presents a very fine book on whitewater paddling – the boat info' is getting dated, but the paddling and safety information is still excellent.

McGuffin, G. & J. (1999) *Paddle Your Own Canoe*, **Erin, Ont., Boston Mills Press**
ISBN # 1-55046-214-8
A fine paddling manual, well illustrated with Gary's own photos, by two of Canada's best known paddlers.

Walbridge, C., & Sundmacher, W.A. (1995) *Whitewater Rescue Manual*, **Ragged Mountain Press, Camden, Maine**
Charlie Walbridge is the "Dean" of North American white water safety, for many years he has been the Safety Chairman for the American Whitewater Affiliation. This or a similar manual should grace the shelf of every paddler who considers paddling on flowing water.

Appendix D: Internet "Web/WWW" Resources:

Alberta Environment - River Basin information / River Flow Information
http://environment.alberta.ca/apps/basins/default.aspx
- this site provides both access to river flow information as a table of recent flows (usually withing 2-3 hrs of actual reporting) or hydrograph with comparison to historical quartiles. In addition one can access precipitation summaries from recent storms, monthly and seasonal summaries, a weekly flow forecast, and flood warnings.

American Whitewater Affiliation www.americanwhitewater.org/
- a good site that contains links to many paddling resources and other paddling groups AND the AWA Safety Code, and incident/accident database.

The Canadian Canoe Museum www.canoemuseum.net/
- North America's only canoe museum, and a comprehensive web site of paddling history.

Canadian Canoe Routes www.myccr.com/index.php
- an online meeting place for those who enjoy exploring the lakes and rivers of Canada by canoe.

Kayakwest Paddlers www.kayakwest.com
- a long series of kayak trip reports for much of Western Canada.

Paddle Canada www.paddlingcanada.com/
- one of the best Canadian starting places for Canadian paddling resources and groups.

Trans Alta Utilities www.transalta.com/transalta/river.nsf/.vwRiverWeb/River+FlowBy+Schedule?Opendocument
- schedule of releases for the lower Kananaskis

Water Survey of Canada / Environment Canada www.wsc.ec.gc.ca/index_e.cfm?cname=main_e.cfm
- the source of hydrology information for the whole country, and the Hydat program used for the development of the hydrographs included in this guidebook.

Appendix E: Canoe Clubs and Associations in Alberta

Alberta Slalom Canoe & Kayak   www.albertawhitewater.ca/asck/

Alberta Sprint Racing Canoe Association www.albertasprintcanoe.com/

Alberta Whitewater Association www.albertawhitewater.ca/

Paddle Alberta www.paddlealberta.org/

****

Borealis Canoe Club (Ft. McMurray) www.borealiscanoe.ca/

Bow Waters Canoe Club (Calgary) www.bowwaters.org/

Bow Valley Kayak Club www.kanpaddle.ca

Calgary Canoe Club calgarycanoeclub.com/

Calgary Kayak Club www.calgarykayakclub.com

Ceyana Canoe Club (Edmonton) www.ceyana.ca

Cottonwood Kayak Club (Innisfail) www.angelfire.com/sports/CKC/

Drayton Valley Paddling Club www.dvpaddling.com

Edmonton Whitewater Paddlers www.paddleewp.com/

Kayak Jasper www.kayakjasper.ca/

Mistaya Paddling Club (Edmonton) www.mistayapaddlingclub.com

Northwest Voyageurs Canoe and Kayak Club (Edmonton) www.nwvoyageurs.com/

Paddle Junkies (Calgary) www.paddlejunkies.com

Pinch-o-Crow Creekers (Crowsnest Pass) www.albertawhitewater.ca/pinchercreek

Red Deer Canoe and Kayak Club www.rdckc.com/

Rocky Canoe Club (Rocky Mountain House) www.rockycanoeclub.org/

United Alberta Paddling Society (Edmonton) www.paddleuaps.ca

Wapiti Whitewater Kayakers (Grande Prairie) www.wapitikayakers.ca

Waterwerks Kayak Club www.waterwerks.ca/

last revised 2009 Aug 27

References

Alberta Canadian Heritage Rivers Consortium (1996) *Canadian Heritage Rivers Systems Study of Rivers in Alberta: executive summary*. Edmonton, Alberta. Alberta Environmental Protection

Alberta Forest Service (nd) *Clearwater River: map/guide for river travel*. Edmonton, Alberta. Energy/Forestry, Lands and Wildlife

Archer, L. (2003) *Northern Saskatchewan Canoe Trips: a guide to fifteen wilderness rivers.* Erin, Ontario. Boston Mills Press

Archer, S. (2000) *Sheep River: paddling outside of time.* in Thomas, A.(ed.), *Paddle Quest:Canada's best canoe routes.*

Buhrmann, H. & Young, D. (1980) *Canoeing Chinook Country Rivers*. Lethbridge, Alberta

Dickinson, D. & Baresco, D. (2003) *Prairie River: a canoe and wildlife viewing guide to the South Saskatchewan River; from Grand Forks, Alberta to Estuary, Saskatchewan.* Edmonton, Alberta. Society of Grasslands Naturalists and the Federation of Alberta Naturalists

Edmonton Park Rangers (nd) *Edmonton River Recreation Guidei.*Edmonton, Alberta, Community Services, City of Edmonton

Hurlbut, D. & Cameron, J. (1996) *A guide to The Little Smoky River: for canoeing, rafting, kayaking and motor boating*. Edmonton, Alberta. Map Town

Kershaw, R. & Lee, C. (1978) *Adventure Guide and Topographic Map of Southwest Alberta: 1:125,000 Scale Topographic and and a complete guide to outdoor recreation adventures.* Pincher Creek, Alberta. Southwest Alberta Business Development Centre

Lund, M. (1997) *Mark's Guide for Central Alberta Paddlers*. Edmonton, Alberta. Mark Lund

MacDonald, J. (1985) *Canoeing Alberta*. Edmonton, Alberta. Lone Pine Publishing

Milholland, B. (2002) *North Saskatchewan River Guide: mountain to prairie a living landscape*. Edmonton, Alberta. North Saskatchewan Watershed Alliance

Parish, K. (ed.) (2006) *2006 Alberta Campground Guide*. Edmonton, Alberta. Alberta Hotel & Lodging Association

Parks Canada (1974) *Wild Rivers: Alberta.* Ottawa, Ontario. Department of Indian and Northern Affairs

Parks Canda (2005) *Canoeing the Bow River.* retrieved 2007-May-02 from http://www.pc.gc.ca/pn-np/ab/banff/activ/activ28c_e.pdf

Parry, B. (ed) (1978) *Canoe Alberta: a guide to Alberta's Rivers, 4th edition*. Edmonton, Alberta. Alberta Business Development and Tourism

Rood, S. & Tymensen, W. (2001) *Recreational Flows for paddling along rivers in souther Alberta.* Lethbridge, Alberta. Chinook Environmental Resources, retrieved from http://www3.gov.ab.ca/env/water/regions/ssrb/pdf_phase2/OldmanR%20Rec%20Flows%20report%20FINAL1.pdf

Ross, J. & Kyba, D. (1995, 2004) *The David Thompson Highway: a hiking guide.* Calgary, Alberta. Rocky Mountain Books (ISBN #0-921102-38-0)

Roth, C. (nd) *Alberta River Guides/Paddler Guides*. Calgary, Alberta. ARCA the Alberta Recreational Canoe Association
    The North Saskatchewan River: Foothills region
    The Athabasca River: Rocky Mountain region
    The Middle Red Deer River: Dickson to Drumheller
    The Lower Red Deer River: Drumheller to the Red Deer Forks
    The Milk River: Wiskey Gap to Deer Creek
    The Middle Bow River: Ghost Dam to Carseland

Saskatchewan Department of Tourism and Renewable Resources (nd) *Saskatchewan Canoe Trips - number 40: Clearwater River - Warner Rapids (Highway #955) to Fort McMurray, Alberta*

Smith, S. (1995) *Canadian Rockies Whitewater: a river guide for canoeists, kayakers and rafters (Southern Rockies)*. Jasper, Alberta. Headwaters Press

Smith, S. (1996) *Canadian Rockies Whitewater: a river guide for canoeists, kayakers and rafters (Central Rockies)*. Jasper, Alberta. Headwaters Press

Thomas, A.(ed.) (2000) *Paddle Quest:Canada's best canoe routes*. Erin, Ontario. Boston Mills Press

Wood, K. (1967) *A Corner of Canada: a personalized history of the Red Deer River Country*. Red Deer, Canada. Kerry Wood